The Americas of Asian American Literature

The Americas of
Asian American Literature

GENDERED FICTIONS OF
NATION AND TRANSNATION

Rachel C. Lee

PRINCETON UNIVERSITY PRESS

PRINCETON, NEW JERSEY

Copyright © 1999 by Princeton University Press
Published by Princeton University Press, 41 William Street,
Princeton, New Jersey 08540
In the United Kingdom: Princeton University Press, Chichester, West Sussex

Library of Congress Cataloging-in-Publication Data

Lee, Rachel C.,1966–
The Americas of Asian American literature: gendered fictions of nation and transnation/
Rachel C. Lee.
p. cm.
Includes bibliographical references and index.
ISBN 0–691–05960–8 (alk. paper). — ISBN 0–691–05961–6 (pbk. alk. paper)
1. American fiction—Asian American authors—History and criticism. 2. Feminism and
literature—United States—History—20th century. 3. Women and literature—United
States—History—20th century. 4. National characteristics, American, in literature. 5. Yamashita, Karen Tei, 1951– Through the arc of the rain forest. 6. Hagedorn, Jessica Tara-
hata, 1949– Dogeaters. 7. Bulosan, Carlos—Political and social views. 8. Jen, Gish—Political and social views. 9. Asian Americans in literature. 10. Gender identity in literature. 11.
Sex role in literature. I. Title.
PS153.A84L44 1999
810.9'895—dc21
99–14575 CIP

This book has been composed in Janson

The paper used in this publication meets the minimum requirements
of ANSI/NISO Z39.48-1992 (R 1997) *(Permanence of Paper)*

http://pup.princeton.edu

Printed in the United States of America

10 9 8 7 6 5 4 3 2 1

10 9 8 7 6 5 4 3 2 1
(Pbk.)

Contents

Preface

SEVERAL YEARS AGO, on a visit to a small northeastern college, I was asked by a musicologist about the importance of my work. "But really," he said, "aren't you just reading a bunch of books?" I was startled by the question because it asked me to speak not just for the significance of my project in particular but for the value of literary studies as a whole. Reflecting back on the incident, I am struck by how often my predecessors in Asian American literary criticism have had to face similar questions regarding the "relevance" of literature to Asian American Studies and its political goals, foremost among them, as a 1975 curricular report phrased it, to effect "fundamental social change" ("Curriculum Committee Report," 13). As Victor Bascara recently pointed out, when Bruce Iwasaki was writing in 1976 he had to counter a widely held view in "the Asian American activist community" that literature was "extraneous to political emancipation" (Bascara, 25). Likewise, Elaine Kim in her seminal survey of Asian American literature implicitly rose to the demand of social relevance by underscoring her deliberate choice "to emphasize how the literature elucidates *the social history* of Asians in the United States," thus rendering literature in the service of social change (Kim, xv, emphasis mine).

Because I work at the crossroads of at least three disciplinary fields—Asian American Studies, American literature, and studies in gender and sexuality—I find that I am continually answering versions of the musicologist's question, and that my answers vary depending upon the particular constituency being addressed. Yet, in each of my answers I am aware of the need to forge a connection between collective politics and institutionalized knowledge production. Thus, the political thrust of my answers is steady and clear: this particular work, as well as the broad disciplinary fields that it presumes and to which it contributes, illuminates the material and ideological conditions that render specific communities what they are. My hope is not only that these illuminations will help bring about social change for these communities, but also that this project will help transform the way in which we think about "social change" and "radical politics" in the first place.

Since the publication of Elaine Kim's book, with its emphasis on literature as an elucidation of social history, Asian American scholars have made different claims for the promise of literary criticism. Their arguments range from viewing critical interpretation as an enhancement of one's understanding of empirical data (Sumida), to claiming literary criticism as a tool for both building communal identity (Wong 1993) and for garnering mainstream recognition (Lim and Ling).[1] Asian American literary criticism can—and perhaps ought to—function in all of these ways. My personal view is that the job of the literary critic is to illuminate individual literary works, not only in relation to the sociohistorical contexts from which they arise, but also relative to the structures of knowledge through which these texts are channeled. In other words, cultural artifacts are never divorced from the way they are received—or made to mean—in accordance with the dominant ideologies of the time. Rosemary Hennessy calls this type of analysis "ideology critique," which is "a mode of reading that recognizes the contesting interests at stake in discursive constructions of the social" (15). It regards the act of reading itself as an ideological practice of making a text intelligible for specific political and economic (power-laden) purposes.

In my examination of particular texts, then, I offer a larger critique of culture and ideology. To paraphrase Michèle Barrett, literary texts are indicators of the bounds in which meanings are produced at a specific historical moment (Barrett 1985, 80). Within various narratives, one can observe an author's negotiation with often conflicting "ways of knowing"—trajectories of interpretation that lend the object of interpretation a specific political valence. For instance, "social relevance" represents one such "way of knowing" to which literary critics of the '70s and '80s were hard pressed to conform. The value of analyzing various narratives lies not least in the articulation of these boundaries within which texts are made to mean.

Therefore, in addition to being a literary analysis of four Asian American novels, this book scrutinizes the ideologies that make possible and favor certain types of readings, by limning which political interests are served when certain narratives and not others are deemed appropriate to the ethnopolitical stakes of Asian American writing. In doing this work of ideology critique, I have my own interested political commitments, particularly to promoting an Asian American collective identity that is attentive to gender issues. In my various chapters, I argue that interpreting Asian American literature in accordance with ethnic-based political commitments often constrains the intelligibility of stories focused on kinship, family dynamics, eroticism, and gender roles. Since the tendency has been to read ethnic or minority literature as exposés of racial oppression, I probe the ways in which Asian American authors negotiate this ethnic prerogative with alternative tales circulating around sexual and gendered identity. Immanent in my "reading of a bunch of books," then, is an examination of the systems of cultural intelligibility that constrain these specific Asian American novels and, I would argue, other contemporaneous American and Asian American narratives as well. The five chapters that form the body of this project thus offer a partial composite of the ways in which multiply-located constituents of collective formations negotiate among the competing claims of communal politics and the competing demands of different audiences.

• • •

> Each one of us is here because somebody before us did something to make it possible.
>
> —Audre Lorde

To admit that there are vested political interests underlying every work of literary, historical, or, indeed, cultural interpretation is not to deny, however, the pleasures involved in reading this particular bunch of books--a pleasure enhanced by the wisdom and guidance of a number of individuals and institutions that have influenced the shape of my scholarly pursuits over the years. The brilliant and pathbreaking works of King-Kok Cheung, Sau-ling Wong, and Elaine Kim have provided fertile feminist ground for exploring through a gendered lens the various critiques of Western and Asian institutions forwarded by Asian American authors--an exploration of which this book is a part. The deftness with which these women interweave several disciplinary conventions and combine their fidelities to Asian American Studies, gender criticism, and literary scholarship has helped me to realize the possibility of making my own work engage multiple audiences simultaneously. I am especially indebted to King-Kok Cheung both for her scholarly example and for the direct and personal ways she has lent me support over the years, from reading countless drafts of my work, to shepherding me through the ins and outs of academia, to providing through each phase of her mentorship an intellectual generosity and companionship beyond compare.

In the writing of this book, I have been blessed with an array of formal and informal mentors. As members of my Ph.D. committee, Valerie Smith, Eric Sundquist, and Michael Salman provided generous and incisive comments that challenged me to craft a project that might aspire to the conceptual originality, historical rigor, and stylistic eloquence displayed in each of their works. Their critical comments have consistently sharpened my thinking, even in those places in the book where I have been unable to incorporate all of their suggestions. I am most grateful, as well, to my informal mentors: Sucheng Chan has continued to inspire me through her pioneering scholarship, her savvy at building institutions, and her tremendous encouragement during the earliest stages of my professional career. And I count myself fortunate to have "traveled" with Caren Kaplan, benefiting from her salient critique of this book and from her sharing with me her own work.

Initial and later drafts of the manuscript benefited tremendously from the discerning readings of Stephen Sumida, Paul Lauter, Susan Schweik, and an anonymous reader of the manuscript. The insights of Mary Pat Brady, Jeanie Chiu, Chris Connery, Chris Cunningham, Alycee Lane, Cynthia Liu, Michael Murashige, Viet Nguyen, and Rob Wilson have helped me rethink individual chapters in relation to current critical debates over race, nationalism, cultural production, and field definition. Equally important to the development of this project have been the time and space provided me by a number of institutions. I have received generous institutional support from the National Endowment for the Humanities, the Office of the Chancellor at UC-Berkeley, and the Center for the Study of Women, the Academic Senate, the Center for Asian American Studies, and the English Department at UCLA.

Because this book delves into the ways various communities are simultaneously and variously making demands upon a particular literary text, it is fitting that I here address the heterogenous yet extremely supportive intellectual community that has enabled me to ask the questions I ask in this book. The supportive environment at UCLA and the discussions and advice of my colleagues in the English department and Women's Studies program have been crucial to the completion of this work. I appreciate particularly the friendship and counsel of Judith Rosen, Richard Yarborough, Helen Deutsch, Arthur Little, Jenny Sharpe, Ali Bedhad, Lowell Gallagher, David Louie, Shu-mei Shih, and Joe Bristow. For comraderie in crossing disciplines and for good dinners and excellent conversation, I thank Dwight McBride, Daphne Brooks, Laura Kang, Oscar Campomanes, Anne Cheng, Gisele Fong, Dean Toji, Cynthia Liu, Roxanne Eberle, and Georgina Dodge. To my students, who are variously touched and inspired upon their first readings of these Asian American novels, I am indebted for their ethusiasm and fresh perspectives that remind me precisely why I entered into this business of "reading a bunch of books" in the first place.

I am grateful, too, for the comments and criticisms of faculty and students at various other institutions across the nation, particularly Lindon Barrett at UC-Irvine and Amy Robinson at Georgetown, whose probing questions ultimately enhanced the conceptual links between fields this book attempts to forge. I would also thank several individuals for providing me with opportunities to present selections of this book to various audiences: Anne Cheng and the English department at UC-Berkeley, Chris Connery and the Center for Cultural Studies at UC-Santa Cruz, and Chris Littleton of the Women's Studies program at UCLA. To my editor at Princeton University Press, Deborah Malmud, who offered me sage advice in the formal submission process, I want to extend my gratitude for her confidence in this work and for her impeccable professionalism.

As an informal editor of all of my work, I am most lucky to have found the companionship of Gabriel Spera. For his wisdom, poetic sensibilities, and for his providing me with peace of mind, this book is a testament to his stamina as well as mine. Finally, I thank my sister, Rebecca Lee, and dedicate this book to my parents, Quinton and Lily Lee, for their love, guidance, and support for my choices, which have oftentimes been quite different from their own.

R. C. L.
Los Angeles
December 1998

The Americas of Asian American Literature

Introduction

> . . . she had considered the great divide of her self's time to be
> coming to America. Before she came to America, after she came
> to America. But she was mistaken. That was not the divide at all.
> —Gish Jen

> Why is it that the advent of the politics of nationalism signals
> the subordination if not the demise of women's politics?
> —R. Radhakrishnan

THE PROPOSITION of this book is that gender and sexuality remain instrumental to the ways in which Asian American writers conceive of and write about "America." The Americas over which these writers ruminate vary widely, appearing as a utopian space of possibility, a violent exclusionary society, a series of assimilationist narratives, a fantasy of wealth and privilege projected onto movie screens, and a center of financial speculation and faddish consumption. It would be misguided to reduce these writers' complex, contradictory, and often ambivalent attitudes toward America to a single unified response. What is consistent across these several narratives is the way in which considerations of gender and sexuality complicate the view of "America" and, conversely, how the view of America often obscures what these novels have to say about family dynamics, eroticism, and gender roles.

Asian American texts bear a special burden in negotiating the incommensurate and unevenly matched topics of America, gender, and sexuality. Already imagined by mainstream presses as appealing only to ghettoized interests, Asian American cultural producers face increased pressure to emphasize the broad value of their works. If, as R. Radhakrishnan suggests, stories that lend themselves to nationalist frameworks have a greater purchase than stories that are interpretable to gendered ones,[1] then Asian American narratives might be said to have a greater appeal when they appear to bear upon national institutions and American character. Those representations couched in a domestic, familial, or gendered framework, by contrast, would seem to address doubly localized and regional concerns. In bringing these two subjects together, I remain keenly aware that the two discourses are unevenly matched in the popular imagination. Does the prospect of writing about America, gender, and sexuality necessarily mean making America into the manifest content and gender and sexuality into the latent one? The mechanics of such narrative negotiations of America, gender, and sexuality form the crux of what this book seeks to explore.

This work is broadly informed by "New Americanist" methods of inquiring into the gendering of America, as found, for instance, in Annette Kolodny's influential work on the feminization of the American landscape that allowed male frontiersmen to conquer and domesticate it; and in Michael Rogin's work on the Indian removal policy that unravels the ways in which hierarchies naturalized in the paternal family were used to justify the displacement, robbery, and genocide of Native Americans.[2] While considerations of race do inform these analyses, their modes of inquiry do not translate so easily to examinations of Asian American discourse. For instance, Rogin emphasizes the way in which Native Americans were characterized by colonial authorities and Jacksonian officials as both racialized savages and children or women needing paternalistic care. His focus thus remains on the dominant discourse of white settlers and on the racial and gendered structures this discourse reveals. By contrast, my study takes seriously the efforts of racial critique from the perspective of minority subjects. Interested not solely in dominant discourse, I interrogate how Asian American subjects, themselves the objects of racialized and gendered projections, end up disavowing the position of women as they contest their own powerlessness.

Feminist critics King-Kok Cheung, Elaine Kim, and Sau-ling Wong have all remarked upon the infelicitous ways in which Asian American racial critiques of U.S. policies have frequently relied on gendered tropes (Cheung 1990; Kim 1990; Wong 1992). Too often, challenges to race-based oppression takes as unproblematic the inequality between the sexes, seeing it as natural, or based on biological differences. My analysis of gender continues in the spirit of these critics, asking how it is that not only in dominant but also in minority discourse, women symbolize dependency—half- or ill-formed subjectivity—and how it is that this gendered imagery naturalizes national policies that deny specific groups voting privileges, property rights, sexual license, and economic independence. Each of my readings is critically informed by the presupposition that gender opposition, gender difference, and gender hierarchy become convenient ways for understanding, enacting, and reinforcing opposition, difference, and hierarchy more generally and in an array of social relationships criss-crossed by racial, class-based, regional, and national differences.

In bringing together the frameworks of America, Asian America, gender, and sexuality, I have also been inspired by the volume *Nationalisms and Sexualities*, which asks "[H]ow is it that the world has come to see itself divided along the seemingly natural lines of national affiliation and sexual attachment? How do these categories interact with, constitute, or otherwise illuminate each other?" (Parker et al., 2). Though I admire the way in which this books' contributors focus on the convergence of two oftentimes skewed discourses of identity, the editors' emphasis on "nation-ness" ultimately limits the usefulness of this framework for my own study of America and Asian America. As recent scholars of American Studies have pointed out, America is not commensurate with nationalism, though a narrowly nationalist framework has been the dominant hermeneutic in the field for over half a century.[3] Exposing the ideological investments in this nationalist outlook, "New Americanists" have urged each other to examine "America" in a broader context, in hemispheric, regional, and global terms (Saldívar; Dirlik; Buell). My own work contributes to this growing body of criticism as it also attempts to bridge the emphasis on gender and sexuality—so well undertaken in the Parker volume—with the flexible geopolitical terrains that now comprise the variegated field of American Studies.

My selection of America as a topic is not without controversy. Asian American critics have recently contested the narrow, nationalist hermeneutic of "America," claiming that it obscures the view of Asia (Mazumdar; K. Scott Wong; Okihiro; Omatsu). In a frequently cited essay published in 1991, Sucheta Mazumdar urges scholars to return the study of Asian Americans to its roots in an international, rather than merely national, framework. She warns that "Asian American Studies has been located within the context of American Studies and stripped of its international links. This nationalist interpretation of immigration history has . . . been a more comfortable discourse for second- and third-generation Americans of Asian ancestry [who have been] reluctant to identify with Asian Studies and its pronouncements on the distinctiveness of Asian cultures in counterpoint to Euro-American culture" (30).[4]

The title of Mazumdar's essay, "Asian American Studies and Asian Studies: Rethinking Roots," indicates the general thrust of her polemic: she wishes to build institutional bridges between disparate fields and thus proposes two main reasons underlying their past divergence, namely, the closet American nationalism of Asian American Studies and the avoidance of politics and racial critique on the part of Asian Studies scholars (30). Despite her efforts to expose the barriers put up by both fields, Mazumdar's essay ultimately focuses on the inadequacies of Asian American Studies, which she describes as revisionist in its intent:

The need is not for a simple revision of American history that would accommodate those who were excluded in the first writing of this history, such as Asian Americans. The need is to define a new paradigm which contextualizes the history of Asian Americans within the twentieth-century global history of imperialism, of colonialism, and of capitalism. To isolate Asian American history from its international underpinnings, to abstract it from the global context of capital and labor migration, is to distort this history.

> In conclusion . . . one has to question the logic of turning to nationalist inter-
> pretations of history. Drawing boundaries and arbitrarily isolating the immi-
> grants' history and culture of the homeland under the rubric of Asian Studies,
> and focusing only on his or her existence after arrival in the United States as
> shaped by the American context, assumes "America" could be understood inde-
> pendently of "Asia" or vice versa. This does not appear to be innovative method-
> ology given international realities. (Mazumdar, 41)

The language, here, mystifies distinct hermeneutical issues: nationalist ru-
brics are not necessarily commensurate with an "Americanist" focus, nor
are works by Asian scholars necessarily productive of a comparative, global
framework (often these area studies' scholars specialize in the study of a
particular Asian *nation*). Through several rhetorical elisions, the passage
associates Asian Studies with an international and global focus, while Asian
American Studies is locked into a narrow nationalism. In accordance with
this reckoning, Asian American scholars are persuaded to turn to Asian
Studies not so much to explore the latter field's "pronouncements on the
distinctiveness of Asian cultures" (quoted above) but to engage in a global
hermeneutics where "America" and "Asia" cannot be imagined independ-
ently. A contradiction thus surfaces in the prose: adopting the rubric of
Asian Studies, with its presumption of "Asian distinctiveness," will hardly
guarantee an innovative methodology emphasizing hybridity and boundary-crossing practices.

The call for better methodologies to emphasize "Asia" and "America"
as interlinked might be better pursued, then, in an essay entitled "American
Studies and Asian Studies: Rethinking the Connections *through* Asian
American Studies." Literary critics in Asian American Studies have long
ago asserted that for them the separation of the two identities "Asian" and
"American" represented a false choice.[5] In the Asian American cultural
texts I examine, the imagining of America is simultaneously the imagining
of Asia, and vice versa, with the two sometimes posed in opposition and at
other times as overlapping.

Before one can judge the validity of the argument that looking to Asia
is somehow a less nationalist preoccupation than looking to America, I
think it is necessary to examine how, exactly, Asian American writers conceive of America.[6] Are these writers imagining America as the domestic
United States to which they wish to assimilate? Are their contemplations
of America much more ambiguous accretions of a number of different concerns? Are they framing America as an exceptional nation, as just another
node on a global playing field, as a cultural imperialist, as a symbol of
utopian society, as the opposite of Asia? These questions are addressed in
the bulk of this book, where I map the ways in which "America" is engaged
in four novels: Carlos Bulosan's *America Is in the Heart*, Gish Jen's *Typical*

American, Jessica Hagedorn's *Dogeaters*, and Karen Tei Yamashita's *Through the Arc of the Rain Forest*. Though part of my purpose is to make visible certain patterns in the Asian American public consciousness regarding what "America" means, I am not trying to construct a closed or unified field that will predict continuing ways in which America will be imagined. Rather my inquiry follows a borderland, hybrid, and multiple mode of inquiry in which I map the contradictory, incongruent representations of "America" across these four novels.

In the sequencing of my chapters, I have implicitly made use of the distinction between America's domestic-national and foreign-imperialist facades. The titles of the first two novels announce their preoccupation with "America," which more or less refers to the domestic United States. Both Bulosan and Jen focus on immigrant characters who contemplate the contradictions of America's promises while living an oftentimes vastly curtailed existence within its national borders. By contrast, the latter two works depict America much more obliquely. "America" in both these texts matters not first and foremost as a national territory but as a cultural style exported to other sites and as a cross-hemispheric term that encompasses both North and South America. In bringing these heterogeneous frameworks on America to bear in my individual chapters, I also undercut the logic of separability that poses America's domestic realm as distinct from its history of empire.[7]

Acknowledging the continued value of "America" as a rubric in Asian American Studies does not make it any easier to find appropriate ways to tackle the oftentimes conflicting politics of interrogating America from an ethnic-racial perspective and critiquing gender hierarchy and deconstructing sexual norms. Too often the practices seem at odds. For instance, some of the most powerful charges leveled at America's exclusionary policies toward Asians come from cultural nationalists such as Frank Chin and Jeffery Paul Chan. They distinguish the United States' "racist love" for Asians, which transforms the latter into "emotionally stunted, dependent [children]," from its "racist hate" for blacks, Chicanos, and American Indians, which contrastively encourages these groups to "develop their own brigand languages, cultures, and sensibilities" that defiantly mock white institutions (1972, 69).[8]

Across several essays, including two coauthored by Lawson Inada and Shawn Wong, Chin and Chan disseminate the idea that the realm of discourse is an important arena in which to fight racism.[9] Embedded in the very structures of language, itself, are pernicious associations of certain peoples with deviant behavior, for instance in the association of yellowness with cowardice and the association of blackness with evil. Focusing their attention on language and the literary arts, Chin and Chan catalogue the ways in which the social oppression of Asian Americans manifests itself in the negative stereotypes of Asians circulated by mainstream writers and in the dearth of resistance literature authored by Asian Americans.[10]

By identifying the discursive realm as one of the most insidious avenues of social oppression and by interrogating the stratification of America's racist policies toward different minority groups, Chin and Chan contribute quite trenchantly to the antiracist critical project of Asian American cultural studies. Unfortunately, along with the saliency of these points comes their less tenable argument that the overall project of Asian American writing is to recuperate Asian American manhood.[11] Binding the "cultural integrity" of Asian Americans with the assertion of a manly style, Chin and Chan universalize what they deem the appropriate preoccupation of male Asian American writers—expressing their manhood—to all Asian American writing and, furthermore, depict the normal configuration of Asian American writing to be one in which Asian American men dominate both numerically and in terms of setting the thematic agenda (Chan et al. 1974, 14–15).[12] Both Cheung and Kim remark on the difficulty—if not impossibility—of excising Chin and Chan's valid points from their cultural agenda centered upon the reinstallation of male privilege. In other words, one of the consequences of the combined antiracism and gender bias of cultural nationalism's critique of America is that Asian American critics, to paraphrase Cheung, feel compelled to choose between feminism and ethnopolitical critique (Cheung 1990).

From a slightly different perspective, Gary Okihiro likewise suggests that an ethnopolitical critique of America and a focus on women are incongruent practices. Claiming that women "have been relegated to the fringes of Asian American studies by men," Okihiro notes the gendered (as well as nationalist) character of Asian American historiography that most often begins in the nineteenth century with the large influx of male coolie laborers to the United States (xii). Defying these geographic parameters, Okihiro's own analysis engages a "transpacific site" formed by the human interactions and social links "between migrant men in America and those of women in Asia" (xii):

> Asian men in America were not solitary figures moving in splendid isolation but were intimately connected to women in Asia. . . . Recentering women extends the range of Asian American history, from bachelor societies in Hawaii and the U.S. mainland to the villages and households in Asia, in an intricate and dynamic pattern of relations. Transcending American exceptionalism is but one of the consequences of a woman-centered history. (69)

While cultural nationalism sacrifices Asian American women to the pyre of their anti-American critique, Okihiro does quite the reverse. Though he similarly constructs an oppositional relation between an ethnopolitical critique of America and a focus on Asian women, he resolves this seeming impasse by risking the former and choosing the latter.[13]

Yet there is also an undercurrent in Okihiro's prose that embraces America. That is, Okihiro does not attempt a history of Asian women in general, but looks specifically at women in Asia who were "intimately connected" to Asian men in America (68). Thus, "America" remains an important defining parameter of the experiences of these Asian women—whose sons, lovers, husbands, and fathers were "sojourning" there—even as "America," the geopolitical entity, is not the concrete environment framing their lives. What does it mean to imply that "America," though not the habitat of these women's daily practices, still materially conditions their lives, economically and socially, if not culturally? "America" is, therefore, used quite flexibly in Okihiro's analysis—as a geopolitical category too limiting for historical scholarship and also as a global economic, social, and cultural agent whose effects are felt outside its national borders.

Thus, Okihiro's defiance of American exceptionalism, in preference for a woman centered history, is not a wholesale abandonment of the "claiming America" rubric. Instead, he diminishes the primacy of this United States' national framework for comprehending Asian American history and culture by placing it next to an alternative explanatory grid, specifically that of a "transpacific" or Pacific Rim region, of which the United States is a part.[14] This work of relativizing "America"—viewing it as one port in an economic system of circulating capital and labor across the Pacific—has ramifications for the political agenda(s) of Asian Americans. On top of contesting racial discriminations within the United States, Asian Americans might be encouraged to tackle the deformations and oppressions of late capitalism. Moreover, feminist criticism reconceived on this terrain would require more than the recovery of women's histories in Asian locations: it would entail, at the very minimum, an account of the enabling or disabling economic and social effects on women circumscribed by such international trade and labor routes and by the gendered terms of kinship reformulated under transnational conditions.[15]

As Okihiro suggests, then, focusing on women can lead one to examine the limits of one's investigative tools. However, it does not follow that the questioning of one's methodological assumptions or political framework will lead to a practice friendly, or even attentive, to women, much less a feminist critique that would interrogate gender hierarchy and gender difference. I earlier alluded to the way in which other Asian American critics have engaged in this work of relativizing the "American" optic by seeking out its limits—examining where and how it closes off other lines of investigation. Instead of emphasizing the long histories of Asian American labor and settlement in the United States,[16] these scholars are more concerned with the particulars of cultural imperialism in former and present

U.S. colonies (Rafael 1995; Campomanes 1997; Diaz; Hall and Kauanui; and Fujikane), and with the changing contours of an Asian Pacific identity in a global society of hybridized cultures, transnational finance, worldwide media links, and de-territorialized cultural flows (Dirlik; Tadiar; Ong; Koshy; S. Wong (forthcoming); and Buell).[17] What troubles me about this exciting debate over the changing grounds of Asian American political critique is that gender issues may take a secondary place, considered irrelevant or less important than these global debates over whether diaspora, exile, postcoloniality, or transnationalism shall replace the nation as an alternative identity formation for border-crossing Asians.[18]

In a recent article, Sau-ling Wong describes the changes in the field of Asian American Studies in terms of a tripartite process of "denationalization" by which she refers to (1) the easing of cultural nationalist concerns, (2) the growing permeability between "Asian" and "Asian American," and (3) the shift from a domestic to a diasporic perspective (1995, 1–2). Wong tellingly locates the site of Asian American gender criticism in the first of these phenomena, describing it as one of several contributing factors to the "easing of cultural nationalist concerns" (2–5). After this brief account, the subject of gender does not intersect in any significant way with the issues broached in the remainder of the essay—namely, the reconfiguration of Asian American Studies under the sign of transpacific, boundary-crossing practices.[19] My point is not to fault Wong's essay in particular but to regard its subdued account of gender as symptomatic of a larger disjunction or relation of subordination between the realm of gender studies and the realm of Asian American Studies—a disjunction that threatens to undermine the vitality of Asian American feminist critique. While Asian Americanists debate the political, cultural, and social consequences of reconstituting Asian America's geopolitical borders in international, transnational, and postnational terms, gender criticism in Asian American literary studies is, to a large degree, mired in a cultural nationalist problematic.

To put it another way, the dominant intellectual frameworks for gender critique in Asian American Studies are aimed somewhat retrospectively—at a particular context when cultural nationalism and its masculinist presumptions were hegemonic. This cultural nationalism, in making broadly public and starkly visible a sexism internal to the community, enabled the emergence of a certain type of gender criticism, one that stressed the dual and interlocking oppressions of racism and sexism visited on Asian American women. An unforeseen downside to this close association of Asian American feminism with a critique of cultural nationalism is that as the authority of the latter wanes so does the urgency of this type of gender criticism. Thus, Asian American feminism risks renewed marginalization as Asian American cultural studies defines its more pressing concerns not through cultural nationalism but through alternative postcolonial and transnational convictions.

One of the effects of the wedding of Asian American feminism with the critique of cultural nationalism is that discussions of gender simply drop out of essays addressing the growing need for frameworks to address transnational or even postnational realities (Appadurai; Miyoshi; Wallerstein; Hannerz; Robertson).[20] Since the embers of cultural nationalism are always threatening to inflame, I would stress the continuing importance of feminist critiques that deconstruct its presumptions. However, I do believe that this sort of gender criticism needs to be supplemented by methods that aim at new critical terrains. In other words, I want to suggest that cultural nationalism is not the only seat of gender oppression in an Asian American context. It may be the case that cultural nationalism is neither more nor less intractable where gender is concerned than postcolonial critique or studies of de-territorialized culture flows.

If a pan-ethnic Asian American identity is only one of many ways in which Asian Americans are identifying themselves—articulated alongside exilic subjectivity and transnational migrant identity—then an analysis of gender must shift to accommodate and scrutinize the new forms of engenderings enshrined in these alternative Asian-Pacific and postcolonial identity formations. One primary purpose of this book is to fill the need for intellectual frameworks with which to comprehend the changing terrains of Asian American gender critique with its new sources in theories of subaltern womanhood and the gendering of international labor. These alternative frameworks do not displace the older cultural nationalist problematic but occur side by side with it. In other words, I would argue for a degree of continuity across Asian American feminist literary criticism rather than a severing of past and present methodologies.

My gendered analysis focuses, then, on the crises and knotty barriers confronting the study of cultural representations of America, gender, and sexuality in contexts informed by the politics of nation-states in oftentimes (neo)colonial relationships upon a terrain increasingly defined as global and borderless. In this way, my project asserts a relationship between Asian America's "older" agendas—of claiming America and combating domestically defined racist and gendered practices—and the "newer" emphases on interrogating both the cultural deracination of colonized Asian and Pacific Islander peoples and the difference that gender and race make to the flow of global capital. An underlying question of this book is whether the alternative frameworks of postcolonialism and theories of global economic and cultural flows are any more hospitable to essaying ethnopolitical and feminist critiques simultaneously. Focusing in my latter two chapters on literary representations that clearly exceed the national boundaries of the United States yet still reflect a context in which America matters, I ask whether their thematic concerns and discursive strategies enable a better view of women—as implied by Okihiro—or whether the alternative (postcolonial and transnational) Asian American political readings to be gleaned from these works merely require even more innovative gendered methodologies.

Each of my chapters is devoted to a single work, which enables me to ground my analysis in the particular ethnic group history and in the critical contexts to which the book is addressed and has been made to address. However, I also share Wong's conviction that establishing intertextual bridges plays an important role in building a sense of Asian American community (S. Wong 1993, 9). The community I am interested in building through this work is one of gender-sensitive coalition, one that both can recognize the stakes of building a common ethnopolitical culture and also scrutinize the ways in which gender significantly mediates identifications based on that common culture.

Chapter 1 examines Bulosan's *America Is in the Heart*, in which the United States appears variously as a place of racial inequality and arbitrary violence yet also of dynamic social struggle and of prospective racial harmony. In the contradictions among these portraits, one sees the outlines of two Americas, one that fails its promise of socioeconomic equality, and the other that endures as a space of idealism and racial coexistence located in the hearts of all peoples who believe in a sense of cross-cultural brotherhood. I examine closely the gendered presumptions of this idealized community sometimes synonymous with America, at other times embodied in a Filipino-American ethnic enclave, and still at other times in a worldwide social-democratic labor movement.

Reading somewhat against the topic of "America," I argue that Bulosan's novel is subconsciously haunted by scenes of eroticism coupled with brutality—of brotherhoods marred and men disconnected by bestial behavior (rivalry) where erotic women figure prominently. However, this narrative structure remains underexplored in Bulosan scholarship, which often enough begins with the question of "America," and then contemplates the text's relevance to migration and labor history in the United States. My analysis of the novel interrogates these portraits of fraternal communities threatened by the presence of eroticized women. If the United States defines citizenship in terms of control over the nation's women, Bulosan's Filipino protagonists negotiate the already gendered terms of state policies not just by opposition—claiming the right to marry white women—but also by practices marked with tremendous ambivalence toward those white, brown, and black women available to them. The idealized (and gendered) collective formation that the narrator ultimately embraces as exemplary of fellowship and the communal spirit not only excludes women but also enables the narrator to resolve the conflicting politics of local, national, and global alliances.

Chapter 2, likewise, focuses on a text, Gish Jen's *Typical American*, in which the manifest plot, focusing on America, occurs alongside a gendered, buried plot, this time centered upon womanly desires and female friendships. A variation on the frontier tale, the manifest plot features a Chinese Davy Crockett, Ralph (Yifeng) Chang, and his adventures with his family in the United States. Jen substitutes a green lawn in the suburbs for buffalo-roaming plains, and, instead of hostile Native Americans, Ralph must grapple with an American-born Chinese man named Grover Ding. Finally, it is not the wilderness that Ralph must tame, but overhead costs and income tax reports. In the mid-twentieth century, the frontiersman becomes an Asian American engineer; the frontiers, a Connecticut residence and venture capitalism.

Jen's satire of "typical American" behavior also contains a gendered subtext. The American models that Ralph imitates are all masculinist models of behavior, from Davy Crockett to Arthur Smith (the gun-owning neighbor) to Grover Ding (self-made millionaire and advocate of making one's own choices). Yet, interspersed in Jen's satire of these masculinist models are suggestions of alternative modes of behavior—the codes that Theresa and Helen Chang adopt. Theresa and Helen's actions emphasize communal balance and strengthening the household. Helen shapes her identity in and through domestic spaces, while Theresa defies gender boundaries and finds a place in a male-dominated medical profession. Theresa's unorthodox behavior, however, seems of a different order than Ralph's transgression, which seems premised upon a killing of the father, or an extinguishing of all precedents, in order to command complete authority (on the model of Harold Bloom's *Anxiety of Influence*). Theresa's transgression, on the other hand, becomes an exercise in finding a place among colleagues and coexisting with others. In my analysis of *Typical American*, I argue that nation and family are two disjunctive paradigms that produce two different interpretations of the novel. Reading in terms of the nation frequently leads to a reduction of the role of the family to that of a resistant ethnic enclave vis-à-vis dominant U.S. culture. However, if one scrutinizes the dynamics internal to the family itself, one perceives rifts within the household, stemming, in part, from the renegotiation of gender roles consequent upon the main character, Ralph Chang, internalizing codes of American masculinity.

From examining two texts that announce their central preoccupation with "America," I next turn to two novels where "America" is more attenuated. For Hagedorn and Yamashita, America is part of wider Western (and transnational) modernization schemes that would "civilize" Third World natives, disciplining their societies to the work rhythms and social structures of the capitalist West and North. Both authors take aim at the ideological apparatus that underwrites the "civilizing" mission by fixing Third World natives in images of purity and savagery.

The first of these, Hagedorn's *Dogeaters*, portrays the cityscape of Manila as being thoroughly infiltrated by American cinema. Everything is like a scene from the movies: characters' dreams and desires mimic the roles of Rock Hudson and Jane Wyman in the American film *All That Heaven Allows*, or Nestor Noralez and Barbara Villaneuva in the Filipino-made *Serenade*. My claim in chapter 3 is that Hagedorn represents not Manila so much as the syncretism of the polycultural globe and a particular Asian American or Americanized Asian manifestation of it. Multiple colonizations—Spanish, U.S., Japanese—complicate what is to be considered native and imperialist in the Philippines. However, critics of *Dogeaters* too often limit their discussions of the book to its imperialist mode of presentation: they charge that it is a sellout to the West, implicitly claiming that there are other modes of presentation that are less westernized, more native, more aligned with the politics of decolonization. Simply overlooked by these critics is the way in which the novel takes as its very subject the politics of representation and how it constrains women, Filipinas in particular. Instead of judging the authenticity of the novel—assessing to what degree it is a native Filipino expression as opposed to an American orientalist portrait—I examine the way in which such a line of inquiry not only understates the capacities of "native" agents to redeploy Western artifacts subversively, but also reduces emancipatory politics to questions of (postcolonial) nationalism—a reduction that further subordinates women to "the" communal cause (which, as Cynthia Enloe and Gayatri Spivak argue [1988b], refers to the cause of native men). The multiplotted narratives of *Dogeaters* do not rotate on the epiphany of nationalist awakening but on the constraints of female embodiment. Hagedorn thus portrays postcolonial political awakening as it occurs through the multiform pathways and trajectories of female empowerment—for instance, through the creative endeavors of Clarita Avila and Rio Gonzaga and through the guerrilla activities of Clarita and Daisy Avila.

My last chapter also engages a text in which the centrality of "America" is diminished. *Through the Arc of the Rain Forest* narrates the story of the *Matacão*, a new territory, a possible resource, a catalyst for miracles, a vast plastic mantle stretching across the former Amazon Basin, and finally an unknown quantity that spurs a scientific revolution. In this novel, set in 1995 and beyond, the author addresses the commercialization of social existence and the tension between consumerism and ecological conservation during a not-so-distant future of rapid change and instant communication. The immediate question posed by such a novel is whether America remains a primary category of analysis in an international marketing age. Rather than dismissing Yamashita's novel as irrelevant or beyond the scope of this study, I wish to explore the ways in which her text complicates the premises of this thesis and revises "America."

One displacement of the United States' optic is represented in the notion of an Asia-Pacific region—itself a subunit of a "world-system" of economic and cultural flows.[21] In this economic region, the United States is theoretically one of many "partners" in a "co-prosperity sphere" in which people are identified not so much by their national distinctions but by their articulation through processes of capital.[22] My chapter examines the imbrication of Yamashita's novel in the Asia-Pacific idea, even as I question the implications of rendering a cultural base for Rim-speak.[23]

Through the Arc of the Rain Forest renders six sets of local storylines converging in a single place—the fictional site of the *Matacão*—that magnetically draws various people and economic interests originating in Japan, Europe, and North America to its locality in Brazil. I probe the ways in which Yamashita negotiates the global and local dimensions of her characters' worlds. On one level, she depicts an Asia-Pacific regional formation structured by the flow of global capital and, on another, she narrates a series of love triangles. Significantly, the two levels of her story intersect by way of crises within households, families, and communities pressured by multiform migrations. These two contexts of local and global, their disjunctions and interrelations, are complexly interwoven in *Through the Arc of the Rain Forest* in ways that the managerial, cybernetic discourse of world systems and de-territorialized culture flows cannot capture.

My general approach in each of the chapters involves juxtaposing various hermeneutics with particular political investments (e.g., proving national fidelity, launching an ethnic critique, deconstructing imperialist discourses, or grasping the de-territorialization of culture) and probing the way in which gender intersects with and alters each of these interested readings. These investments have something to tell us about the salient issues affecting not only Asian American Studies but also U.S. multicultural studies as well. A major impetus of this project has been my desire to construct a way to conduct a feminist critique of Asian American literary works that do not necessarily reflect the traditional ethnic themes of generational conflict and biculturalism. My method has been to limn very distinctly the different political projects with which gender criticism contends for attention. Stories of domesticity, the family romance, and women's desires too often are muted or marginalized by these other political projects. My strategy is to uncover these suppressed tales and to examine the political investments in keeping them suppressed.

By way of conclusion, I would recall the first epigraph to this introduction. The quote is taken from one of the novels covered in the following chapters, *Typical American*, and describes a scene in which Helen Chang watches over the comatose body of her sister-in-law, ruminating on how she has defined her life. Her personal revelation is that "coming to America"—the way in which Asian American immigrants typically mark off their "self's time"—has not been as important a defining moment as finding Theresa. Telling Helen's story from the perspective of a sisterly bond would yield a drastically different kind of tale; yet as Helen's wistfulness suggests, her story has already been recounted with America at its center. The force of "coming to America" has made her—and perhaps author Gish Jen—misread or mistell her own life in those terms.

Like Jen's protagonist, I have thought of this book in terms of seeing Asian American literature pivot on the reconfiguration of "America" by postnationalist critics who emphasize the continuity between America's racialized domestic policies and its imperialist actions abroad. Looking back on the body of my work, I can't help but wonder if what I was seeking to explore was not so much "America" but the manifold configurations of the family romance. Still, the force of reading these novels under the sign of Asian American literature requires an engagement of their "American" themes—whether that be in terms of their critiques of U.S. domestic racial policies or their depictions of the less tangible effects of U.S. economic and cultural dominance on a more globally construed terrain. Rather than following blindly in Helen's footsteps, then, I have attempted to critically assess why she misconstrues her experiences and, analogously, why interested readings about women have to occur in conjunction with other sorts of macropolitical themes. Rather than dismissing "America" as a misreading, then, it would be more valuable to contemplate, as I do in the following chapters, how gender and sexuality intersect with and mediate its contours.

CHAPTER ONE

Fraternal Devotions: Carlos Bulosan and the Sexual Politics of America

> The men brought the girl out and tied her to a guava tree. The angry women spat in her eyes and tore off her clothes, calling her obscene names . . . one of the men rushed out of the tool-shed with a horsewhip. . . . [My brother Leon staggered] toward his bride with blood on his face. He flung himself upon her, covering her bleeding body with his, and the stones and sticks fell upon him mercilessly. Then they tied him to the tree, beside his bride, and the angry peasants, who had been his good friends and neighbors a moment ago, began throwing stones at them.
>
> —*America Is in the Heart* (7)

WITHIN THE FIRST FOUR PAGES of Carlos Bulosan's *America Is in the Heart*, three climactic events unfold: the return of the narrator's older brother Leon, the mob attack on Leon and his bride (as depicted in the epigraph), and the newlywed couple's exile from the barrio. This series sets up a recurrent motif in the novel: a disruption of brotherly unity by the presence of a sexualized woman. Yet the centrality of this dynamic throughout the text is oddly deemphasized by the novel's ostensible and eponymous focus on the American nation. Consequently, this narrative structure remains underexplored in Bulosan scholarship, which often enough begins with the question of "America," and then just as often contemplates the text's relevance to migration and labor history in the United States.[1] In other words, the salience of the book's commentary on American life—especially its exposure of the United States' failed policies with regard to its "little brown brothers"—has produced a noticeable silence from Asian American critics on the sexual politics of the novel, dramatically illustrated in this opening scenario and in other episodes as well.[2]

To remedy this silence, I focus on the way in which gender and sexuality mediate the narrator's vision of America as well as other sub- and supranational forms of brotherly community. Brotherhood in the novel is conceived of literally, in terms of blood relations, and more expansively as a national community, an ethnic immigrant enclave, a transnational class of laborers, and a panracial notion of humanity. What remain consistent in the narrator's depiction of the ever-widening horizon of political affiliations are the gendered limits of fraternity and the tenuousness of brotherly bonds that hinge on the successful regulation of sexuality. My intention, then, in quoting the initial episode above is to draw attention to the primacy of sexual politics in the novel's portrait of U.S.-Philippine relations in the early part of the twentieth century (c. 1913–1941).

To that purpose, I explore Bulosan's "dream of fraternity"[3] articulated through the narrator's past remembrance of kinship but predominantly portrayed as an absent and desired eventuality to be located in various sites, one of which is America. Failing to take hold there, this ideal of brotherhood is otherwise imagined in the labor union, in the Committee for the Protection of Filipino Rights, and in a literary community of progressive writers. Women, who mark the present, emerge as the symptom of lost, fragmented brotherhoods and paradoxically as the face of America's kindness.

The puzzle of America that the novel spends its whole length approximating might be better understood, then, as the projection of a desire for an always impossible, plenary moment of fully inclusive, albeit gendered, community. Bulosan's articulation of the American nation in this particular way requires a critical contemplation of how and why women function so crucially to the narrator's conception of both national collective identity and communal rivalry. The narrator, Allos/Carlos,[4] finds his way around the exigencies of choosing amongst various terrains of political struggle by proposing a homology among "brotherhoods"; yet, his sliding between his various collective commitments remains deeply dependent upon a gender-exclusive notion of subjectivity. Women remain structurally important to the formation and mobilization of these collective identities even as they become markers of loss, absence, and necessity. This paradoxical function that women perform compels my examination into the intersection of gender, eroticism, and national identity.

FRATERNITY UNBOUND

The first ninety-three pages of Bulosan's text appear to belie its American focus. Recounting the narrator's childhood in the Philippines, the novel describes a series of tragedies that befall Carlos's family, leading to the narrator and his brothers' eventual departure for America. Through a mixture of dramatization and exposition, Bulosan underscores a history of class division that underlies the family's poverty: "The sons of the professional classes studied law and went to the provinces, victimizing their own people and enriching themselves at the expense of the nation. . . . [T]hey also took part in the merciless exploitation of the peasantry and a new class of dispossessed peasants who were working in the factories or on the vast haciendas" (24).[5] In Bulosan's novel, Philippine independence, briefly declared in 1898 but quickly thwarted by the United States' "protectorship" of the islands from 1902 to 1946, takes a back seat to the issue of *indio* peasants' exploitation by their elite mestizo landlords.[6]

While the author sidesteps the issue of Philippine independence, to focus instead on class divisions within society, he nonetheless forges a national-societal ideal throughout his book that he most saliently identifies with "America." In other words, America is presented by the young narrator not as an imperialist power that has thwarted the Philippines' own national independence, but rather as the very embodiment of that type of "deep, horizontal comradeship" that Benedict Anderson equates with the nation: "Ultimately," Anderson argues, "it is this fraternity that makes it possible, over the past two centuries, for so many millions of people, not so much to kill, as willingly to die for such limited imaginings" (Anderson 1991, 6–7). It is through this identification with "fraternity" that nations inspire colossal human sacrifice (and that body count, in turn, attests to Anderson's claim that "nation-ness is the most universally legitimate value in the political life of our time" (Anderson 1991, 3). Bulosan's novel, in fact, offers evidence of this kind of sacrificial fraternal devotion: the novel begins with an account of brother Leon returning from soldiering abroad, presumably as an American national (since the Philippines was a U. S. territory at the time), and ends with brothers Macario and Amado leaving for similar tours of duty in the U.S. militia. Yet, despite obvious signs that fraternal community in the novel alludes to the American nation, it would be a mistake to reduce the several portraits of brotherhood—and the different geographic and social landscapes they attempt to take in—as mere allegories of national community. In fact, within Filipino traditions of history and literature exist alternative narratives of fraternal community that are not necessarily commensurate with nationalist imaginings.

For instance, historian Reynaldo Ileto describes a likewise deep, horizontal comradeship espoused by the Katipunan—a religious revolutionary society led by Andrés Bonifacio, whose uprising in 1896 initiated the Philippines War of Independence against Spain.[7] According to Ileto, peasant revolutionaries envisioned Philippine independence as both national liberation from colonial rule and a unity of the people that remained inconsistent with class division and exploitation. He astutely documents the split meanings of *kalayaan* (liberty, independence) as used by peasant and elite leaders. For Bonifacio's Katipunan, *kalayaan* was intimately tied to the ideas of "wholeness" and "becoming one": "In 'kalayaan,' [peasant] revolutionists found an ideal term for independence that combined separation from a colonial ruler (i.e., a mother who showed cruelty instead of love) and 'coming together' of people in the Katipunan. Katipunan is kalayaan in that it is a recovery of the country's pre-Spanish condition of wholeness, bliss and contentment" (Ileto, 87). By contrast, an elite cadre of Filipino nationalists educated abroad, who called themselves *ilustrados* ("enlightened ones"), used the term *kalayaan* devoid of its connotations of wholeness: "Independence had come to be defined in a static sense as autonomy, and unity was formalized in the coming together of men of wealth, education, and social prominence. . . . To the Katipunan, this all gave the appearance of unity, not the experience of unity" that was so essential to the idea of *kalayaan* (Ileto, 183). As an alternative to the *ilustrados*'s singular emphasis on national self-rule, the Katipunan conceived of a more spiritually inspired brotherly condition that may or may not have taken national form.[8]

Literary critic and author N. V. M. Gonzalez also highlights an extranational form of brotherhood by harkening to Filipino folklore and the mythic aspects of brotherly separation and return (Gonzalez 1976, 32). Gonzalez details a story from the island of Samar, wherein two brothers reach a crossroads and leave a needle under a rock to mark the point of separation. The needle memorializes the fraternal connection and provides a reason for each brother to attend to that brotherly connection (they are to check the spot occasionally to see if the needle has become rusty). In Gonzalez's essay, the needle under the rock comes to speak for the ultimate unity of Filipino writers abroad (in America) and at home.

These alternative, non-national discourses of fraternity remind one of the multitiered political resonance of "brotherhood." It is through a lens attuned to such multiple registers that one must approach Bulosan's topos of brotherhood, which is simultaneously a topos of political commitment and gendered community. Attesting to the ephemeral quality of this community, the novel's choice of opening scenarios establishes a sequence of brotherly reunion and separation that repeats itself throughout the narrative. With great anticipation, the narrator watches an unfamiliar man "coming slowly through the tall grass"—a man whom he soon discovers to be his eldest brother Leon returned from the war (3). Though this scene depicts Carlos's meeting his brother for the first time, the narrative also portrays this familial relation as a "reunion," a prior formation brought back to wholeness. Such is the nature of brotherhood in Bulosan's novel—an ideal unity intoned in the past yet also on the verge of prospective realization. As for the present, brotherhood occurs fleetingly, imperiled by circumstances where women figure prominently.

In this instance, Leon's fiancée intrudes upon the renewed sibling covenant and provokes its dissolution. More precisely, an ambiguous interpretation of her failed virginity sends the newlywed couple into exile, effectively terminating the brothers' fraternity. The narrator describes the custom whereby the community "find[s] out" the sexual (im)purity of the bride:

> The ritual was very simple. But it was also the most dramatic of . . . wedding events. My brother Leon carried his wife across the harvested fields to their new home. We followed, shouting with joy and throwing rice upon them. We stopped

in the yard when they entered the house. Then we waited silently, anxious to see the black smoke come out of the house, for it would mean that the bride was a virgin. If no smoke showed, we would know that the groom had been deceived, and we would justify his action if he returned the girl to her people. (7)

An absence or semiotic aporia dominates the unfolding of this scene. In other words, no legitimate sign appears; no smoke spews forth from the chimney. Yet this absence does not so much constitute part of the ritual's testifying action as much as the consequent rage of the crowd does.

The clear sky remains an equivocal sign only *implying* that the bride has failed the test, in that the clear sky does not signify anything until the bride and groom have been alone for a prolonged amount of time. This definition or identification by negation proves characteristic of Bulosan's novel. The lack of appropriate signs approximates but does not tell the reverse of the anticipated meanings. Just as the narrator leaves equivocal the sexual (im)purity of Leon's bride so does he render ambiguous the definition of America. His portrait of the nation presents an abundance of absences and exclusions—that is, one does not have a confirming sign that establishes what an "America in the heart" is. One does not even know what form that confirming sign would take (presumably the Filipino's comfortable life in the United States?). Instead, the novel presents a series of portraits that signal "the absence of America in the heart," signs that can be as ambiguous as clear skies to the virgin.

By recounting this ritual, the narrator ostensibly exposes "a cruel custom" in the Philippines that ostracizes women (7). Yet, I would argue that Leon's bride is not the main concern of this recollected event. Though her body functions as the primary site of action, she herself is repeatedly denied agency over her body.[9] The groom carries her into the grass hut, the crowd of men drag her out and strap her to a tree, and the women tear off her clothes. The specter of the bride's "sexual impurity"—established by various other agents—requires her redemption likewise at the hand of others. Father and son protect the hapless bride from the mob, with Leon using his body to shield his wife from hurled stones and the narrator's father flinging "himself upon [Leon] and his bride" as the whips begin to "[fall] upon him" (8). This drama around the figure of a sexualized woman thus remains pivotal in the chapter insofar as it testifies to male sacrifice and male heroism. The public humiliation, moreover, dramatizes the men's communal sacrifice. Shortly after the public whipping, Leon leaves "the *barrio* with his wife to live in another part of Luzon" (8), abandoning his family for a presumably undeserving wife. The chapter that begins with a brother's return thus ends with his departure.

In Part 1 alone, Bulosan recounts several of these brotherly separations. Fraternal bonds appear fleetingly, either already located in the past, or on the verge of disappearing. Brotherhood, in Bulosan's text, thus exhibits this distinct temporality wherein the future is marked with a pastness or loss. Hence the narrator describes another of his brothers, Amado, just as he is leaving home: "He raised his dirty right hand and waved lovingly at me. 'Good-bye, Allos!' he shouted. I watched him disappear behind the tall grass in the river, his bare feet pounding in the mud as the rain swallowed him" (17). If brotherhoods dwell in the past as well as recede into the future, then the moment of separation marks the present.

One can imagine this moment of separation as a turning point where eroticized women act as the fulcrum. For example, when brother Macario returns home, he too has to flee the family fold due to the wedding ambitions of a "strange young girl." The prospect of losing Macario, however, presents the family with a greater sense of tragedy than did either Leon's or Amado's departures. The novel early on establishes Macario as the family's "hope": "It was for Macario that we were all working so hard, so that he could come back to Binalonan to teach school and, perhaps, to help us support our large family" (10). Besides being the family's hope, Macario also represents the nation's dream of a more egalitarian society to be forged through popular education:

> Popular education . . . was a new and democratic system brought by the American government into the Philippines, and a nation hitherto illiterate and backward was beginning to awaken. In Spanish times education . . . belonged exclusively to the rulers . . . [and] the peasants were denied even the most elementary schooling. When the free education that the United States had introduced spread throughout the islands, every family who had a son pooled its resources and sent him to school. (14)

In addition to "open[ing] up new opportunities" for the peasants, this national system of education forges a greater sense of a horizontal, sibling community (14). Sons from every barrio merge into high schools and universities, where they become metaphoric brothers.

Yet Macario, as the local agent of this horizontal community, cannot complete his brotherly work upon his return home. (Such work includes his educating Carlos, his instructing the local schoolboys, and by extension, his forging at the ground level the type of popular education through which a democratic society arises.) A young girl—nameless, like Leon's wife—interrupts Macario's pedagogy by insisting that he marry her. When Macario refuses, she goes "to the school principal, and before we knew it my brother was asked to resign his job" (44). After fleeing to another island, Macario writes to the family, telling them that "the strange girl had followed him to Mindanao, and he had escaped to Manila. Now he . . . was contemplating going to America" (48). Macario's departure signals yet another severed fraternal link galvanized by an eroticized woman. In contrast to Leon who chooses to stay in the Philippines with his wife, Macario escapes by traveling to the United States, where women presumably cannot follow.[10] The text begins framing America as the site to which brothers flee and wherein a lost brotherhood might be recovered.

Like his elder sibling, Carlos also finds himself fleeing home in order to avoid a forced marriage. Though he wishes to stay with the family "until the rice is all planted" (78), his innocent dance with a peasant girl transforms into grounds to entrap him in marriage. Consequently, Carlos cannot help his mother with the crop but must flee to Lingayen if he doesn't "want to be married to a mud-smelling peasant girl" (78). From there he departs for America, chasing after a dream of freedom which is contrasted to the lives of both women and toiling peasants.

By subtle turns, the author forges two mutually reinforcing connections: one between freedom and brotherhood, the other between imprisonment and women. Because they signal a lack of personal liberty, women cannot participant in a free community but can only act as the equivocal sign of its absence (akin to the clear sky that ambiguously indicates the absence of virginity). Not surprisingly, the narrator's farewell to his brother Luciano furthers the association of women with enslavement:

> I went to Binalonan to say good-bye to Luciano. His wife had just given birth to another baby. I knew that he would have a child every year. I knew that in ten years he would be so burdened with responsibilities that he would want to lie down and die. I was glad that I was free from the life he was living. . . . "Don't come back to Binalonan, Allos!" he said. . . . "Don't ever come back, please, little brother! . . . Don't come back as I have done. See what happened to me?" (89)

To avoid a similar lifestyle, Carlos heeds his brother's words to "never come back." Oddly, then, the narrator's separation from his brother (who has effectively married out of brotherly community) is framed as a truer enactment of fraternity (and its implied freedom) than his continued proximity to Luciano would be. The coupling of freedom and fraternity thus implies both *freedom in fraternity*—that freedom can only be achieved through collective effort—and *fraternity in freedom*—that brotherly ties made "unfree" by the presence of sisters-in-law are not true fraternities, only degraded versions.

The narrator's dream of brotherhood, thwarted in the novel's first part, finds a new location in America.[11] Encouraging Carlos's identification of fraternal community with the United States is the aforementioned popular education "spreading throughout the archipelago" (14), a system which the narrator imagines to be the doorway to democracy but which one can also describe as a colonial apparatus that constructs freedom and equality as "American" ideals. According to Ronald Takaki, Filipino youths (in the Philippines) attending schools established by Americans "looked at pictures of Washington and Lincoln, studied the Declaration of Independence, and read about the 'home of the free and the brave' in their English-language textbooks" (Takaki 1990b, 57). Given this context, one understands Carlos's perception of the United States as an ideal site for democratic brotherhood to flourish.

The transplanting of brotherhood onto American soil also finds a historical parallel in the formation of American branches of Filipino fraternal orders such as the Caballeros Dimas Alang. According to Sucheng Chan, "[O]ne reflection of the influence that American culture had on Filipinos was the existence of many American-style fraternal organizations within the Filipino immigrant communities" (75). Thus, one such "popular" organization, Dimas Alang—which was founded in Manila in 1906 but which set up a branch in San Francisco in 1921—both disseminated "the ideals of nationalist heroes José Rizal and Apolinario Mabini" and strove to achieve "'human brotherhood under the Fatherhood of God' through a love of country, justice, dignity, decency, freedom and equality" (76). The coupling of "human brotherhood" with patriotic zeal would seem to suggest a homology between brotherhood and country. However, Dimas Alang's purported goals also expose the discontinuities between brotherhood and nation. Is one's "love of country," in the passage above, directed at the Philippines, at America, or both? Is "love of country," then, a sectarian interest detracting from the formation of "human brotherhood"? The confusion results in part from the peculiar "American" status of Filipinos, who, during the period that Bulosan recounts, were considered neither aliens nor citizens but "nationals." The later granting of independence to the Philippines, moreover, rendered Filipino immigrants residing in the United States "aliens"—destabilizing their national identities once again.

This shifting definition of national-societal borders may partly account for the novel's supranational focus even as the narrator tries to couch his embrace, search, and nostalgia for brotherhood in terms of the nation. Interestingly, this inexact homology between brotherhood and nation enables the narrator's endorsement of many types of "humanist" action that often have conflicting political agendas. For example, the struggle for Filipino rights in the United States and the rights of workers all over the globe are both couched as fights for "brotherhood."

Just as Carlos recounts in the novel's first part the disappearance of his sibling relations, so does the narrator depict "aspects of American life" which conflict with the America he has been seeking (104): two police detectives "without provocation" shoot a Filipino in the back (128); a posse of railway detectives chase after Carlos's friend José, who ultimately loses a leg under a speeding train (147); union busters and their henchmen set fire to Filipino bunkhouses (145–46). Racist vigilantes, policemen, and the hired hounds of farm owners belie the notion of kinship between Americans and Filipinos. Despite the viciousness and impoverishment that Carlos witnesses, he still insists on a better "America" lurking behind the "terror and ugliness."[12] Though he can produce no positive evidence of this "more perfect union," the narrator nevertheless insists on a better "America" that he has not yet seen (i.e., one that is not vicious and not impoverished). This America—which I will distinguish as the "America in Carlos's heart"—emerges as both a site of desire and an unfolding narrative to which Carlos has yet to find the "door." Yet, even in his observations on its current absence, the narrator has already begun inscribing this "America in the heart" vis-à-vis its alterity. To reiterate, the text makes visible not so much what "America" *is* as what it *is not*. This definition-by-negation leaves the "door" to America perpetually open. That is, by virtue of its slipperiness, this definition-by-negation enables—even requires—supplementary narration, for the cumulative descriptions of what an entity is not helps approximate but does not reveal what that object is. Thus, the "America" of Bulosan's title emerges in contrast to the social formation limned by the narrative's accounts of violence, flight, racial persecution, and regulated sexuality.

The aforementioned instances of violence that bespeak the absence of this better "America" are all examples of white-on-brown violence. Less explicable and hence more troubling to the narrator, however, are instances of intra-ethnic violence that do not neatly dramatize racial enmity but instead suggest a self-destructiveness that centers, significantly, upon erotic needs.[13] Following the pattern constructed in Part 1, these episodes pose sexualized women as the cause of brotherly separation. For instance, during his season in the Alaskan canneries, the narrator describes his burgeoning friendship with "two oldtimers who were not much older than I"—Paulo Lorco and Conrado Torres (101). Their fellowship appears congruent with the development of progressive politics: "[It] was the beginning of a friendship that grew simultaneously with the growth of the trade union movement and progressive ideas among the Filipinos in the United States" (101). This congruency suggests a homology between social fraternities and labor collectives.

The brotherhood ends when Conrado's Indian girlfriend, La Belle, claims Conrado is the father of her child and tries to force him into marriage (102–103). For reasons inexplicable to the narrator, Paulo steps in to save Conrado by telling the cannery officials that he is the father. "I'll stay here for seven years, all right," Paulo says to the narrator. "I'm in a mess in Los Angeles anyway—so I'll stay with this dirty Indian girl" (103). Carlos never sees Paulo again.

Whereas the breakup of this trio occurs without physical injury, numerous other occasions depict the violence which accompanies scenarios of male companionship interrupted by eroticized women. Most memorable, perhaps, is the narrator's depiction of the "Manila Dance Hall," where a fight over "a tall blonde in a green dress" ends with one man clubbed by a lead pipe, and another gunned down (105–106). Violence similarly erupts in Helena, where Carlos boards with "a small Filipino called Pete" and Pete's common-law wife, Myra, "a young Mexican girl who was always flirting with the other men" (149). Myra tries to run away with one of these men, Poco. However, Pete brutally prevents her from leaving: "He dragged her to the parlor like a sack of beets, beating her with his fists when she screamed for Poco. . . . Pete pulled off Myra's shoes and started beating the soles of her feet with a baseball bat, shouting curses at her and calling her obscene names. . . . 'So you want to run away!' he kept saying. 'I will show you who is going to run away!' (150). Poco finally goes into the house—where Myra now seems resolved to remain with Pete—and starts shooting them (151). Marking another fraternal separation, the narrator and Poco's cousin leave the scene with the latter weeping, "The damn fool . . . is going to be hanged—and all for a prostitute!" (151). According to Poco's cousin, Myra is the cause of this violence rather than its victim.[14] What is lamentable in this episode, then, is not the murder of "a prostitute" but the loss of a friend and cousin, Poco. Such eroticized women emerge as expendable foes—catalysts who set into motion the real tragedy: the loss of male companionship.

Even though these women are, at best, peripheral characters, they remain crucial to the text's representation of decaying male friendships. Like the degraded America that inspires Carlos's ameliorated re-vision of the nation, these prostitutes and dance-hall girls fuel the narrator's desire for a less hostile and fragmented community that seems possible only by way of excluding their eroticized presence. Interestingly, these women take the lion's share of blame for inciting internecine sexual rivalry. For example, though Luz brings home "a Mexican woman [from] the street," she appears the instigator of brotherly dissension:

> Luz and his woman made love all night. The woman was very drunk, and she screamed and laughed alternately, depending on what they were doing. Now and then José, who was constantly cursing, threw something at them. Once Luz went to the bathroom in the hall. . . . José, seizing his opportunity, jumped into the couch where Luz's woman was waiting. I got up hurriedly and bolted the door, hoping to avoid a scene. Luz started pounding on the door, shouting threats to the woman. . . . Nick . . . opened the door. But José was already back in his bed, feigning innocence when Luz switched on the lights to see which one among us had gone to his woman. (135)

The woman, rather than Luz, embodies an offending sexuality. *Her* laughter and screams both narrate the sex act and aggravate José. When Luz returns to a closed door, he "shouts threats *to the woman*" (emphasis added), again identifying her as the affronting agent. Through such turns, the narrative assigns culpability to the woman, not only for being the embodiment of erotic need but also for inspiring a "sickening scene" of brotherly discord (135).

In the passage above, the author also sets up a series of associations linking the erotic, the unbrotherly, and the bestial. In response to the Luz-woman-José triangle, Carlos says, "I died many deaths in these surroundings, where man was indistinguishable from beast" (135). This bestial or inhuman behavior describes an atomized sense of self where each man is pitted against the other in order to claim woman as his exclusive territory—a process which makes brotherly collectives impossible. This antagonistic relationship (where women are symptomatic) contrasts the type of male friendship associated with trade unionism and progressive socialist ideas typified in Conrado, Paulo, and Carlos's fellowship. One begins to see how all-male societies in Bulosan's text emerge as precursors to labor activism, which presupposes that women do not labor. The fact that women toil as prostitutes and entertainment workers does not appear an issue over which they can bond with the properly laboring subjects of the novel, the Filipino migrant workers. Female sex workers are literally "viewed" outside (male) work settings in places such as the Manila dance hall—a leisure site which doubles as a labor site for women. Though many of the Filipino men are sexual in their dealings with these women, they nevertheless remain possible candidates for Carlos's dream of a progressive social formation. By contrast, women are depicted as the cause of brotherly dissension and not as prospective members of a social formation in which they are considered laboring subjects rather than consumable objects.

Squelching any doubts over the gendered contours of these nascent labor unions, Bulosan also portrays two women whose primary purposes are to prevent coalitions of labor. The text's portraits of Lucia Simpson and Helen underscore the inevitability of female treachery when women become active in either the trade-union movement or socialist politics. Lucia Simpson, a middle-aged American woman with an "insatiable thirst for the company of men," uses her Communist Party affiliations and her participation in the CPFR (Committee for the Protection of Filipino Rights) as a "front" with which to satisfy her "emotional demands" (290–92). Helen, posing as a labor sympathizer, seeks out José, "the ablest organizer among Filipinos in California," in order to betray their striking strategies to the police (198–203). Both women use sexual intimacy to infiltrate labor fraternities and promote their internal fragmentation. Women are not only unrecognized as labor but appear the Other of labor—the abject identity against which male labor defines itself.

The symbolic construction of woman as the Other of labor does not mean that the narrator entirely omits positive portraits of working women. The novel's glowing accounts of Marian and Carlos's mother come readily to mind as two instances which would seem to belie this construction of women outside of labor. However, I would argue that the approving portraits of these two women do not ultimately validate their heroic, laboring feats as much as their capacities for feminine self-abnegation. Marian, a prostitute who labors for Carlos, gives the narrator nearly three hundred dollars before she dies from syphilis (215, 218). She enters Carlos's life because she desires "someone to care for . . . even if it were only a dog or a cat. . . . What matters is the affection, the relationship, between you and the object" (212). The novel heralds this feminine "caring" that manifests itself in self-sacrifice (even martyrdom), as exemplified by both Marian and the narrator's mother. Carlos recalls his mother "serving [food to] my brothers and sisters" but refusing to eat herself: "She was starving herself so that her children would have something to eat" (281–82). The text lauds such feminine self-denial that appears "natural" in mothers. That is, it would seem implausible for mothers to launch an organized resistance against their children—those for whom they labor. Instead, such labor is not regarded as labor but as maternal care. Similarly the novel's emphasis on Marian's desire to "care," which clearly involves her working as a prostitute, oddly conceals the fact of her labor and thereby refrains from establishing her as a legitimate working member of organized labor. Not surprisingly, then, Marian's work as a prostitute occurs offstage, whereas her handing her money over to Carlos and her dying in the hospital (i.e., signs of her "care") are centrally played out. The female laboring subject gives way to the female nurturing subject—the all-sustaining mother who endlessly provides to the detriment of her own health.[15] Rather than being incorporated into a labor fraternity, Marian becomes sacrificed to the *narrator's* articulation and promotion of a workers' collective. One might conclude that Marian remains the sole sympathetically-depicted sex worker precisely because she subordinates herself to Carlos rather than fomenting discord among men.

In similar fashion, Carlos's mother's labor is overridden by her symbolic potential as Mother, the wellspring of brotherly bonds. However, the narrator does not efface his mother's toil wholesale. In fact, the book's emphasis on her incessant sacrifice for her family eclipses alternative portraits of Carlos's mother as a desiring subject. For example, Carlos notes his mother's fascination with the beauty and finery of the bourgeois shoppers at the Puzzorobio market. When an elegantly dressed woman stops at his mother's stall and purposely topples the beans his mother is selling, Carlos's mother scoops up the mess, saying, " 'It is all right. . . . It is all right.' " The narrator contrasts his mother's acceptance of bourgeois disdain with his own response: "I was one peasant who did not crawl on my knees and say: 'It is all right. It is all right.' " (38). His mother's contrary example acts as the medium through which Carlos renounces a backward, peasant admiration of the bourgeoisie. In addition, this portrait highlighting the mother's *nonmaternal* desires stands out as one of the few (if only) places in the novel where the narrator does not laud his mother's example.

The text, then, does not often depict Carlos's mother as she appears in Puzzorobio: a woman with her own needs and desires, emulating the bourgeoisie through her petty mercantilism. Her specificity as a female subject (which may include her longing for fine dresses to replace her rags) as well as her labor as a merchant (rather than as a caregiver) becomes textually subordinated so that she can be placed in the foreground as a symbol—Mother—whose value proceeds directly from her womb and her breast, the means by which she develops and sustains others. Thus, as the father in Bulosan's *The Laughter of My Father* states, "A woman isn't measured by the books she has read, but by the number of sons and daughters she has produced" (126). In other words, the merit of woman lies in her maternity.

In contrast to these maternal women are those eroticized females who are ignored as laborers and who seem incompatible with worker's fraternities because, unlike Marian, they do not bend to manly will. What remains bestial about these women is their thwarting Luz's, José's, or Pete's "proprietary" claims. Thus "Luz's woman" is not just "his" but "theirs" and "no one's" at the same time. In other words, improper eroticism comes to refer to sex acts that do not secure women as singular possessions.[16] One might surmise, then, that "bestial" eroticism remains so described because it implies the heterosexual male subject's dispossession. Tautologically, then, to be properly *human* guarantees the right to *hold property*, even as the ability to hold property under the law becomes evidence of one's humanity. Moreover, both physical property and what constitutes the politically proper become articulated in heterosexual erotic terms, with women mediating the connection between those two types of claims.

The distorted view of eroticized women may be a function of the sexual politics of America, by which I refer to the codes of sexual conduct that both restrict the behavior of the nation's members and regulate who counts as a citizen-subject. Unlike other Asian immigrants, Filipinos of this period were not officially considered aliens. Prior to the Tydings-McDuffie Act (1934), the United States could not restrict Filipino immigration as they had other Asian immigration, since Filipinos were deemed "nationals" moving within the vast (overseas) territories of the United States rather than foreigners moving to a different country. However, state legislatures could, and indeed did, restrict the social and sexual intermixing of Filipinos and American citizens.

The mixed blessing of "national" status comes to light in Bulosan's depiction of Carlos's shipboard journey to America as a steerage passenger. Interestingly, this incident provides one of the novel's few examples of interracial male sympathy. Pleasantly sunning himself on deck after being confined for weeks in the ship's hold, Carlos hears the outraged comments of "a young white girl wearing a brief bathing suit":

> "Look at those half-naked savages from the Philippines, Roger! Haven't they any idea of decency?"
>
> "I don't blame them for coming into the sun," the young man said. "I know how it is below."
>
> "Roger!" said the terrified girl. "Don't tell me you have been down in that horrible place? I simply can't believe it!"
>
> The man said something, but they had already turned and the wind carried it away. I was to hear that girl's voice in many ways afterward in the United States . . . an angry chorus shouting:
>
> "*Why don't they ship those monkeys back where they came from?*" (98–99)

As "nationals" but not "citizens," Carlos and his Filipino companions are constantly under the threat of being repatriated "home"—a strategy which effectively pronounces America as always already not the home of Filipinos. This illegal status, which articulates an improper *national* identity, also connotes *sexual* impropriety, even as a presumably prior sexual illicitness becomes the excuse for denied legal status. The scantily clad girl proves instrumental in splicing these lines of sexual and national impropriety. Her "terror" justifies white men's (national) armed response—they must protect her from the supposed sexual menace of Filipino men. However, Bulosan portrays Roger's unexpected sympathy with the Filipino men whose situation he "understand[s]." The narrative suggests that all Rogers have experienced some form of imprisonment, whether literal or metaphoric, and on that level can empathize with enslaved men of all races. Preventing men's "natural" sympathy, then, is this woman who holds up the specter of "unnatural" sexuality—interracial couplings that by great ideological effort imply cross-species couplings.

The girl's description of Filipinos as "monkeys" provides the keystone to this ideological work. Their supposed beastlike status would render Filipino-white intercourse a form of sexual border crossing that must be regulated by national laws. A syllogistic logic is at work here: only decent human beings can become national citizens and, conversely, national legitimacy affirms one's humanity (as well as sexual propriety). Not surprisingly, then, the construction of Filipinos as non-Americans involves antimiscegenation laws that deny Filipinos both a proper sexuality and *human* subjectivity, characterizing them as beasts whose coupling with Americans would be sexually and socially unnatural. Thus, a 1933 article in the *California Law Review* quotes a popular claim of antimiscegenation proponents that mixed intercourse results in " 'unnatural amalgamations productive of sickly and effeminate offspring' " (W.I.C., 117). Constructing effeminacy as a disease, the very language of such arguments reveals the core misogyny also at work in antimiscegenation laws.

In *Roldan v. L.A. County*, to which the novel refers, Salvador Roldan challenged the application of existent antimiscegenation laws to his own prospective marriage to a white woman. In 1933, a Superior Court upheld the legality of this proposed union, ruling that Filipinos—as Malays—were of a separate category from Mongolians, Negroes, or Mulattoes, who were the stated races forbidden intermarriage with whites. The California State Assembly responded to the Superior Court decision by amending the Civil Code on April 21, 1933, "to include Malayans among those who could not contract marriages with white women" (Cordova, 117). Antimiscegenation laws were overturned in *Perez v. Lippold* (1948), where they were deemed unconstitutional; however, such laws remained part of the Civil Code for ten more years, with California legislators withstanding "four attempts to have the law formally repealed" ("Anti-Miscegenation Laws," 65).

While purporting to preserve a *human* Order against the threat of bestial contamination, such antimiscegenation laws have in view a *national* Order limited to the Caucasian race (as well as a gendered order, as revealed by the bans on effeminacy). Thus, U.S. laws both withholding American citizenship from Filipinos and preventing Filipino men's sexual mixing with white women work toward the same end: to exclude Filipinos from properly belonging to the body politic. Economic motives clearly underwrite denied citizenship. As Colleen Lye remarks with regard to more recent debates over illegal immigration, "[T]he generation of [capitalism's] extraordinary surplus value derives precisely from the illegalization of a large sector of this country's labor demand" (Lye, 52). That is, only citizens have a right to draw upon the nation's resources; thus laborers who are noncitizens massively contribute to national productivity precisely by exacting little in return for their labor.[17] Antimiscegenation laws also keep Filipino laborers from acquiring citizenship. Yet they do so by revoking the national rights of American women. Takaki notes that the federal district director of naturalization proposed that "American women marrying Filipinos would lose their U.S. citizenship" (Takaki, 342). In their capacity as childbearers, women become tantamount to the nation's border police.[18] If they produce interracial, "monstrous" children, then they have failed to protect the nation's racial boundaries and, therefore, are not worthy of remaining citizens.

Highly significant, then, is the narrator's designation of nonerotic, maternal women as "undeniably the *America* I had wanted to find" (235). This description refers to Eileen Odell, who embodies an "America [which] was human, good, and real" (235). Her "almost *maternal* solicitude" (234; emphasis added) mirrors the kind regard of other female faces of the nation: Miss Mary Strandon, Doris Travers, Alice Odell, and the aforementioned

Marian. Two young girls also hold a strictly platonic relationship to the narrator and are also remembered with reverence: Judith, a young girl in Buelton who lends Carlos her books (173), and Mary, who lives with Carlos and his companions and becomes "the delicate object of our affections. She was an angel molded into purity by the cleanliness of our thoughts" (301). Excepting Marian, all of these women remain distinctly nonsexual—a quality that indirectly affirms their national status. By being sexually unavailable to the narrator, these women remain official American citizens. By contrast, the various white women in the novel who *have* married Filipino men—the woman who enters a Holtville restaurant accompanied by her Filipino husband and child (144), and Macario's roommate's bride, whom the narrator characterizes as "old enough to be his mother" (131)—are not hailed by Carlos as "the America I had wanted to find."

Only proper American women (i.e., legal citizens) emerge as the face of the nation. Their legal status, however, is not the sole reason why Carlos identifies them as the America he has been seeking. Part of their appeal lies in their speaking an American inclusiveness that remains synonymous with the narrator's dream of brotherhood. Like Marian, then, these women in their "maternal solicitude" underscore the primacy of the male subject and the importance of his forging brotherly bonds with other men. As Jonathan Goldberg in another context suggests, within homosocial communities "women are predictably enshrined as The Mother, a 'trope of ideal femininity, a fantasmatic female that secures male-male arrangements and an all male history' " (Parker et al., quoting Goldberg, 6).[19] The narrator's reverent accounts of his mother's great sacrifice reverberate with a nostalgia for the way that she recalls to the narrator his indisputable fraternal relations—that is, she unites Carlos, Macario, Leon, Luciano, and Amado via her single womb. Her name, in fact, becomes a code word through which brothers renew their fraternal connections. Brother Amado, who, after his years in America, doesn't recognize Carlos, asks his younger sibling for their mother's name: "to [Amado], and to me afterward, to know my mother's name [Meteria] was to know the password into the secrets of the past [and] it was also a guiding star, a talisman, a charm that lights us to manhood and decency" (123). The siblings' blood bond through Meteria's body secures the two men in their future "manhood and decency." She therefore acts as an inspiration, a channeling mechanism or "charm," that enables the remembering of brotherhood.

As surrogate mothers, Mary Strandon, Doris Travers, Marian, Alice and Eileen Odell likewise remind Carlos of his extended brotherhood with men of all races. Introducing him to a world of books, these women encourage his intellectual affiliation with (male) authors who share his vision of cross-racial tolerance. Though instrumental in nurturing his literary aspirations, these women, like Meteria, function as passageways through which the narrator discovers a socialist politics that prizes men as its proper subjects.

Carlos's casting America's "kindness" in the bodies of women would seem to belie the nation as a gender-exclusive brotherhood. However, the mere presence of women does not contradict the thesis of Carlos's "America" as an all-male collective. In fact, more persuasive (because harder to unravel) is the specter of women speaking male privilege, advocating political agendas set by men, and inadvertently securing brotherly bonds even as they remain marginal to that bonding.

The narrator's description of Alice Odell illustrates the elision of women's issues even when the category of Woman takes center stage. Carlos interprets Alice's intention behind her writing her autobiography:

> She wanted to say that she had been made stronger and more courageous; that she was *not like other women* who are afraid to break through the walls of prejudice. But although she felt that way about other women, Alice believed in their essential dignity, because she herself had it, so simply, so strongly.
>
> This, I believe now, was what she actually wanted to say. (231; emphasis added)

The narrator recovers Alice from her condemnatory statement with regard to "other women" by interpolating "what she actually wanted to say" but didn't. In fact, the narrator emerges the hero of women, asserting "their essential dignity" against what might be construed as Alice's misogynist words (she implies that women, in general, are a prejudiced lot). The gauge of women's dignified or undignified nature, however, is the degree to which they exhibit racial prejudice. Heralding women, then, becomes tantamount, not to antisexist work but rather to finding in the *essence of woman* this impulse toward cross-racial tolerance.[20] Thus, in the passage above, Carlos hails woman, not to address her circumscription by patriarchy but to applaud a cross-racial tolerance that she embodies.

If women are subordinate members of a community—not the Subjects of society but only the vehicle across which proper male Subjects bond—their presence in fact mediates the community as an all-male collective.[21] Ironically, the Filipino immigrants of Bulosan's text suffer a similar subordination to America's all-white community, yet the novel depicts their fight for more than nominal inclusion in the nation. Part of that struggle involves exposing the United States' racial bias. In parallel fashion, part of the fight against gender oppression involves illuminating the male exclusivity implicit in the "America of Carlos's heart." Carlos can assert his brotherly formation as a free and equal society only by considering men as the "proper" subjects and rendering antisexist work irrelevant. Moreover, those claims that "rank" racial oppression over gender oppression (instead of conceding their equally important though uneven effects) remain unable to acknowledge their privileging of the male subject in much the same way that racist discourse does not see itself as racist but as merely focused upon its "proper" (i.e., most important) subject: white people.

Though the novel exposes the falsity of America's egalitarian rhetoric by pointing out the United States' exclusion and active persecution of Filipinos, Mexicans, Indians, and African Americans, it perpetuates a similar (gender-based) exclusion in its imagining of an alternate community. Thus Macario's speech, which perhaps most clearly limns Carlos's replacement "America," defines the nation as a community of men:

> "It is but fair to say that America is not a land of one race or one class of *men*. We are all Americans that have toiled and suffered and known oppression and defeat, from the first Indian that offered peace in Manhattan to the last Filipino pea pickers. America is not bound by geographical latitudes. America is not merely a land or institution. America is in the hearts of *men* that died for freedom; it is also in the eyes of *men* that are building a new world. America is a prophecy of *a new society of men*: of a system that knows no sorrow or strife or suffering. America is a warning to those who would try to falsify the ideals of *freemen*.
>
> "America is also the nameless foreigner, the homeless refugee, the hungry boy begging for a job and the black body dangling on a tree. . . . All of us, from the first *Adams* to the last Filipino, native born or alien, educated or illiterate—*We are America*!" (189, emphases added)

One might excuse the heavily gendered language as a convention of the times; however, such a dismissal would overlook the productive contradictions between the masculinist bias of this vision of national community and the nation as embodied in the essence of woman. Moreover, one might assert that this masculinist bias is most evident, not in the gendered language but in the construction of masculine enterprise as work and in the simultaneous omission of working women from Bulosan's catalog of laboring "Americans." The Filipino pea picker, the Indian peacemaker, the lynched black man, the impoverished boy looking for a job, and even the illiterate man with writerly aspirations are all exclusively male members of the narrator's newly proclaimed society. Seeming to embrace all readers in its use of the first-person plural, the last sentence proclaiming "*We are America*" leaves women out of its introductory clause, wherein "us" is delimited to the first "Adams" through the last Filipin*o*, with the masculine declension quite significant here. Overlooked by Macario are the Mexican prostitutes and the white girls in the dance hall, who remain glaringly absent because of their overwhelming presence in the rest of the novel. Women who labor in the sex trade, as well as women who labor in public service, domestic households, skilled trades, or industry, are specifically not included in the "We" of working men who can claim national legitimacy.

Interestingly, the passage above appears verbatim in Bulosan's previously published "Letter to a Filipino Woman," written upon the unverified report of Salvador P. Lopez's death at the hands of Japanese occupation forces.[22] Thus, Macario's speech, excerpted from the "Letter," originally spoke to the context of World War II and, specifically, the Japanese occupation of the Philippines. The author's reprinting these sections as words from a journal editor who was concerned with the labor movement in America circa 1934 suggests that Bulosan was trying to speak to various terrains of struggle through an overarching notion of "the battle for democracy." For instance, in the "Letter" he likens Lopez's heroism in the Philippines to his own efforts to build "a new America. Whatever we are doing, we are all working toward a democratic society" (Bulosan 1943, 646). This incorporating of various resistance movements under the vast umbrella of democracy bespeaks Bulosan's universalizing vision that oftentimes occludes the specificities and differences among various political movements. In this respect, Bulosan was not unlike his contemporaries in the American literary radicalism movement, who conjoined their support of the working class with the battle against fascism (Rabinowitz, 19).[23]

In the original letter, Bulosan furthermore drapes feminine symbolism over the exclusively male contents of America in order to give the appearance of gender inclusiveness. The epistle to the widow Lopez, though specifically addressed to a woman, details Salvadore Lopez's and Bulosan's own heroic struggles against fascism in both the Philippines and in the United States. In the only section that focuses upon Mrs. Lopez, the author imagines her "frail, childlike body, hiding in dangerous mountains"—an image designed to "inspire continued resistance against the enemy" (Bulosan 1943, 645). Mrs. Lopez, in other words, is to inspire resistance fighters, as she has inspired the narrator to write his own narrative of resistance.

A similar letter to a Filipino woman acts as a stylistic device in *America Is in the Heart* . While recovering from lung surgery, the narrator befriends a young boy named John Custer who requests Carlos to write a letter to his mother in Arkansas:

> I started writing to an American mother in Arkansas. She had never heard of me, and I had never seen her, but her son was a common bond between us. I was writing to her what I had had in my mind and heart for years. The words came effortlessly. I was no longer writing about this lonely sick boy, but about myself and my friends in America. I told her about the lean, the lonely and miserable years. I mentioned places and names. I was not writing to an unknown mother any more. I was writing to my own mother plowing in the muddy fields of Mangusmana: it was the one letter I should have written before. I was telling her about America. Actually, I was writing to all the unhappy mothers whose sons left and did not return. (247)

The similarities between the letter's contents (the lean, lonely years; the recording of places and names) and the novel's own narrative details suggest that the first person testimony in *America Is in the Heart* is, in itself, a letter to Carlos's mother. That the American vision he forges may implicitly exclude her (by virtue of her gender) becomes mitigated by the fact that he writes this narrative of "America" on her behalf. Moreover, the mother figure becomes a way for Carlos to conceive of a fraternal community across racial lines (e.g., writing to a mother in Arkansas is writing to his own mother—hence the white boy in the hospital and Carlos are symbolic brothers). Thus, women become incorporated into the narrator's American revisions as inspirational muses and epistolary addresses.

In his analysis of Bulosan's novel, E. San Juan Jr. pinpoints women's inspirational function, attributing to them "the creative principle of the imagination" (San Juan 1972, 95). Though seeming to assign women a positive valence, San Juan oddly distinguishes their merit through effacing the feminine:

> [The creative principle of the imagination] is embodied by a cluster of sponsoring Muse figures: the mother, Marian, Mary and other female models of selfless devotion, solicitude, understanding. They represent the collective democratizing principle of self-fulfillment through the exercise of one's generative powers, the free creative imagination. Innumerable scenes can be adduced to prove the compelling nature of *this urge to sympathize or collaborate with other men*. This force finally directs Bulosan to a reasoned affirmation of the people, the working masses, as the heroic protagonists of his own personalized annals. (San Juan 1972, 95; emphasis added)

These female models represent a democratizing principle, also synonymous with the "urge to sympathize . . . with other men." This passage elides the feminine, directing the reader to perceive "generative power" in manly collaboration (rather than in female reproduction). The paragraph only evokes reproductive capacity in order to denude it of female agency. Thus the passage progresses: female muse figures symbolize a democratizing principle that the male subjects of the novel enact; the latter's formation of a brotherhood of men, also synonymous with "the people," becomes the proper subject of Bulosan's text. Once again, men compose the people—the subject—with woman as a vague principle lying somewhere beneath the text.

San Juan's attempt to reinscribe the feminine as imaginative principle largely falters because of the problems of relegating women to a principle rather than pursuing them as self-sustaining subjects. Perhaps unwittingly, San Juan's reading follows closely Bulosan's own subordination of female subjects, overtly celebrating women in order to disguise their underlying expendability. Thus, the eschewing of sexualized women but platonic embrace of "decent white women" in Bulosan's text allows for purposely conflicted readings of the narrator's relation to women: his kind regard toward maternal figures seems to mitigate the virulent portraits of nondecent women. The narrator's reverence for Eileen, Alice, Marian, and Mary

Strandon also legitimates Carlos's sexuality on two accounts: it assures the audience of the hero's heterosexual preference and it attests to his ability to transcend the sexual "beastliness" ascribed to Filipino men.

A nationally enforced abstinence, resulting from antimiscegenation laws and disparate sex ratios between Filipino men and women, may partially account for Bulosan's occlusion of sex workers from his brotherhood of labor. The Filipino workers seem unable to acknowledge the prostitute or dance-hall girl without somehow being both attracted and repulsed by her sexuality. In order not to be viewed as "unmanly" (read asexual or homosexual), Carlos constructs only one dynamic between the male subject and the sex worker—one in which the virile heterosexual man, desiring the eroticized woman, contracts for her services and figuratively "consumes" her.[24] The nonsexual regard perhaps necessary to viewing sex workers as laboring subjects is made less tenable by antimiscegenation laws, disproportionate sex ratios, and heterosexual mandates. All three factors overdetermine the interaction between laboring men and female sex workers, so that dominance rather than coalition frames their social intercourse.

While national directives on sexuality may underlie Bulosan's textual subordination of women as laboring subjects, it may also be the case that this cross-racial, egalitarian brotherhood (of labor) is secured by the objectification of women. In essence, I am proposing to read the U.S. history of antimiscegenation laws and ideologies of male privilege as overlapping and partial explanatory grids rather than as totalizing metanarratives. This supplementary methodology would propose, then, that the objectification of women results from male supremacist ideological work that is also evident but not wholly contained within U.S. antimiscegenation laws.

Carlos desires a homosocial community of male-to-male links, not across power differentials but across power commensurabilities. However, such power commensurabilities are made possible by the distinguishing power differential between women and men. The free male subjects of this imagined community exist in nonhierarchical relations to each other by virtue of their shared gender privilege. America's classless society, then, is not one in which all men are similarly *dispossessed* but one in which each man has equal opportunity to claim "America" as his own. Thus Filipino men, black men, Mexican men, Indian men, white men are all part of Carlos's "America in the heart," in that they are all allowed to hold America as property and are all permitted to hold American women "properly."

The platform of the Committee for the Protection of Filipino Rights reveals the way in which recuperated property and recovered claims upon women form the basis of Carlos's more inclusive vision of America. The narrator lists "ten important points" that articulate a "broad generalization of [Filipinos'] difficulties in California":

"How come we Filipinos in California can't buy or lease real estate?" . . .

"Why are we denied civil service jobs?" . . .

"Why can't we marry women of the Caucasian race? And why are we not allowed to marry in this state?"

"Why can't we practice law?"

"Why are we denied the right of becoming naturalized American citizens?"

"Why are we discriminated against in relief agencies?"

"Why are we denied better housing conditions?"

"Why can't we stop the police from handling us like criminals?"

"Why are we denied recreational facilities in public parks and other such places?" (268–69)

The first six points are interesting for their mapping the overlapping terrains of national legal residence, property, and matrimonial rights. Implicit in these ten questions is the presumption that if Filipinos—as American "nationals"—are part of the body politic (explicitly not "foreigners"), they should not be denied the most saliently identifiable signs of national legitimacy: the license to own property, marry American women, serve the country in civil sector jobs, write laws, and become citizens. (The last four points identify other signs of national legitimacy, primarily the ability to claim government assistance and not be harassed by state agencies.) National identity would seem to imply the immanence of national rights. Yet while these entitlements seem to be neutral and objective (e.g., the natural rights of freemen), they represent a set of exclusive privileges reserved for a specific racial and gendered group. The ability to buy real estate, occupy civil service jobs, practice law, and so forth, are not the rights of black, Mexican, Indian, or Malay men but implicitly the rights of white men. To what extent, then, do these ten points express the desire for a joint ownership in whiteness?[25] The appeal of these ten points proceeds in part from their exclusiveness: attaining such rights would be tantamount to belonging to America's privileged racial group. The discourse of national rights, then, masks to a certain degree the way in which the above claims are racialized as well as gendered.

Question three, for instance, implicitly posits a male subject whose constitutional prerogative to marry a Caucasian woman has been abridged. If attaining a Caucasian woman as one's legal spouse is a sign of national inclusion, then women are not the subjects of citizenship but merely the measure of it. One might pose, then, some correlative questions to the one above: to what extent does attaining the aforementioned privileges reestablish men's rights over women? Does a joint ownership in whiteness presume upon or have its foundation in a shared male privilege?

It might be useful here to recall the claim of antimiscegenation proponents that mixed unions result in "unnatural amalgamations productive of sickly and effeminate offspring." As previously stated, such national man-dates—under the guise of preserving a human Order—construct specific racial identities (Negro, Mongolian, Mulatto, and Malay) as inhuman, bes-tial, and alien (or nonnational). From this prohibition, one can also see that a specific gendered identity—that of the effeminate or feminine—is also constructed as diseased, unnatural, and implicitly undesirable in the nation (hence the need for antimiscegenation laws to prevent the germination of such a population). In the production of national identity, then, certain bodies are marked as alien—what should be excluded from the nation in order to protect the purity of its citizenry. Such rhetoric allows for the denial of certain "rights" or privileges to those alien bodies, thereby en-abling their exploitation as cheap labor to the (material) benefit of those defined as the nation's proper citizens.[26] By focusing on these Others, the nation avoids looking at its own race and gender, seeing itself in "neutral," "natural," and "national" terms. One must scrutinize, then, the way in which the debate over "national" entitlements obscures the way in which civil liberties are granted only to those people who qualify as subjects on the basis of race and gender.

As the "ten points" also make clear, if one is devoted to the cause of Filipino rights, one is in a sense arguing for the same opportunities to achieve possessive individualism as has every other white male citizen. This "end" remains at odds with the narrator's socialist politics, which eschews the processes of objectification and ownership. A tension thus develops between a politics aimed at attaining American citizenship and property for Filipinos and a politics of international socialism working toward a global collective of labor. By the end of the novel, then, there is a split in brotherly causes: Macario goes to fight for a global collective of antifascist peoples, while Carlos stays in America. The discontinuities among broth-erly commitments would seem to shift the novel's focus from a national to a global arena. That is, one can chart the novel's progression in terms of Carlos's developing socialist consciousness: he begins looking to reunite his family, then widens his vision to work toward an American society of cross-racial tolerance, and then—after discovering labor activism as well as progressive literature—he commits himself to the struggle of laboring men all over the world. From imagining first his family, then America, as the embodiments of fraternal good will, the narrator discovers the many different geographies upon which laboring men resist capitalist exploita-tion (also vaguely conflated with fascism or fascist politics). Brotherhood inhabits the globe, rather than a single nation. Yet even as Carlos's class consciousness exceeds national boundaries, the novel insists on embracing the nation in its final pages, thus redrawing the book's patriotic outline.

How does one account for this resolution? Several critics have suggested that the resurgence of nationalism during World War II, the time of the novel's publication, proved favorable to an American-faithful ending.[27] The context of the war transmuted the socialist politics of other works by Bulosan in this period. For instance, Bulosan authored the text for "Freedom from Want"—one of Roosevelt's four freedoms that were collectively designed to explain the reasons behind America's military engagement. There, Bulosan defines "freedom from want" as the right of laborers to use what they produce—in effect offering a socialist interpretation of "freedom"; however, Norman Rockwell's accompanying portrait of a grandfather carving a turkey at an abundantly laid table distorts Bulosan's attempt at making socialist politics a national (and international) cause. Instead, Rockwell's portrait implicitly portrays America's national family as a white, upper-middle-class family. It is this scenario and this family for whom the boys abroad fight and for whom the workers of Bulosan's accompanying text (as well as the author himself) are made to labor.

While taking into account the wartime context of the book's publication, I would also argue that this retrenchment back into nationalist discourse must be placed within the context of the brotherly dynamic symptomatic of the rest of the novel. The concluding two chapters repeat the structure of the first chapter, where brotherly farewells lead to fraternal remembrance. Having just received advance copies of his first book of poetry, the narrator wishes to celebrate with his brother Amado, whom he discovers in a bar drinking with two girls. One of the girls mocks the book of poems and tears out its pages. Amado defends his brother's literary feat by clobbering the girl (321). No longer in the mood to celebrate, Carlos leaves his brother in the bar with his female companions. Shortly after this incident, Amado enlists in the army and says a final good-bye to his brother. At that time, he asks Carlos to give a dime to the Negro bootblack whom he has forgotten to pay. Upon receiving the payment, the bootblack tells Carlos: " 'I'm joining the navy tomorrow, so I guess this is good-bye. I know I'll meet your brother again somewhere because I got my dime without asking him. But if I don't see him again, I'll remember him every time I see the face of an American dime. Good-bye, friend!' " (325). The bootblack speaks about the possibility of a reunion with Amado even as he dismisses the need for actual contact because of the way he will recall Amado in the face of an American coin. In this episode, which testifies to a more inclusive, cross-racial fraternity, the Negro bootblack becomes the last figurative brother to whom Carlos says good-bye. The penultimate chapter thus ends with the narrator walking to his hotel "filled with great loneliness" (325).

The plot sequence complete, the concluding two pages act as the book's epilogue, proclaiming the narrator's indestructible faith in America:

[T]he American earth was like a huge heart unfolding warmly to receive me. I felt it spreading through my being, warming me with its glowing reality. It came to me that no man—no one at all—could destroy my faith in America again. It

was something that had grown out of my defeats and successes, something shaped
by my struggles for a place in this vast land, digging my hands into the rich soil
here and there. . . . It was something that grew out of the sacrifices and loneliness
. . . out of our desire to know America, and to become a part of *her* great tradition,
and to contribute something toward *her* final fulfillment. I knew that no man
could destroy my faith in America that had sprung from all our hopes and aspirations, *ever*. (326–27; emphasis on the word *her*, added)

The face of the America landscape—akin to the face of an American
dime—holds the promise of a warm embrace, imagined here as a female
embrace but which in keeping with the rest of the novel would be more
appropriately identified as that feminine spirit synonymous with the "urge
to sympathize . . . with other men." Like the bootblack, Carlos renounces
the need to reunite physically with his departed siblings because of his
having this symbolic representation of their brotherly love. America is thus
embraced within the final pages of the book to counterbalance the finality
of fraternal separations in the preceding chapter. The patriotic emphasis
of the novel's finale can therefore be less dramatically interpreted as a re-
framing of brotherly commitment in the many vistas of America—its soil,
its currency, its national symbols—precisely because fraternity is moving
beyond national confines.

The overt national discourse of this final proclamation again obscures
the gendered exclusivity implicit in the vision to which Carlos remains
faithful. Because America is evoked as a "her"—feminine symbol of male
homosocial networks—love of country conceals the narrator's "ever"-last-
ing attendance to an all-male collective. Taken together, the last two chapters depict brotherly bonds pressured by women even as familial links give
way to more universal, though no less fraternal, devotions. Both scandalous
and maternal female figures inspire the novel's conclusion, with women
again mediating the narrator's portrait of prospective male community.

The final irony of this steadfast commitment to brotherhood may lie
precisely in the transhistorical, gendered bridge it imaginatively creates
between men of all races, even those formally situated in a colonizer/colo-
nized relationship. Drawing upon popular socialist terminology circulating
in the thirties, Bulosan's narrator astutely echoes as well as transforms
tropes of brotherhood and fraternity to make labor organizations recognize
racism within their own ranks. Yet the delay in publication until 1943
meant that this sentiment in the novel was received at a time when all-male
alliances evoked not so much the unity of labor but more readily the ranks
of enlisted soldiers from several different countries that militarized in solidarity. The war machinery is, of course, deeply gendered and nationalistic.
Bulosan's emphasis on homosocial alliances, while written in a socialist
spirit, nonetheless tapped into a powerful U.S. mythos of masculinized,
military patriotism to which the author may have been ideologically op-

posed (especially as that masculine military nationalism took shape in the "taking" of the Philippines). Somewhat contradictorily, then, Bulosan's protagonist embraces an idealistic brotherhood between brown and white, rather than shattering this sibling discourse in order to denounce the dominant familial ideology that figures the U.S.'s foreign intrusion into the Philippines as the benevolent acts of an older sibling. One has to wait until the rise of postcolonial nationalisms and, correlatively, Jessica Hagedorn's quoting verbatim of McKinley's rationalization for colonizing the islands, to see the near absence of family feelings in the decision to invade and "enlighten." Carlos is, thus, poised between wanting somewhat "extravagantly"[28] a homosociality that doesn't exploit or terrorize, and necessarily exposing brotherhood as an ideology that conveniently obfuscates the United States' role as both invader and expeller. It may come as an odd revelation that Carlos, while being driven by necessitous conditions throughout his narrated life, chooses to believe in a fraternal balm.

• • •

Like America's soil and her dimes, Bulosan's novel stages itself as another national symbol that represents the continuity of brotherhood. From a sentiment of loss, of brotherhoods rapidly disappearing, the novel moves into a sentiment of desire—with its positive and perhaps compensatory response toward absence or loss. Brotherhoods symbolically beckon in the warming embrace of the land, rather than being sought in a physical reunion between Carlos and his brothers. From viewing America as continually escaping his reach, the narrator articulates a degree of certainty by novel's end concerning the type of national democratic society that will emerge in the future, perhaps even after the narrator's own death. Thus, instead of seeing organic unities becoming foregone, Carlos asserts that a fraternal goodwill *will be realized* in America—a goodwill that imitates his own affiliating spirit toward the nation and its various members.

Such goodwill, however, does not extend to the female subjects of the novel. Significantly, women do not appear as (laboring) Subjects in this ideal brotherhood but only as the symbol for the generative spirit in man or as the erotic object at the heart of fraternal divisions. Women also remain essential to the novel's portrait of potential homologies as well as incongruities among the multiple (familial, national, transnational) levels of brotherhood. Maternal figures become vehicles through which the narrator can claim "brothers" across these communities. By contrast, sexualized women who exceed male property claims become markers of the hierarchy between communities and of inviolate racial difference. Thus, women in their maternal aspect encourage a homology among levels of brotherhood; women in their sexual capacities express and maintain the boundaries between these levels of brotherhood.

The rearticulation of brotherhood in national terms, moreover, masks the gendered bias in Carlos's model society. Though America can be conceived as a great "she" to whom the narrator is devoted, his final embrace of the nation only confirms the inevitability of homosocial bonds. From one perspective then, the text's problem with women arises from its striving for wholeness based on a paradigm of brotherhood and by its inadequate framework of a society that can cope with difference (of which gender is just one type). Looking for a "common denominator on which we could all meet" (147), Carlos laments the divisions across which sectors of society separate as he similarly decries the disintegration of manly companionship across the bodies of woman. However, those divisions across which various communities separate are necessary to articulate distinct political agendas, and in that function they remain desirable even as the narrator finds them lamentable. Instead of seeking the nation in homogeneous terms, perhaps the task is to mine the heterogeneity of identities in any collective and *not* to privilege certain identities over others by the very denial of their differences.

CHAPTER TWO

Gish Jen and the Gendered Codes
of Americanness

GISH JEN's *Typical American* chronicles the adventures of a Chinese American immigrant, Ralph Chang, and his family in the United States. With its opening line, "It's an American story," the novel both characterizes the Chang family as part of U.S. history and alludes to the ways in which national narratives are to inscribe the Changs (3). On the one hand, Jen emphasizes the timelessness of national myths that represent Americanness to these immigrants. Drawing upon a hodgepodge of eighteenth- and nineteenth-century literary references, Ralph Chang emulates Benjamin Franklin, believes in Emersonian Romantic individualism, encounters a Melvillian confidence man, and lives a rags-to-riches life made familiar by Horatio Alger. On the other hand, the Changs' path toward Americanization remains very much bound to the particular historical period that the family experiences first hand—the Cold War era of suburbanization, acquisitive individualism, coercive conformism, and *Leave It to Beaver* family idealism.

During the fifties and early sixties, in which the preponderance of Jen's novel is set, metaphors of brotherhood and sibling alliances have been displaced by that of the male-headed household (e.g., the *Father Knows Best* family) as the favored trope of kinship and, by extension, social organization. Instead of starting out with fraternity as an originary, wholesome state or as an image of egalitarian horizontal alliance to which one must both aspire and return, Jen conjures up a vertical and heterosexually configured family structure where gender and generation determines one's hierarchical standing in this social unit.[1] The distinct gendered and sexual dynamics of the fictional Chang family are very much a reflection of changes in immigration laws during and after World War II, when the United States passed a series of acts that ended bans against female Asian immigration and thus allowed for a greater degree of Asian family formation on American grounds. Placing the immigrant, middle-class family—rather than the male proletariat—at the center of her narrative, Jen takes on American myths of equality and economic abundance, not by proposing an alternative labor-based, socialist vision of what America could be, but rather, her parodic series of tales detail the distortions to a particular immigrant family as they remake themselves into typical (petty capitalist, heterosexual) Americans. It is through their earnest and sometimes manic aping of American bourgeois codes of social ascent that Jen exposes the violences underlying "the American Dream," specifically the progress narrative of limitless expansion that lies at its core. Importantly, this exposure of America's mythical superabundance takes on the form of a gendered critique, with women's bodies and perspectives instrumental to Jen's depiction of what is trampled upon and suppressed in the pursuit of self- and economic limitlessness.

After rehearsing postwar changes in U.S. immigration laws that significantly alter the gendered and sexual organization of Asian arrivals, I examine Jen's strategy of parodic imitation, through which the narrative leaves ambiguous whether the Changs are the "typical Americans" named in the title or merely imitative of typical American behavior. Throughout my examination, I pay close attention to the novel's negotiation of two political agendas, an exposure of America's exclusion of Asians as a group and the revelation of violence within the Asian American household. By detailing rifts internal to the Chang family, Jen underscores issues of gender subordination and heterosexism at the same time that she details the racial barriers that deter the Changs' efforts to become American. I propose, therefore, to read the novel's performative send-ups of "typical American" behavior with an eye toward the novel's simultaneous deconstructions of national (U.S.) mythology and of an idealistic imagining of the immigrant family and home.

ATYPICAL AMERICAN?

During the period in which *Typical American* is set (c. 1947–1965), changes in U.S. immigration laws radically transformed the gendered and economic composition of Asian American communities. With the onset of World War II, the United States looked to Asian nations, not just as a source and scourge of cheap labor, but as strategic military sites and potential allies in, first, the war against the Axis powers, Japan in particular, and, second, the Cold War between communist Russia and capitalist America. As early as 1943, U.S. immigration policies toward the Chinese reflected this shift toward international alliance, when Congress passed the Chinese Repealer, ending prior exclusion laws and allowing Chinese to naturalize and become citizens.[2] Also marking a distinct change in immigration policy, the United States subtly allowed for family formation by granting "nonquota immigration status to Chinese wives of citizens [thus reversing] the long-standing practice of excluding Chinese women. . . . Now citizens could petition for their spouses to come join them and form families" (Hing, 36). Filipinos and Indians were extended similar immigration and citizenship opportunities, as well as the extension of nonquota status for spouses and children, in 1946 (Hing, 36–37).[3] Such policy changes clearly affected the character of Asian immigration in the postwar period: Chinese, Filipinos, and Indians might settle permanently in the United States, become legal citizens, and establish families on this side of the Pacific.

In addition to these policy changes producing shifts in the gendered and temporal character of immigrant communities, Congress eventually approved, in 1965, several preference categories that favored immigrants of a more privileged economic strata, namely professionals and foreign nationals with capital to invest in the United States (Hing, 40–41). However, even before the 1965 amendments were enacted, global political events and Cold War politics created a category of political refugees that enabled some five thousand Chinese college and graduate students, predominantly from the upper and middle classes, to seek asylum in the States. When communist forces toppled the nationalist Chinese government, "some of China's brightest intellectuals, most of them from well-to-do families [were allowed] to remain in the country" (Chan, 141). According to Sucheng Chan, "these men and women sought work in universities, research laboratories, and private industries, bought homes in the suburbs, and had little to do with the old-time Chinese immigrants except for occasional meals in and shopping trips to various Chinatowns in America (Chan, 141). It is this more economically privileged and educated strata of Asian America upon whom Jen focuses her readers' attention.

Because of this new immigrant group's lack of association with the "old-time Chinese immigrants," one might expect Jen's novel to offer an entirely different kind of narrative than that produced in "classic" Asian American literature such as Bulosan's depiction of Filipino migrant laborers or Maxine Hong Kingston's account of the backbreaking work done by her ancestors on the sugar plantations and railroads. These latter texts emphasize the century-old presence of manual Asian labor in the United States, a history that implicitly argues for subsequent generations' rightful place in America, despite being perpetually assigned the status of "foreigner" (see my later discussion in chapter 4). Jen's novel shares the impetus to establish Asian Americans' rightful place on American soil, but rather than establishing that claim by highlighting the instrumentality of Asian labor to U.S. industry and agribusiness, Jen emphasizes how culturally alike the middle-class Changs are to "typical Americans." By portraying the Changs' embodying the tenets of American character—especially as mythologized in the national literature—the narrative suggests that the Changs would be considered all-Americans if not for the color of their skin. *Typical American,* in short, does not testify to the rightful place of Asians in American history by virtue of their collective labor as much as it exposes the racial bias of American cultural scripts.

From the outset, then, Jen's audience observes the Changs' reiteration of the contents of American classics. For instance, the narrative introduces

Ralph producing his own versions of canonical American literature, such as Ben Franklin's *Autobiography*. As Franklin sets down thirteen "Virtues" in order to acquire their "Habitude," so Ralph designs a list of aims, the first item of which encompasses Franklin's whole project: "1. I will cultivate virtue" (6). Not only does Ralph twice mention resolutions to refrain from overeating, echoing Franklin's number one priority—"Temperance. Eat not to Dulness. Drink not to Elevation"—he also vows chastity and promptly breaks that vow as has this founding father (Franklin, 464, 452). Franklin furthermore drew his list of virtues from his own reading, rendering Ralph's imitation of a literary imitation a copy of a copy.

Through such exponential mimicry, Jen stresses the Changs' duplicating not the unique persona of Franklin but more widespread scripts of behavior labeled "American." That slip from imitating an individual to parodying a whole set of representative characteristics becomes clear upon Ralph, Helen, and Theresa's aping of their delinquent building superintendent, Pete:

> Ralph took to imitating Pete's walk. He'd slump, a finger cleaning his ear, only to have Theresa gamely cry out, "*No, no like this,*" and add a shuffle. . . . They studied the way Pete blew his nose . . . the self-important way he flipped through his calendar. "Well, now, let me have some look-see," growled Theresa. "Typical Pete!" Ralph roared in approval. . . . And pretty soon, no one knew quite how, "typical Pete" turned "typical American." (66–67)[4]

Pete is not individually important, only exemplary of a broader behavior pattern. By reverse logic, the Changs, mimicking "typical American" codes, might also be supposed indistinct in their adoption of representative Americanness. However, throughout the novel, Jen pursues the idea that the Changs are not representative national types. Their visible efforts to imitate or avoid American cultural signs as well as other people's insistence that they are poor or impossible performers of "typical American" pastimes suggests that, indeed, the Changs are not like Pete. They do not instantiate American behavior; they only perform its representations and, even then, at a slant.[5]

The Changs' simultaneous distance from and similarity to Americanness, in effect, lends a dual character to Jen's political critique. Their distance from being American reminds the reader of U.S. exclusionary sentiment that continues even beyond the official dissolution of the "Asiatic barred zone." In other words, the lessening of racial exclusion on the level of official state policy does not translate into a lessening of informal exclusions that occur in American civil society; and it is in this informal realm where Jen registers her critique. Despite the Changs' impeccable adoption of American social, economic, and cultural behaviors, they are nonetheless considered racially different and, therefore, un-American. This critique raises the very specter of Asian difference from Americanness as a type of disenfranchisement to Asians as a group. At the same time, the narrative's emphasis on the Changs' following closely "typical American" pursuits allows Jen to forward a more general critique of American narratives, not so much because they exclude Asians, in particular, but because their mythology of self- and economic limitlessness overlooks the labor of others and wreaks a terrible gendered violence (see my discussion later in this chapter). Somewhat paradoxically, *Typical American*'s critique of America is both particular to an Asian perspective and not particular to an Asian perspective.

Beyond Franklin's *Autobiography*, then, Jen provides her audience ample opportunities to witness the Changs' cleaving to broad American narratives, most notably the paths of moneymaking and self-making. However, before Ralph, in particular, performs these master narratives that stress individualism, he is joined by his sister Theresa and wife, Helen, who together acquire signs of Americanness—the body mechanics akin to Pete's shuffle and nose-blow—that precede their acting out of the national drama. Obtaining U.S. citizenship provides the first of these signs. After nine years in the States, Theresa, Helen, and Ralph have "studied up on the three branches of government, and so advanced from permanent residents to citizens" (123). Jen emphasizes the process of the Changs' legally becoming American as a performance of sorts—a test in memorization. Thus, the narrator lists under this testament to their Americanization other instances of the family's acting out American rituals: "They celebrated Christmas in addition to Chinese New Year's, and were regulars at Radio City Music Hall. Ralph owned a Davy Crockett hat. Helen knew most of the words to most of the songs in *The King and I*, and *South Pacific*" (123). The light-hearted tone of the passage masks the difficulty of performance. Only through slight details (e.g., the nine years before legal status) does the reader surmise an uneasiness behind the Changs' role-playing. Though it doesn't appear unusual that the Changs should memorize the United States' tripartite governing structure, it does seem odd that Helen hums tunes that memorialize Western incursions into Asian domains. Certain American narratives, it would seem, can be performed more easily than others.

Through the Changs' prodigious copying of American behavior, Jen questions the American myth of a raceless society. Helen performs what first appear to be innocuous cultural texts—popular Broadway tunes—yet in doing so, she unconsciously endorses both the alien difference and cultural inferiority attributed to "Orientals" in these stage dramas. Helen's Americanization thus involves a violation to herself. Such split significance colors each sign of the Changs' Americanization. As they engage in "typical American" pursuits, they and the reader are reminded of the Changs' estrangement from the typical, as in the case of their admiration for baseball. Calling themselves the "Chang-kees," Ralph, Helen and Theresa simultaneously affiliate and disaffiliate with that national pastime and the national team whose name acts as a metonym for Americans as a whole:

> Theresa explained how the Yankees had lost the Series to the Dodgers the year before; they rooted for a comeback. "Let's go Chang-kees!" This was in the privacy of their apartment, in front of their newly bought used Zenith TV; the one time they went to an actual game, people had called them names and told them to go back to their laundry. . . . [Now], they preferred to stay home and watch. "More comfortable." "More convenient." "Can see better," they agreed. (127–28)

The designation "Chang-kees" distinguishes the family from those other "typical Americans" (e.g., the Yankees) who are not told to "go back to their laundry." Though the Chang-kees first appear to be mocking the sports enthusiasm of "typical Americans," their superlative devotion to baseball becomes a shade compensatory. Though they discursively embrace their distance from typical Yankee fans, that distance has been foisted upon them by racist catcalls.

The family responds to the hostility of the ballpark by withdrawing to their home, a constrained choice given the history of Chinese Americans told to "go home."[6] "Home," in the latter case, refers to China, with the order to "go home" preserving the nativist dream of America as "home" to whites only. "Home" thus emerges as a conflicted trope within the novel, appearing variously as a safe domestic space for the Changs, as a Far Eastern realm to Yankee fans, and as a national fantasy defined against racial others (the United States, the national Home, as distinctly not home to "Chinamen"). Within this mix of meanings, Jen shows the Changs performing the great American narrative of home buying: "What had they understood about America? Evenings, they shook their heads at themselves. *We didn't realize.* . . . It was as if the land they had been living in had turned out to be no land at all, but a mere offshore island. . . . Whereas this New World—now this was a continent. A paradise, they agreed" (157–58). By purchasing an enormous "split-level, with an attached garage" (156), the family participates in a legislatively sanctioned mode of citizenship, one explicitly unavailable to the Filipino laborers of Bulosan's text. Thus, the family's real-estate purchase resonates with "Chang-kee" difference: unlike Yankees (i.e., white, middle-class families), they buy a home partly as a bunker against drivings out.

At first, the narrative associates the acquisition of the house with the miraculous production of familial unity: "A top-quality family was growing out of a top-quality house; . . . [Helen] couldn't help but wonder—could a house give life to a family?" (159–60). Helen highlights a generative image of the house, through which the national narrative of home ownership taps its persuasiveness. Capitalizing on the domestic image of home as a place of comfort and family values, this national narrative deliberately confuses home ownership with homemaking, so that the home one buys seems to confer automatically domestic comforts. Jen, however, depicts the labor that produces such tranquillity. It is not the "four walls and a roof" (154) that cause miracles to happen but the actions of women.[7]

For instance, Helen makes the "house hold" through her attentiveness to others: "[She] thought in terms of matching, balancing, connecting, completing. In terms, that is, of family" (56). Her balancing aesthetic takes concrete form through her work on the family's first apartment. While Ralph rages at the building superintendent to fix the cracks in the walls, "Helen, meanwhile, hired a plumber, scraped the loose paint so it wouldn't hang, walked Ralph's file cabinet into the back bedroom to hide the crack" (66). In fabulist style, Jen portrays the house as an affective structure that mirrors the stability of the family. As Helen works to literally cover over the rifts in their home, so does Theresa secretly labor to preserve the household. Cracks widen and leaks gush as Ralph becomes more resentful of the two women's successes. When Theresa announces news of a scholarship she has won, a chill takes over the apartment, the building furnace having broken down. The two women repair the trouble, Helen by fixing the furnace and Theresa by faking the loss of her medical scholarship.

Making home, then, is not reducible to political gestures on a national scale, such as contesting biased zoning and housing practices or lobbying for the repeal of Alien Land Laws—in short, winning the right to own property in the United States. It also involves negotiating conflicts within the family, with Jen underscoring the way in which American incorporation, while involving collective ethnopolitical action against state practices, also requires the reshaping of immigrants within gendered domestic configurations.[8] Thus, in addition to portraying the family confronted by a larger adversary—racial prejudice—Jen encourages her narrative to be read in terms of divisions of labor within the family.

Domestic tranquillity, seemingly inherent in that product called "home," is forged by women's labor, specifically their accommodating to the rule of the patriarch.[9] Moreover, Helen and Theresa's arduous efforts to make stable the home becomes a Sisyphean task: making Ralph "at home" is already an impossibility by virtue of a national Home narrative that excludes "Chinamen." Asian American women thus labor against a double exclusion—they are those whose silences enable an Asian American "home" already disabled by America's "Home," which is the exclusive terrain of whites.

Making home and making oneself at home have subtle distinctions that become clear upon attending to gender and race. Making home signifies an investment in communal living space and the concessions one allows to ensure the stability of that shared space. By contrast, making oneself at home signals rendering the home comfortable for the self—in other words, building a place where each man can be king. Jen underscores this sense of making oneself at home in her portrait of Ralph's tyranny:

> "*This way,*" Ralph demonstrated, inhaling, exhaling. "*Even. Do you see? You should breathe this way.*"
> Helen mimicked him, timidly. "*That one right?*"
> "*Right,*" pronounced Ralph. "*Again.*"
> Helen did it again.
> "*Again,*" he commanded. "*Again.*" (71)

Helen plays the obedient wife, imitating Ralph's breathing technique, just as Theresa has acted as the dutiful sister by faking the loss of her scholarship. Cultural scripts do not cease making demands on the Changs; only the locus of their enactment shifts. Instead of performing Americanness for Yankee fans or for the naturalization service, the Changs masquerade for each other. This intrafamilial masquerade illuminates the power differentials within the household that racial or ethnic paradigms often elide. The choice, however, is not to choose between racial and gendered critiques (i.e., to view them as mutually exclusive); rather, the task is to explore how racial disparity and gender subordination collaborate with each other.

In the passage above, Helen memorizes Ralph's prescribed breathing technique in much the same way that the Changs have memorized their citizenship scripts. Ralph wishes to make Helen part of his domain just as national narratives prescribe and make uniform the behavior of those within America's Home. What is striking, then, about the national narrative of Home is its ability to confuse making home with making oneself at home. The national script of Home requires those who will accommodate to the structure of their new *patria* (usually women and minorities), and those who will revise, transgress, and break current structures, to forge their personal vision of society (usually white males). Yet even as the national narrative endorses both these roles, it masks the concessions of the former by highlighting the "freedom" associated with the latter. Building a communal home of the nation relies deeply upon such an uneven division of labor and rewards across gender and race.

Even though the domestic image of the home is part of the nationally sanctioned narrative, home *ownership* provides the crux of nationally encoded norms: "Why," asks Gayatri Spivak, "is the housing index something that's always cited in the business pages? Because it's the largest amount of capital that an individual releases into the circuit of capital" (Spivak 1990, 85). As the business pages would indicate, homemaking remains less important to the national narrative of industrial capitalism than home ownership. However, romantic notions of the home as a secure space or sign of a loving relationship obscure the nation's underlying endorsement of home buying as increased capital expenditure.

Interestingly, during the Cold War era in which Jen's novel is set, homemaking emerged as a crucial component of America's national ideology. Blanche Linden-Ward and Carol Hurd Green record the way in which homemaking was cocooned in nationalist discourse in the early sixties: the Future Homemakers of America saw themselves as "launching good citizenship through homemaking" and *Time* magazine hailed the suburban housewife as " 'keeper of the American Dream' " (Linden-Ward and Green, x). As early as 1964, Eve Merriam proposed economic reasons behind this renewed emphasis on women's place in the home: "Technologically, there is no reason for so many women to stay home. Ideologically, however, there is every reason under the capitalist sun. There are simply not enough profitable jobs to go around" (Merriam, 142). Merriam furthermore identified the way in which a new consumerist patriotism was enlisted to convince women to stay home:

> Stay right here indoors, because there's nothing wrong with our economy that a red-blooded housewife can't fix. . . . As the nation's Number One, all-purpose, conspicuous consumer, the full-time housewife is not the queen mother of our economy. She is the patsy. She is the lucky little lady on whom products can be unloaded. Since the stuff can't be dumped onto Cuba and other unmentionable areas any more, and as the blanked out areas increase, she becomes ever more vital to the American way of life. (Merriam, 145)

Merriam asserts a direct relation between the nation's heralding household consumerism and the United States' inability to persuade other nations to its capitalist economy (and thereby to buy American products and keep the United States profiting from international trade). In essence, Merriam radically suggests that America's increased preoccupation with homemaking has everything to do with the nation's Cold War anxieties. While the United States was ostensibly concerned with communism's expansion abroad, much of its energies went toward ferreting out Red Party members "in [the nation's] own backyard" and enshrining the patriarchal family as the core of American values (Kaledin, 5). One might characterize the fifties, in particular, as a decade in which international politics became studiously ignored through an extensive focus on "the home."[10]

Jen herself reproduces that willed blindness to global politics in a novel ironically profiling "typical American" responses. While linked with the turmoil of world events, the Changs' story seems to occur without relation to the international scene. Rather than invasions or wars, births and household purchases establish the novel's watershed dates. In essence, Jen recalibrates time according to a domestic calendar, with events of familial importance becoming the reference points of history.

While this domestic chronology may be Jen's method of posing feminist alternatives to masculinist history, it may also be the case that Cold War events are so much part of the novel's subtext that they are taken for granted and told only through mundane details. Thus, one might complement Jen's history of the household by noting that in the same year that Ralph emigrates to the United States, Mao's Red Army defeats Chiang Kai-shek's nationalist forces, rendering Chinese students abroad with no home, or at least not the same home, to return to. The United States' rivalry with the Soviet Union, the demonizing of communism, and America's attempt to persuade other nations and their members to follow its model of "democratic" free enterprise all clearly contribute to the Changs' prolonged sojourn and eventual resettlement in the States. Yet Jen chooses to relegate world events to the novel's background. Thus, only through dinner conversation does the reader learn of the Changs' concern over "whether the United States was doing the right thing in Korea" (111). Political occasions—such as Kennedy's election, the attempted invasion at the Bay of Pigs, the civil rights protests of the mid-sixties, and the United States' increased military aid to South Vietnam—serve as chronological footnotes to the narrative's primary focus on family history (e.g., the Changs' becoming citizens, Ralph's launching his own business, Helen's job hunt when the restaurant fails). Through this muffling of the fifties and sixties' Cold War context, the author reproduces the American fantasy of a secure, nuclear family living in suburbia—an image that prospered in the same decade that saw the flowering of the Red Scare. It is this exaggerated focus on the home, as a response to perceived threats from outside, that Jen's novel both corroborates and critiques.

The Changs, like millions of Americans in the postwar era, move into their suburban split-level where homemaking—the feminine industry responsible for comfortable images of the home—appears the necessary consequence of home buying. However, Jen undoes the conflation between homemaking and home buying by introducing the character Grover Ding. A veritable home breaker (he attempts to ruin Ralph and Helen's marriage), Grover also remains a consummate homeowner: "Grover was whole or part owner of any number of buildings and restaurants," including the Changs' first apartment house (105).

Interestingly, Grover remains the most "American" of Jen's Chinese American characters. Janis Chao establishes Grover's "Americanness" by citing his ancestors' long history in the United States as well as Grover's own wealth:

[Helen:] *"What does he speak?"*

"English," said Janis. *"This is America. His family has been here for so many generations, I don't think he even knows what province he's from. And what does it matter anymore? He's rich. . . . [H]e has a maid, this one. Think of it—no housework!"* (86)

Grover's Americanness explicitly proceeds from both his wealth and his having lost touch with his Chinese origins, less explicitly—though no less importantly—from his having mastered American home ownership as a profit-making scheme.[11] In line with Spivak's observation, then, I would argue that the American national narrative of "home" encourages home ownership as part of capitalist production. This national narrative enlists the male home owner as its "hero," with the female homemaker-consumer as his patriotic counterpart. In other words, proprietorship and consumerism, rather than the production of a communal living space, underwrite the American Dream, even as communitarian values enshrined in the discourse of "family values" masks this underlying economism.

Unlike Ralph, Grover does not operate within a communal living space; he never inhabits houses and commercial buildings but only acquires them for investment purposes. Grover's conspicuous lack of home, then, emerges as a peculiar prerequisite for his self-made status. He owns houses without having to compromise within a home. He is self-possessed without a familial inheritance or a boss to take credit for his achievements. He exists only in the present, in whatever design he choose, and distinctly rejects identification by "hometown." To Ralph's question, "So where you from. . . . Your hometown is where?," Grover responds, "Hometown! You've been here how long? And still asking about people's hometown." He shook his head. "I'll let you in on a secret. In this country, the question to ask is: 'So what do you do for a living' " (105). Grover makes explicit the codes of Americanness that govern identification itself. Americanness is a function not just of content but of form, so that Ralph's calling himself "American" has less weight than the way he tells others about his (national) identity. While in a protocol of "hometown," one's definition remains stable, inherited, locatable, and presumably unchanging, in a protocol of occupations, one's identity derives from the market and can be anything one construes it to be. For instance, Grover, who has "labored" as a slumlord, an actor of sorts, a recycler of stolen fats (to make soap), and a land developer, identifies himself as "a millionaire" (106). Through these multiple and speculative self-portraits, Grover introduces Ralph to an itinerant sense of self—a self not already defined by ancestral legacy or even by one's current familial relations, but several selves to be realized through one's own imaginative leaps. The result is a version of radical individualism, of limitless self-will and creative imagination at its most positive applications, or of shysterism and con-man tactics at its worst.

In his parroting of radical individualist tenets, Grover appears to exemplify the model minority myth, which, in itself, represents a specific reworking of American individualism reconfigured for immigrant types. Grover's economic achievement would seem an illustration of how, by dint of hard work, improvisation, and charm, the Asian American protagonist can become a "millionaire." The novel, however, reveals this narrative as only part of the story. Grover succeeds through exploiting his tenants, business partners, and ethnic confreres—the Changs. *Typical American* thus retells Grover's tale of "self-made" success from the perspectives of the losing parties. Even though the Changs contribute massively to Grover's rise in fortunes, they do not share in his wealth. Thus Jen suggests that the stratification among Asians in the United States, coupled with their reliance upon each other—due in part to the larger racism of mainstream society— become the very enabling conditions that produce certain Asian American "success stories," at the cost of other hidden stories of "failure."

Everywhere There Are Limits

Grover's economic wealth proceeds from his insider's knowledge of both Chinese and American ways: more specifically, he knows how to make American bucks by preying upon the naiveté of more recent Asian immigrants. Grover makes himself essential to Ralph by constantly pointing out the latter's greenhorn blunders, and, whereas formerly Ralph looked upon American ways as blunderous, after he befriends this self-invented Chinese American character, he begins to imagine his own desire for limitless possibilities as an admirable American trait. In fact, once Ralph meets Grover, he recommits himself to the American individualist narratives that he first embraced as a solo student, recently arrived in the States and removed for the first time from family influences. One might recall that Franklin's autobiography provided the contours of Ralph's earlier self-definitional efforts.

After the pivotal introduction to Grover, Jen shows Ralph's indebtedness to many other manuals of self-making enshrined in the national literature. Briefly, self-making relies upon an effacement and replacement of origins: "self-made persons" claim to be unencumbered and unentitled by an ancestral inheritance, thereby seeming to be *self*-originating. As a supreme form of egoism, self-making seduces via its promise of self-evaluation. The myth of self-making is that one can assess one's value according to one's own standards rather than someone else's. This independence from judgment has been memorialized in Thoreau's *Resistance to Civil Government*,[12] which proposes a radical freedom from social obligations, most emphatically the law, and Emerson's "Self-Reliance," which acts as a manifesto on answering to no one but oneself.[13] Clarifying the ideological work that "self-making" myths perform for the United States as whole, Stephanie Coontz remarks on how the self-referentiality of such myths denies the very founding of the American nation on the dispossession of Native Americans:

[T]he tendency of Americans to overestimate what they have accomplished on their own and deny how much they owe to others has been codified in the myth that the colonists came on an 'errand into the wilderness' and built a land of plenty out of nothing. In reality, however, the abundant concentrations of game, plants, and berries . . . had been produced by the cooperative husbandry and collective land-use patterns of Native Americans. (70)

I would argue, then, that the American idiom of self-making becomes the subject of extended satire in Jen's novel precisely because of the ways in which this individualist ethic eclipses the hidden labor performed by others (with these "others" composed of both racial minorities—as in Coontz's example—and women).

In scrutinizing the trope of self-making, Jen probes the irony behind a canonized myth of origins. Self-origination emerges several times inscribed in the annals of American literature. As Grover himself instructs Ralph, "[A] self-made man should always say he was born in something like a log cabin, preferably with no running water [and] all self-made men found what they needed to know in bookstores" (107). Self-making, often synonymous with a boundless individualism, appears a mere commodity stocked at Barnes and Noble. Ralph's learning of the idiom of (self-) limitlessness from textual interpolations highlights the paradox of limitlessness as already encoded within narrative limits.

Ironically, Grover is not the first person to introduce Ralph to the script of self-making. An undergraduate advisor, Professor Pierce, gives Ralph *The Power of Positive Thinking*,[14] from which he first learns of the limitless self: "As per the author's instructions, he'd written down a statement to carry in his wallet: 'I can do all things through Christ which strengtheneth me.' He could do anything! . . . [A] man was what he made up his mind to be" (88). Ralph abbreviates this notion of self-making as being "a mangod . . . able to do what he would" (88). The narrative inscription of these American idioms implies a contradiction in form and content. Limitlessness would seem to defy encapsulation; yet Ralph consistently comes across American texts that formulate boundless individualism as a step-by-step method.

Jen allows the paradox of an already inscribed, self-originating narrative to speak for itself. In essence, she makes "a parody of the very notion of an original," to borrow from Judith Butler's account of drag queens' subversions of gender through repetitive excess. As "gender parody reveals that the original identity after which gender fashions itself is an imitation without origin," so do the multiple allusions to other accounts of self-making reveal this narrative of national identity "an imitation without origin" (Butler, 138).

While her intertextual references bespeak the collapsed origins of self-making, Jen's own novel plots the "de-formity" of this trope through its narrative turns:

> [Ralph] stared up into the multicolored air, and knew: he wanted to be like that man-god. . . . He pictured himself able to do what he would.
>
> And to an amazing extent, his imagineering worked. . . . [H]e noticed that his bit of athlete's foot had gone away; that he thought more clearly; that he could will certain foods to appear in the icebox. . . .
>
> The day of the dinner, though, he got stung by a bee . . . right between the eyes. How was it possible? He was an imagineer! Yet when he held his hand to his face, the skin was pounding hot. . . . His whole brow was swelling as though with a third eye. (88–89)

Something so small as a bee interrupts Ralph's self-deification. A symbol of man's lack of control over fate, the bee sting derives its enormous significance from Ralph's former musings upon *The Power of Positive Thinking*. In other words, the narrative of self-making itself sets up the conditions for its unmaking, bearing out in slight variation Butler's statement regarding gender parody.

The discontinuities of scale between the bee sting and its massive consequence also remind the reader of Ralph's distance from "self-making." His exaggerated performance of "do[ing] what he would" takes American "can-do" spirit from the loftiness of grand achievements, such as the transcontinental railroad, into the realm of groceries and athlete's foot. His success at willing "certain foods to appear" also reminds the reader of the hidden labor behind America's "self-made" enterprises. Evidence of Ralph's formidable character requires his willed blindness to Helen's behind-the-scenes work, just as the building of a national transportation system—as testament to America's pioneering spirit—cannot acknowledge the labor of Chinese coolie workers.

Jen's comparison of the bee sting to a third eye—presumably, an instrument of enhanced perception—occasions further ironies. Ralph's forehead literally grows larger, his swollen-headedness becoming an apt metaphor for his search for a godlike stature, yet also posing a barrier to any increased insight into the self. Given that Ralph is ostensibly searching for the very mystery of his own being, his third eye ironically punctuates a myopia that Ralph acquires once he commits himself to expanding his self-perception:

> Who was he? It was years before Ralph even knew to ask himself [that question]. . . . [H]is own nature eluded his grasp. . . . What could be more frustrating? Why try? It was a uniquely low return enterprise. And yet he found that in America, in practical, can-do, down-to-earth America, he had much company in

this activity—that a lot of people wondered who they were quite seriously, some of them for a living. It was an industry. (177)

Jen satirizes a whole field of valorized subjectivity (i.e., questions of being) by exposing it as a national preoccupation. Again, a textual example gives testimony to this American "industry": *Calorie Counters: The 1-2-3 Way to an All-New You*, given to Ralph by his daughters, capitalizes upon a national desire to make oneself over. As a grocery-store version of subjectivity studies, *Calorie Counters* articulates the practical applications of the field, in essence by guaranteeing its profitable return—"an all-new you." Jen allows the two styles of self-examination to illuminate each other: the product-oriented self-help narrative reveals the low-return solipsism of seeking one's own nature; conversely, the abstract narrative of subjectivity exposes the teleological necessity of the practical, "1-2-3"-step version. Depicting both the theoretical and practical narratives, the author touches upon that schism between script and performance. The script of subjectivity gains much of its appeal by divorcing itself from the trivial ways self-exploration is practiced. But which narrative bespeaks the preponderance of Americans' self-making? While a national narrative couches self-making as a valorized endeavor in self-discovery and self-reliance, Jen depicts the most often practiced version of self-making as moneymaking.

The elision between making self and making money is forged through repeated couplings of the terms. In identifying himself to Ralph, Grover terms himself "a self-made man. A millionaire," as if the two conditions followed upon each other. Previously, Ralph had been primed to this homology between self-making and moneymaking by an early encounter with an old man at a luncheonette, who tells Ralph "what was wrong with America": " 'Dough,' said the man. He gripped his sandwich so hard, its contents bulged. 'That's all anyone understands in this country. Dough, dough, dough' " (17). In the United States, one's facility with communication and commerce is a function of one's capital assets.

To be "self-made," then, reveals itself as a misnomer. Instead of finding a means of valuing himself that is self-sprung, Ralph measures his worth against the profit-making standards prescribed by the script of American capitalism. The more swiftly he conforms to its outline, the more quickly he discovers himself as a "self-made" nonconformist.[15] Thus Ralph "frees" himself from all dependencies and communitarian sources of judgment: he gives up his professorship in mechanical engineering and flaunts his older sister's extramarital affair so that she removes herself from the family home. The impersonal form of money replaces both sister and university official as arbiter of Ralph's self-worth. Moreover, cash appears more manipulable than either Theresa or the chairman of the engineering department, Old Chao. Ralph can re-ring the restaurant's register tape every night to underreport on his taxes, thereby inflating his net profits—his measure of self-worth. It is this intensified focus upon profit making that causes Ralph to lose sight of his familial relations. Thus, while he locks himself in the basement ringing up the phony register receipt, Grover seduces Helen upstairs on the couch. In essence, Ralph chooses self and profit over family and home.

Jen scrutinizes the commitment to money making in the same way that she scrutinizes the narrative of self-enlargement. As the bee sting acts as a literalization of swollen-headedness without positive effects, so do Ralph's visions of upward mobility take on the form of escalating steps that lead nowhere:

> The mechanism [to close the convertible car roof] was stiff; between the wet vinyl and his raw hands, he could only get it to straighten halfway before it stuck. Struggling, he pinched a finger, which bled pink in the rain. He gave up. But then he couldn't get the roof to fold back down, either. Pull as he might, it remained a luminous rising in the twilit air, like a stairway to nowhere, or the headless incarnation of a jack-in-the-box. (184)

The gaping roof of Ralph's broken-down car reverberates throughout the novel as a symbol that mocks the desire to build the tallest building, break the limit, or go "up, up, up" without some other defining purpose. Setting the record for the highest achievement (breaking the limit) serves only the purposes of self-aggrandizement.

Ralph's strenuous efforts to become a self-made man thus take a tragic turn. In his search for greater profits, Ralph expands his restaurant by an additional floor—literally breaking open the old roof; the entire structure begins to collapse, forcing the restaurant to close. With this second "stairway to nowhere," the author critiques profit making and self-aggrandizement as a supposed infinite quest.

Jen underscores "the ending" of the Changs' success story with other architectural correlatives. First, Ralph throws a vase out his home's living room window, creating "a black hole in the center of the household" (261). Secondly, when some shingles blow off the roof, Ralph hires a cheap, nonprofessional roofer who subsequently breaks "his uninsured ankle": "The fight Ralph and Helen had then broke them both. How was it that she went sailing, like a human version of their brass vase, out the bedroom window? . . . [Ralph] shoved her back away from himself, out of his murderous hands. . . . Glass tinkled; she felt the impact afterward, the firm, cool, glass, breaking through" (262–63). Flaunting the affective fallacy, Jen depicts Ralph's divergence from the narrative of self-making through the failed integrity of the home's enclosure. Black holes represent a transgression of material boundaries as well as a violation of the "success-story" outline. In essence, Jen breaks the limits of the limit-breaking narrative by not conforming to its trajectory of success. Instead of boundlessness resulting in abundance, the author shows boundlessness resulting in vacuums. Transgressions, rather than forging an ever-widening domain of civilized behavior, are portrayed, both flatly, as the mere limning of an outer boundary (black holes representing the theoretical limits of empirical knowledge), and negatively, as a violence to women's bodies. Jen thus highlights de-privileged transgressions—criminal trespass rather than ego-expansive limit breaking.

By emphasizing negative transgressions, the author offers a skeptical perspective on the individual's ability to craft his/her personal success, much less solve the problems of the world. Instead, she focuses upon the limits of American national narratives, not least by revealing their gendered and racial biases. While idioms of radical freedom and boundless individualism stress the agency of each American to make his or her own fate, stories of criminal transgression remind and reassure the citizenry of a social order ranked in accordance with gender and racial privilege. Paradoxically, valorized narratives of transgression reinforce racial and gendered hierarchies by justifying a subject's lower class status as his or her just desserts. The argument might proceed: because each individual has equal access to transgressive, boundary-breaking behavior, those who cannot transcend the limits of their inherited situation are responsible for that "failure." Yet, even as everyone might have access to transgressive behavior, only certain people have access to privileged transgressions, while others have access only to criminal ones. To extend the theatrical conceit, the scripts of normative and deviant transgressions are not open to everyone but typecast their potential players.

A certain type of transgression, then, belongs to "typical" or privileged Americans, their privilege in fact enabling relatively safe transgressions. The transgressions that the Changs commit, while partly determined by their individual agency, is also indicative of their condition as already transgressive of the racialized spaces they inhabit. Driving them in their journey "up, up, up" is not only an American sense of progress but an imperative to have something special—or as Theresa puts it, "to be nonwhite in this society was indeed to need education, accomplishment. . . . A white person was by definition somebody. Other people needed, across their hearts, one steel rib" (200). Beneath Ralph's stirring to "be his own boss" lies a fear of humiliation, which might be characteristic of Americans, but is particular to Ralph's situation—his failure to comprehend American sayings, American protocol, and American ethics. One might read Ralph's transgression of his limited sphere of movement, then, as both a statement on "typical American" will (assuming the homogeneity of the United States) and a counterstatement about the atypical American's need for one steel rib.[16]

The notion of compensatory performance also helps clarify Ralph's cleaving to male privilege. By adopting certain models of masculine behavior, Ralph hopes to be accepted as American. The national trope of self-making thus reveals itself as male self-making. Emphasizing the gendered violence interwoven into this narrative, Jen depicts the "start of [Ralph's] success story . . . the start of a self-made man" (193) through his communing with Grover against the desires of his family and over the bodies of women.[17] Ralph would seem to follow, then, the type of canonical male bonding detailed by Nina Baym, who takes to task the masculinist bias, not of American literary works themselves, but of the members of an American literary critical establishment who have canonized the theme of beset manhood, wherein the implicitly male individual divorces himself from a specific set of social circumstances and becomes the embodiment of a "pure American self" (131). "The problem," Baym correctly identifies, "is with the other participants in his story," who are depicted "in unmistakably feminine terms"; thus "the encroaching, constricting, destroying society is represented with particular urgency in the figure of one or more women" (133).[18] The "pure American self," defined against these feminine constraints, thus takes on a distinctly misogynist character.[19]

The homosocial bonding of Ralph and Grover takes on a similar misogynist cast as the two men commune through the objectification of women. At a Pennsylvanian diner, for instance, Grover shares not only food with his new friend, Ralph, but also a more troubling "item"—the restaurant's waitress. The narrative casts this nameless woman as a figurative final course to the two men's meal: "Grover, getting restless, suggested that they simply go back into the kitchen to see what was left that they hadn't tried. . . . The waitress reappeared. . . . Grover caressed her earlobe. . . . She giggled. He pulled her to him. 'What do you say?' Grover winked at Ralph again. 'To the kitchen?' " (104). The waitress becomes that last item in the kitchen that the two men seek. Ralph, "suddenly polite," does not enjoy this final entrée (104); however, the waitress becomes for the two men a body over which to exchange glances, a food and sex service rolled into one.

This sexualizing and objectifying of women becomes the modus operandi of the two men's homosocial bonding. Women act as the terrain upon which the two men "discover" their collusive appetites, which have as their ostensible object the bodies of women but which have more to do with the two men's developing brotherhood, than a desire for women. For instance, a prospective matchmaking for Theresa occasions Grover's introduction to the Chang family; yet, this initial meeting animates *Ralph's* "love at first sight" for Grover as the embodiment of American manhood (90). One should note that the chapter title, "Love at First Sight," possesses an ambiguous referent. While clearly the title describes Ralph's newly kindled feelings for Grover, the heading might also refer to Grover's lusty appraisal of Ralph's wife, Helen (92–93). The scene unfolds with Grover dismissing Theresa as a possible mate after eyeing her physique:

> Theresa lifted her head shyly.
> Grover craned his solid neck up, then down. His hand curled like a cooked shrimp. "Nice shoes," he said finally.
> "New ones," Helen volunteered.
> "Very darling," said Janis. . . .
> "Very darling, indeed," agreed Grover. . . . [H]e winked again, a gleam in his eye, at Helen. (93)

The passage testifies to the two men's shared predilections, not only to desire the same woman (Helen) but also to denigrate and objectify women. Grover's rejection of Theresa, moreover, appeals to Ralph's "self-making," which requires his "liberation" from genealogy, from family, and from powerful women—all of which can be achieved through his contesting Theresa's elder authority.

Theresa and Helen both reproduce a family life in which Ralph—the official male patriarch—finds himself somewhat of a loafer and freeloader compared to his sister and wife.[20] One might recall Helen and Theresa's laboring to make the house hold even as Ralph attributes to divine intervention such miraculous events as the heat resuming and his own "rise from the couch" (87). In short, Ralph misrecognizes the agency of these women, even as actions such as commanding Helen to breath "this way" hint at his subconscious and anxious awareness of their leading the way. Instead of showing himself equally or more capable of maintaining the home, Ralph aspires to head the household by exercising his gender privilege and subordinating his wife.[21] Later, he colludes with Grover to expel Theresa from the house. First Grover violates her sexually: "[Grover] leaned across the table, so close [Theresa] could smell his aftershave. . . . From her plate he picked up the oil stick she hadn't eaten yet, dipped it in the soybean milk. 'Delicious,' he said, taking a bite. . . . It dripped onto the boomerang tablecloth. Then he kissed her on the mouth. Or was it a kiss? . . . [W]hat he'd actually done was run his tongue over her lips—he'd licked her" (206). Like rape, Grover's sex act is not inspired by desire but rather by misogynist contempt. Interestingly, Jen portrays this scene of violation from the narrative perspective of the profaned woman. It is as if, in the larger scheme of self-making, such infringements go ignored by the male heroes. Consequently, the author writes in the blank spaces from the perspective of the violated, those who have been deleted from the official "success story." Reiterating the outrage, Ralph taunts Theresa: "My *Jiejie* [older sister] with two boyfriends! Kisses everybody! Everybody!" (208).

The repeated humiliation ultimately drives Theresa, not Grover, from the house (210).

Though male homosociality seems to raze vertical hierarchies enshrined in genealogy, it achieves its horizontal camaraderie by way of asserting all men's similar and equal privileges over a distinct subordinate group—in this case, women. This mechanism of fraternal equality as a function of shared gender privilege, though similar to that postulated in *America Is in the Heart*, is nonetheless much more transparent in Jen's text, in part because of the heterosexual family at the center of *Typical American* that allows one to see plainly Ralph's anxieties about female agency and his tyrannical attempts to head the household. Only by highlighting Ralph's rejection of family as a break from vertical constraints—that is, the younger and presumably weaker escaping the oppressions of primogeniture—can one construe Ralph's ouster of Theresa as a narrative of liberation rather than tyranny. If one reconstrues this rejection of family as a rejection of already embattled female authority, then homosociality as familial transcendence exposes itself as merely the extension of male privilege. Toppling Theresa and regulating Helen's breathing are not so much levelings of generational hierarchies as much as they are sexist objectifications of generationally equivalent family members (siblings, wives) as lesser, due to their gender difference.

With Theresa out of the picture, Helen becomes the supple body over which Ralph and Grover bond. Both men require her complicity with their masculine rule, so that Helen willingly breathes a certain way as she willingly fondles Grover. Jen forges the connection between the two men's modes of persuasion by entitling the story of Grover's seduction, "Helen, Breathing." To recall that earlier event, Helen plays along with Ralph, asking him to "*Show me once more?*" his correct breathing method (71). Though Helen consents to this "game," the author makes explicit the "manly tyranny" that circumscribes this role playing (71). Grover's seduction of Helen, likewise, necessitates her collusion. He leads her astray by framing his own interests in terms of her desire. That is, he creates a narrative of Helen's marital situation that serves his own purposes: " 'You did the right thing. You did not think, This is America, I can marry who I want. . . . You did not think'—he mimicked an American girl—'I'll choose. I'll pick' " (223). Using the appeal of a national narrative of self-determination explicitly tailored for women, Grover manipulates the rhetoric of free will to fit his needs. Helen four times attempts to halt this narrative saying, "Stop . . . Stop . . . Stop . . . Stop!" throughout which Grover both proceeds with his story and continues undressing her (223).

Helen's choice not to concede to Grover arrests the homosocial entrepreneurial narrative (229). That is, unbeknownst to his business "partner," Ralph, Grover conned him into buying a restaurant situated on unsuitable land that clearly cannot support the weight of a second story. Grover allows Ralph to build a second story to revenge himself of Helen's ultimate rejection of his sexual advances. It is Helen's choice "not to continue" their affair that instigates the turn of events.

Rather than performing another narrative of American "success," Helen reveals what happens to the narrative of masculine self-making without the presumed obedience of women. In her portraits of Helen and Theresa, Jen depicts ruptures in the American script through women's choice "not to continue"—in essence to put a temporary stop to the narrative's unfolding. This strategy of discontinuity arises as a peculiarly feminine and Asian tactic that intervenes into American garrulousness:[22]

> In later years, when Helen taught the girls *how to talk*, she'd teach them when *not to continue*, as she put it. It was a polite way of making a point, she said, but the way she said it, the girls knew that by point she meant barb. How come, though, when they fell silent, no one seemed pricked? "American kids, their mothers teach them nothing," Helen said. "Typical American, what can you say."
> In their household, on the other hand, silence had teeth. (135)

As King-Kok Cheung suggests, equating silence with passivity and inaction relies upon ethnocentric, gendered, and logocentric presumptions. Accordingly, Cheung unsettles "the Eurocentric perspective on speech and silence, which [she sees] as polarized, hierarchical, and gendered, especially in regard to Asians and Asian Americans" (Cheung 1993, 23). Dovetailing Cheung's critique with my own, I propose a reading of female interruptions to the masculine narratives of self-making via a radical, deconstructive lens that attends to "not continuing." Interrupting the narrative and highlighting its black holes emerges as Jen's particular radical practice. Her female characters do not embark on fundamentally other narratives, nor do they assume the part of the questing hero(ine) in the traditional narrative. Instead, they halt narration itself, with *halt* here signifying a temporary cessation. Clearly, women's "not continuing" does not effect a literal closing of Jen's text. However, these provisional stops enable a critical glance at what is discontinuous—unwritten, unspoken—in the national narratives of self-making, home ownership, and entrepreneurship.

"Unlearning Our Privilege as Our Loss"

My examination of the Changs' transgressive performance of American national scripts has emphasized their paradoxical deviance from already written narratives of societal transgression. I have tried not to blanket the Changs' deviance as a failure, despite the temptation to interpret Jen's novel as a failed "ethnic success story." The reasons for my care in this matter are manifold. In talking about the role of "typical American," I have been suggesting not only that Americanness is a text that can be read and therefore critiqued but also that it is imperative to read any deviance from that text, not as evidence of un-American behavior (unassimilable behavior), but as a symptom of what the current narratives cannot allow. This might include women's resistance and women's desire outside the desires of men, a subject to which I will return shortly.

Instead of puzzling over why certain groups do not assimilate according to ethnicity paradigms, I would underscore the volitional fallacy underlying this line of thought. The focus changes from questions of immigrant choice to an emphasis on how ideological, discursive structures such as Americanness interpellate multiple subjects differentially. Rather than implying that agency is a foregone possibility, I subscribe to a third possibility between "the self-determining subject" versus "societal codes determining the subject," to use Butler's phrase. Butler locates agency in the possibility of a variation or repetition of the rule-bound discourses that constitute the subject: "[I]t is only *within* the practices of repetitive signifying that a subversion of identity becomes possible" (Butler, 145).

Additionally, the bracketing of positive and negative judgments allows for a critical practice that uses simultaneous narratives to illuminate each other, rather than one that implicitly chooses a single narrative as the standard against which to assess a specific text's conformity (success) or deviation (failure). Such a practice, even if correctly "positioned," remains dogmatic rather than critical, apropos of Gayatri Spivak's formulation of the terms: "What is the relationship between critical and dogmatic philosophies of action? By 'critical' I mean a philosophy that is aware of the limits of knowing. By 'dogmatic' I mean a philosophy that advances coherent general principles without sufficient interest in empirical details" (Spivak 1993, 25).[23] In other essays, Spivak speaks about deconstruction as such a "critical movement" that "suggests that there is no absolute justification of *any* position" (Spivak 1990, 104).[24] A critically sound analysis thus requires an "unlearning of our privilege as our loss," to use another of Spivak's phrases—in other words, a continual shifting of the grounds of assessment. A dogmatic practice, by contrast, would choose its ground of assessment, privilege it, and never question that privilege, while subjecting various texts to its dogmatic scrutiny. While my "practical" alliances rest with Asian American scripts of resistance, my critical commitment to coalitional politics and allied readings requires that I look at how a dogmatic use of Asian American scripts loses a feminist dogmatic script, and vice versa.[25] My alternative practice then is to employ both scripts critically, for mutual illumination and mutual diminution as well as supplementation (neither script representing a total field of critical approaches).

Such a lens of mutual and complementary illumination allows for the reading of success in failure and failure in success, so that Ralph's drop in profits, and his consequent deflation of ego, also results in Theresa's "profitable" return home. Failing the national, and implicitly masculine, narrative of success, then, results in a return to women—a literal return, in the case of Theresa's homecoming. Her return to the Chang household, however, does not signify a recovered security in the home. Instead, after her homecoming, Ralph continues to wreak havoc on the family, running Theresa over with his speeding car. A return to women, therefore, does not imply a traditional notion of women's victory, such as their moving into the protagonist role. Rather, this return renders visible the hidden violences to them.

A return to women serves to focus attention upon their seeming absence in already written narratives—their relegation to black holes. A black hole, as the theoretical limit to physical knowledge, provides a boundary, signifying, in essence, "that which we have not yet narrated" or "that which we do not yet know." In the history of orientalist academic knowledge, as Edward Said details, Asia has traditionally functioned as that boundary which provides the literal outline for the real subject of study, the West (Said, 32 and 72).[26] Revisionist or nonorientalist practitioners have responded by trying to write a positivist history of the East—one not in relation to the West, one before Western colonization.[27] Such practitioners, in sum, respond to orientalism by posing counternarratives. Offering a third alternative, Spivak poses deconstruction's critical intervention into both Western humanist narratives and Third World postcolonial counternarratives. She suggests that the impulse to narrate itself must be interrogated through a critical practice she attributes to both deconstructionists and poststructuralists but which describes Jen's efforts as well:

> The post-structuralists . . . imagine again and again that when a narrative is constructed, something is left out. When an end is defined, other ends are rejected, and one might not know what those ends are. So I think what they are about is asking over and over again, What is it that is left out? Can we know what is left out? We must know the limits of the narratives, rather than establish the narratives as solutions for the future. (Spivak 1990, 18–19)[28]

Clarifying her statement, Geoffrey Hawthorn elaborates, "[T]hey're not objecting to the very idea of producing narratives, they are . . . pointing out the silences . . . the undescribed others that are implied in each of these narratives. They're not themselves concerned to put a stop to narration itself" (Spivak 1990, 19). Sharing the sentiment that "we cannot but narrate" (Spivak 1990, 19), Jen does not escape national narratives but rather repeats and critiques them, limning what they repeatedly exclude.

As an interventionist glimpse into that exclusion, I return here to the subject of women's resistance and women's desires outside the desires of men. Alongside Jen's reiterative plots that seem to feature Ralph as protagonist, runs the parallel track of Helen and Theresa's unnarratable story of female intimacy and suppressed lesbian desire.[29] However, suggestions of their romantic intercourse can only emerge via heterosexual institutions. For instance, in expressing her feelings for Theresa, Helen refers to the already written, heterosexist legend of the red ribbon:

> "*You know that saying about a wife's ankle?*" she put in softly.
>
> "*What?*" said Ralph.
>
> "*Don't interrupt,*" said Theresa. "*She's talking.*"
>
> ... [Helen:] "*Do you know that saying, about a wife's ankle? Being tied to her husband's?*"
>
> "*Of course,*" encouraged Theresa. "*With a long red string. From the time she's born.*"
>
> "*Well, I think maybe my ankle was tied to my husband's and sister-in-law's both.*"
>
> "*Ah no! To both? To my ankle too?*" Theresa protested, laughing. Then, in English. "Are you trying to pull my leg?" (65)

Helen almost doesn't voice this muted declaration of love because of Ralph's interruption. Moreover, the scandalous nature of this declaration is smoothed over by a joke, all three parties avoiding what would rupture the patriarchal home—precondition for the American success story. Instead, Helen learns to sever the tie to her sister-in-law so that the "leash" to her husband might tighten.[30]

Ralph's presence thus changes the tenor of the two women's relationship. Whereas they formerly delighted in each other's company (52), now they come together only to talk about Ralph. Even so, these conferences, in which they cannot say what they mean, occur in the closet, subject to multiple repressions:

> Helen pulled Theresa into the hall closet. "*What should we do?*"
>
> Theresa ... responded carefully—"*Whatever we can*"—and when Helen didn't say what that was, thought hard. Her relationship with Helen had always depended on silence. Restraint. Only now did she appreciate how much it depended on sight as well. How else, after all, to know how to read those silences? For instance, this one, now, coalescing in the air like a queer humidity.... [E]xperimentally, she said, "*You know, I've been thinking of getting married.*"
>
> "Really!" said Helen. Her voice burst with surprise....
>
> Later, though, Helen clopped down to the basement in wonder. All she'd wanted had been for them to throw up their hands together. At Ralph; at the cold; at the rain. It had been a feeling she'd been after, a convivial solidarity; she'd hoped to murmur to one another, as if sitting at the edge of one of their beds. But instead look what had happened. (79)

As opposed to male homosociality, women's conversation, much less their romantic intercourse, cannot be represented easily. Even as Theresa and

Helen still make decisions together, neither of them desires the choices they make. The heterosexual mandate that results not only in Helen's marriage but also in both women's subservience to the patriarchal family requires the two women's separation (their concluded conviviality) to facilitate their singular devotion to a male head of household.

Only when Helen is in danger of permanently losing Theresa does she admit the latter as a watershed in her life:

> Now, now, Helen realized: *Theresa had made that world possible.* . . . In one thing, Grover had been right—Helen had understood nothing about love. She had understood nothing about how people could come to mark off her life. For example, she had considered the great divide of her self's time to be coming to America. Before she came to America, after she came to America. But she was mistaken. That was not the divide at all. (288; emphasis added)

Helen's realization at the bedside of Theresa's comatose body occurs eight pages before the novel's end, leaving the two women's transgressive love for each other largely unnarrated. Instead, both Theresa and Helen's sexual transgressiveness becomes scripted as extramarital affairs that flout marital monogamy but keep intact heterosexual coupling.

For example, Theresa's erotic passions find expression in her relationship with Old Chao:

> [She was] surprised at how soft his lips were as he pressed them up and down her neck. She was surprised that the wet point of his tongue at her ear could make her whole body shiver, as though with fever. The firmness of his touch surprised her too, and how many parts of her body could be cupped, and what bursting tenderness was this in her nipples? She found she liked roughness and gentleness both, and that kissing back made her tingle more; and that when the time to stop came, she ached. (173)

The passage turns from Old Chao's sexual stimulation to the pleasures contained within Theresa's very body. She discovers herself as a site of pleasure, in contrast to her former anxiety over her own desires.

Watching the other medical students sleeping together peaceably, Theresa worries that these overwhelmingly male interns might see her inadequately repressed libido:

> What was hardest about training, for Theresa, was having to sleep in that dank, little room the interns all shared, with men. "If there were more women . . ." someone had explained with a shrug. . . . She thought about how soundly the men slept. She thought about how the men snored and tossed. They cried out. They moaned. They farted. They scratched themselves, and worse. Even the still ones, who slumbered soulfully, who curled up neatly, even they disturbed her. . . . So peaceful, but what dreams they might stir up in her if she slept, all throbbing,

and sliding. A spinster's hot heaves; how pointed her needs were, it was impossible to sleep. It was impossible to think about people witnessing her sleep. What if she moaned, and cried out, and scratched herself, or worse? (147)

The near repetition of the concluding phrase, "moaned, cried out, scratched themselves, and worse," paradoxically emphasizes Theresa's difference from the men. Her unconscious desires, unlike theirs, cannot be publicly witnessed. Theresa understands the implicit script that allows for the public expression of men's reposing with each other and permits women's entrance into that group only as a sexualized presence. In the end, Theresa does not sleep. She cannot rest with her desires.

Helen's sexual transgressiveness also expresses itself through heterosexual formulas. Rather than marrying Theresa, Helen marries Ralph. Instead of residing with Theresa, Helen has an affair with Grover, who all but moves into the Changs' home. One might conclude from these examples that Jen reinforces compulsory heterosexuality. Her novel does not, in fact, offer an alternative space in which to conceive of women as the subjects and objects of female desire. However, I would suggest that this reinscription, through hyperbolic repetition of both the heterosexual romance plot and the American quest narratives, exaggerates and therefore exposes these patterns as formulaic and prescriptive. As Trinh T. Minh-ha suggests,

> When repetition calls attention [to] itself as repetition, it can no longer be reduced to connote sameness and stagnancy as it usually does in the context of Western progress and accumulation. . . . When repetition reflects on itself as repetition, it constitutes this doubling back movement through which language . . . looks at itself exerting power and, therefore, creates for itself possibilities to repeatedly thwart its own power, inflating it only to deflate it better. (Trinh 1991, 190)

Traditionally, repetitions compound the importance of what is repeated; yet Trinh highlights the way in which this consequent exaggerated significance jars the audience into a realization of disproportionate emphasis. Repetition thus leads to diminishment. Clearly, Jen reflects on her own repetitions of the "American success story," working Ralph to extravagant reenactments of his heroic national predecessors.[31] It is arguable whether she considers as well her reinscription of the heterosexual romance. Despite the author's equivocal intention,[32] *Typical American*'s coding of language through hyperbole and repetition paves the way for critical reflections on the power of these national narratives.

At the novel's conclusion, Jen finally abandons her parodic mode to deliver a sobering summation of the limits of America's self-making narrative: "[Ralph] could not always see, could not always hear. He was not what he made up his mind to be. A man was the sum of his limits; freedom only made him see how much so. America was no America. Ralph swallowed" (296). Ralph's conclusion that "America was no America" balances the performance and script of the nation in an axiom of non-equivalence. That is, American narratives appeal through their abstraction—their ideological dress of lofty idealism, wherein "boundless individualism" signifies human freedom, and self-making implies class mobility and social equality. Jen depicts Ralph performing these ideals and in their practical application, exposing their dogmatic violences. Narrative itself becomes part of the culprit: in the narration of self-making there is an abstraction of its value.[33] Yet in the performance of the narrative, there is a specifying or demystifying of this value; one sees the violences hidden in the narrative abstraction. Performance thus necessarily fails the narrative and in doing so mines the narrative's limits and violences. Thus, Ralph cannot equal a "typical American," not merely because he lacks business acumen but because the script of Americanness excludes Chang-kees along with cumbrous, desiring women.

Interestingly, the place where Ralph acknowledges his limits becomes the site from which women's stories can emerge. The novel's final image, depicting Theresa and Old Chao beckoning to Helen to join them in a wading pool, follows immediately upon Ralph's "bleak" realization. Theresa and Old Chao's illicit relationship stands in for the more elusive and unrepresentable romantic relationship between Helen and Theresa taking place offstage at the hospital. Will Helen join the two bathers? The novel ends before the reader can know—in essence, limiting itself to the "typical American" tale.

• • •

> It's not a question of waging war on narratives, but [of] realising that the impulse to narrate is not necessarily a solution to the problems in the world. So what [Derrida and Lyotard are] interested in is looking at the limits of narration, looking at narrativity, making up stories that tell us, 'This is story,' or making up stories that tell us, 'This is the programme to bring about social justice.' They're looking at that in a certain way as symptomatic of the solution.
>
> —Gayatri Spivak (1990)

Typical American does not offer positivist solutions to the oppressions of past narratives. In rehearsing American tales of success, Jen pressures the limits and teases out the blind spots of these narratives, rather than posing a radically other narrative, if indeed there is one, that would resolve their prior omissions. By limiting herself to those "codes of Americanness" already available, Jen offers a profound critique of the racial and gendered presumptions embedded in national scripts of success. Rather than reassuring the reader that Americans live in a merit-based society, privy to endless opportunity, Jen suggests that power inequities between groups differentiated by race and gender are thickly woven into the fabric of America's national narrative of "opportunity." Though the Changs can approach a "typical American" identity, their stories become remarkable precisely because Americanness is always a limit that they cannot reach—an infinitely receding identification. It is through their attempts to repeat Americanness and their falling short of identical outcomes that Jen initiates her series of critiques.

Her effort thus follows the kind of deconstructive or "critical" practice that Spivak articulates as a posthumanism that acknowledges the limits of human effort to conquer the world and solve its "problems." Spivak writes, "[The poststructuralists have] waged a war of deconstruction against all the 'grands récits' with which we find our way around the world. . . . Scientific rationality, the unification of knowledge, the emancipation of humanity" (1990, 18). Revising Spivak's statement on poststructuralists to apply to Jen's novel, I would assert that "without destroying these [humanist] narratives . . . [Jen] takes a distance from them and shows what incredible and necessary crimes are attendant upon them" (1990, 102). As postcolonial studies and Third World feminisms have asserted, humanism, as the ideology behind Western nations' "civilizing" mission, means something quite different to colonized Asians and colonized women than it does to Western male colonizers. In asserting man's ability to solve the problems of the world, humanism justifies the arrogance of imperialism and patriarchy by draping them in the language of amelioration. A poststructuralist emphasis departs from the arrogance of seeing the West's progressive mission as the only mission.

In a fashion somewhat similar to the way in which Bulosan's novel exhibits a split advocacy of particularistic Filipino rights on the one hand and of a worldwide coalition of labor on the other, Jen's narrative also struggles to negotiate two seemingly incommensurable tasks: an exposure of the United States' racial inequalities, specifically the exclusion of Asians as a group from mainstream national narratives, and a depiction of gendered stratification within the Asian American household, a representation that underscores Asians as heterogeneous and differentially excluded from national privileges. This pursuing of multiple, oftentimes conflicting political agendas has had a wider enunciation in what Stuart Hall calls narratives of "new ethnicities," a body of representations that depict both the subordination of racially defined classes and the "heterogeneity" within such groups. Rather than giving voice to a monolithic racial subject, narratives of new ethnicities emphasize that race "cannot be represented without reference to dimensions of class, gender, [and] sexuality" (Hall 1988, 28).

Finding that several simultaneous perspectives exist on the same issue, a corresponding criticism of "new ethnicities"—forged at the juncture between feminist and racial perspectives—intervenes into narrow conceptions of progress that ignore how one's (man's) achievement may be another's (woman's) exploitation. *Typical American* associates the humanist quest specifically with an American pursuit, portraying its several refractions in the narratives of male self-discovery, male entrepreneurship, and the patriarchal household. Magnifying their black holes, Jen limns the bodily violences required by these narratives and chooses not to wage a similarly outfitted counterattack. She suggests that the impulse to narrate itself must be interrogated. Through performative excess, Jen urges her audience to look upon "typical Americanness" with all seriousness and humor.

CHAPTER THREE

Transversing Nationalism, Gender, and Sexuality in Jessica Hagedorn's *Dogeaters*

> [Hagedorn's novels are] the kinds of novels that will be
> written in the next century. They make the typical American
> novel look very gray.
>
> —Ishmael Reed

DOGEATERS BEGINS in the air-conditioned darkness of Manila's Avenue Theater where the American release "All That Heaven Allows" plays in Technicolor and Cinemascope. Like the narrator, Rio, and her cousin Pucha, Hagedorn's readers sit enthralled to the movie's "perfect picture-book American tableau, plaid hunting jackets, roaring cellophane fires, [and] smoking chimneys" (3). Not until the second paragraph is the reader momentarily interrupted by the sound of noisy lovers stealing kisses in the theater's darkness; yet quickly the focus returns to "Jane Wyman's soft putty face, Rock Hudson's singular, pitying expression . . . [and] the virginal, pastel-pink cashmere cardigan draped over Gloria Talbott's shoulders" (3). The screen stretches across the audience's imagination until Hagedorn pans back to remind them that they are also voyeurs in this scene—both observers of and participants in the seduction of American film.

It is this enticing quality to Hagedorn's narrative reproductions of American film that critics of *Dogeaters* find both captivating and irksome: the representation of American movies—symbols of the United States' colonial legacy—ought to instruct the reader on the continued cultural imperialism being effected in the Philippines rather than delight him/her with reproduced, spectacular details. In so effectively portraying the allure by which cultural imperialism operates, Hagedorn's text itself undergoes scrutiny as to whether it is "Filipino" or "American" (Gonzalez 1991, 191), expression of indigenous talent or the rearranged debris of an American entertainment industry. The author's emigration to the United States (in 1961) almost three decades before *Dogeaters*'s publication fuels charges that she misrepresents Manila by overemphasizing a colonized mentality and by not portraying a nonbourgeois nationalist counterculture adequately.[1] One might answer such critiques on the grounds of representation alone: while the author's putative subject is Filipino society during the Marcos

regime, her book might be better read as a creative document from a Filipino American perspective that emphasizes America's cultural dominance
on the islands in order to critique that dominance, even as the author
reinscribes it. Yet, I would further argue that it is through the attributed
"weakness" of Hagedorn's novel that her narrative conducts such a powerful critique of neocolonialism and late capitalism. By illustrating the seduc-
tiveness of American film, Hagedorn challenges her audience to sympathize with the journey toward political "awakening" and the colonial
mentality that both precedes and coexists with it. Like Fanon, she refuses
to rank her Filipino characters according to their degree of revolutionary
consciousness and instead legitimates the perspectives of colonized peoples
in their various aspects (i.e., in their rejection and embrace of Western
artifacts and technology).[2]

Moreover, for Hagedorn, "revolutionary consciousness" in a postcolonial context involves not only nationalist but also feminist and gay awakenings.[3] Yet critics of Hagedorn have left unremarked the fact that Hagedorn
depicts the Marcos years, not from the perspective of elected officials and
their military henchmen, but from the perspective of these leaders' mistresses, sisters, daughters, and wives. (The large exception to this rule is
the gay male character, Joey Sands, a half-"black American" prostitute.)
That such stories are deemed repetitive rather than radical has implications
for our assessments of radicalness on the whole.

In this chapter, I survey the specific debates around Hagedorn's novel
and place these debates in the context of the postcolonial, feminist, and
spectatorship theories which they inform and by which they are informed.
First I explore the issue of Hagedorn's style of narration, specifically how
critics have negatively responded to what they construe as the novel's regressive politics by focusing on her "postmodern" writing practices—that
is, her nonrealist mode of narration. A major plank of my argument is that
a gendered subtext underlies these representational critiques, especially
those that find fault in Hagedorn's "repetitive" aesthetic. Therefore, I deconstruct the multiple (feminist and gay) subject positions that lend "originality" to Hagedorn's "cinematext of the Third World" (San Juan 1992,
118). In placing women at the center of her narrative, Hagedorn contributes to an evolving tradition of literary works that detail Asian/Pacific
feminine postcoloniality, such as Wendy Law-Yone's *The Coffin Tree*, Theresa Hak Kyung Cha's *Dictée*, Ninotchka Rosca's *State of War*, Lois-Ann
Yamanaka's *Wild Meat and the Bully Burgers*, and Sara Suleri's *Meatless Days*.
The final part of this chapter attends to Hagedorn's portrait of the constrained choices offered to postcolonial female subjects, whose sexual desires are too often channeled into programs of good citizenship. Hagedorn
probes the ways in which the unruly sexual desires of Filipinas are nationally disavowed.

With this discussion of *Dogeaters*, I also shift focus somewhat toward a work set beyond official U.S. territorial borders—yet not beyond the reach of American and Asian American imaginings. While Bulosan's, Jen's, and Hagedorn's novels are all ostensibly concerned with cultural institutions exemplifying "Americanness," they nevertheless differ quite substantially in their choice of settings and forms of political critique. Both Bulosan's and Jen's novels alert their readers to the perils of exclusion on a domestic terrain by critiquing, to varying degrees, the gendered and racial terms of the United States' social, political, and cultural institutions. By contrast, Hagedorn's narrative concerns itself with the perils of "inclusion," so to speak—of U.S. territorial encroachments upon sites outside its borders. Becoming legitimate members of the U.S. nation-state is not necessarily the goal of postcolonial subjects.

THE POLITICS OF POSTREALISM

Though *Dogeaters* ostensibly portrays Filipino society during the Marcos regime (c. 1965–1986), its recollection and restaging of American cinema suggests that the author's concern is not so much with the varied and complex communities inhabiting the Philippines as much as with a particular encounter between U.S. popular culture and Manila's metropolitan society. In this respect, the novel appears to underscore city resident Paul Dumol's sentiment that "the strongest single influence on the Philippines is that of mass culture. . . . We are the province, the outlands for the big city which is across the Pacific" (Denton and Villena-Denton, 180).[4] The encounter that both Dumol and Hagedorn describe, rather than overtly condemn, is one in which Manila residents take pleasure in and identify with icons of U.S. popular culture.[5] In that identification, Filipinos alter the significance of these iconic acts, making it difficult to determine where the American cultural markers end and the Filipino ones begin.

That blurring of Filipino and American identities has a genealogical corollary in the ancestral backgrounds of the novel's first-person narrators, Rio Gonzaga and Joey Sands. American bloodlines and the persistent allure of the U.S. entertainment industry overdetermine both their identities. For instance, the opening chapter introduces Rio's maternal grandfather, an American named Whitman Logan. Almost an icon of the United States, Rio's grandfather sports the famous American poet's name and hails from the heartland of that nation, the Midwest. However, Rio knows relatively little about her grandfather and has to "invent [her] own history" from a mosaic of Hollywood clips (259). When her comatose grandfather yells in his sleep, "*Chicago, Chicago, Chicago*," a "movie projector goes off in [Rio's] head. . . . June Allyson descends from a winding staircase, wearing a ball-gown made of gold-flecked, plastic shower curtains" (16). Through cinematic iconography, Rio makes sense of her familial relations. Scripts of American entertainment thus provide Rio with a syntax—an enabling and constraining structure—with which to understand her midwestern past.

Joey's American ancestry likewise reminds the reader of the United States' lingering presence on the islands. Only by indirection does the narrative reveal Joey's paternity. The German filmmaker Rainer inquires of the narrator: " 'Your father—he was a black American, yes? Andres told me.' 'Andres talks too much,' I say, though I don't really mind. 'He was stationed at Subic Bay—that's all I know about him. Not his name. Not anything'" (146). Only half way through the novel does Hagedorn reveal that Joey's father is a guardian of the U.S. military bases on the islands. This textual submergence of the militia's presence mimics the subdued infiltration of the islands by an American neocolonial presence.

Though Joey knows little about his paternity, he strives against national anonymity by proposing his own American last name. When Joey's former lover Neil returns to the United States, he sends Joey a postcard from the "Sands" Hotel: "That's where I got my last name. . . . 'The Sands.' A casino in Las Vegas" (72). The choice of surname both memorializes Joey's relationship to Neil and represents a prospective avenue of escape: "It's gonna be good. I know how to get to Neil. He'll send for me: We can live in Vegas or L.A." (77). Naming himself after a monument of American entertainment, Joey locates his origin and destiny in U.S. celluloid space.

As these examples indicate, Rio's and Joey's ties to the States are both "real" and imagined. "Reality" seems to inhere in the body—in one's bloodline. Imagination, by contrast, remains a sur-real exercise in recalling and repeating what are themselves reproduced images—postcard photographs and movie clips. Yet in accepting these labels unquestioningly, one is in danger of locating the "real" in America and of privileging a Western site of "production" over and against an Asian (and Asian American) site of "reproduction." The fixing of the "real" in bloodline suggests that reality rests in an (American) patriarchal dissemination of national identity. Reality springs from Western seeds rather than from native self-invention. That both practices yield an American(ized) identity illustrates Hagedorn's use of the West as determining text of her novel (i.e., after colonialism, there is no "outside" to the text of Westernization). Yet, the difference lies in whether reality is to located in a Western implantation of genetic material—in a historical past—or whether it is to be located in the native's interpretation and performances of Western images—in a postcolonial, performative present.

Hagedorn tacitly questions the reductiveness of oppositional politics that couch any signs of Americanness as evidence of the ethnic, minority, or Third World subject's co-optation (that measures resistance in terms of "pure" native identity, or by the purity of one's native sources). The

Americanness of her protagonists' identities is something they cannot avoid, making their desire for America all the more complex. Does this desire indicate their consent to dominant ideologies, or is it an inevitable effect of their ancestry? Clearly, for the two first-person narrators of American extraction, the United States, its cinematic imports, and its cultural modes for ordering the world are concepts they cannot entirely reject. But even for those characters not directly descended from American stock, the narrative suggests an overwhelming magnetism toward the brutality and seduction of America. As one character, Senator Avila, puts it, "[We are] a complex nation of cynics, descendants of warring tribes which were baptized and colonized to death by Spaniards and Americans. . . . [We are] a nation betrayed and then united only by our hunger for glamour and our Hollywood dreams" (101). America is not only an enticing entertainer but also a possible, though suspect, ground for the collective identity of Filipinos. That is, the commonalty of American "betrayal"—violent conquest, that is—is one definitive experience that the disparate archipelagic peoples share.[6]

If, in Bulosan's narrative, America was the promise of brotherly equality and the reality of capitalist exploitation, and if, in Jen's text, America is the promise of an economic and subjective limitlessness that is undergirded by gendered violence, then, in *Dogeaters*, America is both the imperial power that colludes with native leadership and the cultural wash that forms Filipino/Filipina subjectivity and desire. It is this contradiction—that America can comprise both an oppressive enemy as well as a formative component of Filipino identity and desire (most emphatically through the influence of Hollywood film)—that fuels much of the controversy surrounding the novel as to whether it "sets back the race," misrepresents and exoticizes Filipinos, cleaves to a regressive socioeconomic message and style, or even tells a well-written story.[7] In fact, it is oftentimes difficult to separate critical disdain directed at the entertainment industry and, by extension, at Hagedorn for peopling her novel with celebrity personas, from political critiques aimed at the novel's supposed exoticization of Filipinos that might also be derivative of Hollywood stereotypes. I take as a fundamental premise of this chapter, then, that in the assessment of several of Hagedorn's critics, scenes, tropes, and stylistic innovations borrowed from the American film and broadcasting industries are integrally linked to—even serve as synecdoches for—the evils of the United States (i.e., in their readings, "cinema" stands in for imperial dominance and/or capitalist ideology).

In his review of *Dogeaters*, Leonard Casper expresses an implicit desire for a more realist narrative that hinges on believable characters and narrators that will demonstrate class conflict in Philippine society so as to propel and resolve the narrative in an affirmation of the ideal of "communitarianism" (Casper, 153).[8] The literary critic objects to the superficial wash of dreams, desires, and images that comprise *Dogeaters*'s style and that, more-over, parallels a thematic focus on "loss of memory, a loss of destination and direction, and then . . . a loss of reality altogether" (Casper, 153). Both Casper and E. San Juan Jr., two critics vastly different in their political stances, share a highly critical view of "postmodern" writing of which Hagedorn's novel is only one example. From an aesthetician's perspective, Casper comments on Hagedorn's risking "what many a postmodern author risks: negligible characterization; discontinuity, in place of causality" (157), "the impression of drift and shapelessness" (154), and a puzzling "lack of accurate, sequential chronology in the narrative" (154). Despite his quarrel with *Dogeaters*'s flaws, Casper avoids dismissing the narrative's politics wholesale, as San Juan does in his Marxist evaluation of the novel's repeti-tive style, upon which I will elaborate.[9] Both critics seem to desire a greater degree of realism, if by realism one means a style of writing committed to the representation of contemporary social issues, where "characters de-velop in relation to entrenched institutions and the struggle between classes" (A. Kaplan 1988, 2), as opposed to a tradition of romance, where "the creative power of the mind [shapes] its own reality within the limits of moral ambiguity rather than the field of social relations" (A. Kaplan 1988, 4).[10] In tracing the historical context of this literary movement in America, Amy Kaplan characterizes realism as an idiom or cognitive princi-ple of ordering a world made somewhat "unreal [by] intense class conflicts which [produce] fragmented and competing social realities, and [by] the simultaneous development of mass culture which [dictates] an equally threatening homogenous reality" (A. Kaplan 1988, 9). Thus, realism con-fronts a chaotic (unreal) world of social upheaval by promising a transpar-ent vision of the material world and a spectatorial position from which one can "control and produce the real world by seeing it *without being seen in turn*" (7; emphasis added). Though Kaplan is describing a body of texts and mode of writing particular to turn-of-the-century America, her obser-vations on realism's politics that lie *precisely within its representational capaci-ties* can be most illuminating to the type of narrative mode that *Dogeaters* violates and that critics of the novel hold up as an implicit standard of comparison.

Dogeaters's postrealist style is not "post-" because it avoids limning social relations but because it defies conventions of objective recording. Rather than conveying the upheaval of the Marcoses' rule through a panoptic, godlike vision, Hagedorn steeps her narrative in questionable recordings and skewed looks. She continually highlights the subjective viewpoint from which one observes an event, constantly switching perspectives and, in doing so, suggesting that social relations also inhere in who looks, who writes, who represents—determinations that are plural rather than singu-lar. Several critics have remarked on Hagedorn's calling into question the veracity of the primary storytellers' narratives, those of Rio and Joey, through the contesting voice of Pucha Gonzaga in the penultimate chapter of the book (Balce-Cortes and Nguyen). Pucha demurs, "Rio, you've got it all wrong. . . . You like to mix things up on purpose. . . . I'm no *intelektwal* as you've pointed out loud and clear, but my memory's just as good as anybody's." (248). Pucha insists on the legitimacy of the nonintellectual's perspective, the perspective of those who are often the observed rather than the official observers, those whose memories are characterized as too subjective or to be valuable.[11]

Rather than adopt a third-person "intelektwal" narration that constructs an observing subject position that is not observed, in turn, by others, *Doggeaters* proceeds from narrative perspectives that stress the positions of both the anthropological "pure native" who is habitually seen through the lens of Western expertise (see Trinh 1989) and the urban "native" or Third World celebrity constructed by media reports and gossip, whose reality is part lived, part made up, but always under view. Both types of "natives" share the quality of "to-be-looked-at-ness," a phrase coined by feminist film scholars to describe the spectatorial position women occupy on the screen (Mulvey, 33). Hagedorn takes seriously the perspectives of the watched, the gazed upon, the icons of spectatorial pleasure (and contempt) who offer counternarratives to the official "information" produced about Filipinos by political and intellectual authorities such as the nineteenth-century French traveler Jean Mallat and the American president William McKinley. Rather than offering a single perspective on "reality," Hagedorn presents several conflicting and simultaneous narratives that exist in a horizontal relationship to one another.

Narratives like Pucha's effectively jolt the reader, taking him or her out of the story and into a consideration of who is telling the story, whether the story is "true," and what economic and political ends motivate the story's construction. The "jump-cuts" from one perspective to another that Hagedorn employs effectively halt the narrative—a strategy, as detailed in the last chapter, that opens that narrative up to critical reflection. The impression of "discontinuity" that Casper discerns in the sequential unfolding of events might register precisely this critical awareness in the narrating subject not just of seeing but of being seen, a pause where the speaker considers his or her subjective space and its difference, as well as relation to those other social actors and forces in view. Rather than dismissing this discontinuity as an aesthetic glitch in the story line, we might consider it a critical juncture, allowing one to question the ideological narrative by which one unconsciously operates, whether that be faith in Western progress or faith in transparent discursive access to the "real."

It is this innovation of reproducing well-worn screen images from the position of the nonintellectuals, those people "to be looked at" rather than thought also to be looking back, that critics of Hagedorn's postmodern style seem to miss in their dismissal of how it recycles cinematic staples. The novel's style of narration—its heterogeneous presentations of an event from one perspective and then picking up the story from another perspective—comes under direct criticism from E. San Juan Jr., whose review of Hagedorn's novel is part of his broader enunciations of Filipino identity politics and U.S. racial politics.[12] Driving the essay is San Juan's critique of liberal pluralism and its celebration of cross-cultural contact and hybrid identities. Emphasizing the imbalances of power that structure such exchanges, San Juan claims that one cannot define hybrid identities, such as "the Filipino American subject-position" without "elucidating what the problematic relation is between the two terms which dictates the conditions of possibility for each—the hyphen or nexus which spells a relation of domination and subordination" (San Juan 1992, 125). In other words, transnational, hybrid identities such as the exiled Filipino or the American-born Filipino, must be articulated as a problem, a vexing allegory of international policies and America's global hegemony, rather than a dual heritage that can be remembered with pride. While agreeing with San Juan's critique of a facile pluralism and identity politics, I would demur from several other of his points, most emphatically the leaps his argument takes from pluralism to postmodernism to Jessica Hagedorn's *Dogeaters*, in order to condemn the latter two through guilt by association. Three sentences testify to these leaps, but I quote the preceding sentence for clarification:

[It is easy to take] pride in the fact that we are beneficiaries of both cultures, East and West, and that our multicultural awareness, our cosmopolitanism, enables us to partake of the feast of humanity's accomplishments—from Egyptian funerary art and Plato's ideas to the latest IBM computer. This is in fact the fashionable axiom of postmodern theorizing. The postmodernist technique of pastiche, aleatory juxtaposition, virtuoso bricolage carried to its logical culmination, is what presides in the first part of *Dogeaters*—a flattening of heterogeneous elements approximating Las Vegas simultaneity—until the introduction of Joey Sands, symbol of what is actually meant by "special Filipino American relations," forces the text to generate a semblance of a plot (cause-effect sequence, plausible motivation, etc.) whereby the scenario of sacrifice—Joey's slaughter of [the dog] Taruk, iconic sign for the surrogate father who also functions as castrator/betrayer, and for all the other patriarchs upholding the code of filial piety—is able to take place and the discourse to end in a prayer to the Virgin "mother of revenge." But that vestige of the traditional art of storytelling, in which irreconcilable victims of a neocolonial regime end up in a revolutionary camp plotting retribution, finds itself embedded and even neutralized by a rich multilayered discourse (exotic to a Western audience) empowered by what Henri Lefebvre (1971, 1976) calls the capitalist principle of repetition. (San Juan 1992, 125)

I would first contest San Juan's characterization of liberal pluralism (i.e., "our multicultural awareness. . .") as "the fashionable axiom of postmodern theorizing." San Juan focuses purely on formalist symptoms of postmodernity rather than connecting discursive tools such as "bricolage" and "pastiche" to the political critique of which they are a part. By contrast, David Harvey paraphrases this "positive" account of postmodernism given by the editors of the architectural journal *Precis 6*:

> [P]ostmodernism [is] a legitimate reaction to the "monotomy" [*sic*] of universal modernism's vision of the world. "Generally perceived as positivistic, technocentric, and rationalistic, universal modernism has been identified with the belief in linear progress, absolute truths, the rational planning of ideal social orders, and the standardization of knowledge and production". . . . [By contrast,] fragmentation, indeterminacy, and intense distrust of all universal or "totalizing" discourses (to use the favoured phrase) are hallmark of postmodernist thought. (Harvey, 8–9)

"Fragmentation," which *Dogeaters* exhibits in quantity, is not merely the sign of Hagedorn's "virtuoso" writing skill, but an expressive tool through which the author contests absolute truths and narratives of progress such as they are exhibited par excellence in McKinley's speech justifying the "taking" of the Philippines as an act of Godly inspiration (71). In other words, Hagedorn's novel, though sharing some stylistic hallmarks of postmodernism, might be better characterized as " 'decolonizing' writing," as defined by Lisa Lowe: " '[D]ecolonizing' writing, which may include features associated with postmodernism (such as nonlinear, antirepresentational aesthetics), emerges not from a terrain of philosophical or poetic otherness within the West but out of the contradictions of what Bipan Chandra has called the 'colonial mode of production' " (Lowe 1996, 108). Hagedorn's thwarting of traditional linear, realist narratives that purvey the "truth" stylistically parallels her text's thematic critique of U.S. imperialism.

Digging deeper into San Juan's rhetoric, one discovers the critic's reluctant concession of "a semblance of a plot" that stars the hero, Joey, symbolically killing the father and then joining "a revolutionary guerrilla camp plotting retribution." Leaving aside the argument that "killing the father" cleaves to its own principle of repetition, one might raise an eyebrow at San Juan's finding the *only* residual plot in the story that features one of Hagedorn's few male protagonists. The *dozen* or so story lines that feature female protagonists clearly do not qualify as "semblances of plots."[13] Moreover, in San Juan's estimation, Joey's narrative isn't quite "plausible" until he becomes an enemy of the state (i.e., when he is forced to become part of the underground resistance movement). Thus, the narratives of Joey's homosexual desire, his objectification by Western johns, and his capitalizing on Western tourists' curiosity about native sexuality are also merely distractions from the "traditional art of storytelling."

A gendered subtext drives San Juan's critique of Hagedorn's "repetitious" narrative: the traditional story featuring a nationalist politico is "embedded" and "neutralized" by the pastiche of the novel's first part, which precisely focuses upon female desires and homosexuality. Gender and sexuality mediate for San Juan what counts as a story and what registers as "trivia" (118). His critique of Hagedorn's pastiche, then, remains blind to the revisionist qualities of her several stories: they may be re-limning the frame of a postcolonial, transnational culture but they are doing so from the perspective of the perpetual nonsubjects of history. *Dogeaters* thus retells the story of the Marcos years, not from the perspective of political and military leaders, the Western press, or subaltern historiographers, but largely from the viewpoints of Filipina mistresses, sisters, daughters, and wives. (Thus, turning Jen's strategy on its head, Hagedorn text returns to women quite literally, placing them in the protagonist roles.)

That the predicament of such women cannot be "resolved" solely through native, nationalist liberation becomes clear upon examining Hagedorn's portrait of *bomba* star, Lolita Luna. Though she is the object of mass audiences' adoration, Lolita Luna possesses relatively little power and agency over her body as "exploded" to watchers around the nation. In his article "Patronage and Pornography," Vicente Rafael examines the circumscribed role of the *bomba* star by correlating her emergence with the rise of Ferdinand and Imelda Marcos's politics of spectacle. According to Rafael, *bomba*—literally meaning "bomb"—became synonymous with impassioned political rhetoric where the speaker would "reveal something about another politician that the latter would have preferred to keep secret" (291). Associated with scandal, *bomba* came to refer to the spate of soft- and hard-core pornographic films produced in the Philippines during the late sixties and early seventies. The *bomba* star, like Imelda, represented a new sort of ambitious female who aspired to what seemed a powerful position in the limelight. However, according to Rafael, these women were the vehicles through which government leaders and film producers "taught" the viewing audience to enjoy their passive recipient position. Attending campaign rallies became an opportunity to hear Imelda's singing performance rather than to assess Ferdinand's political promises. Women thus emerged as both a lure and a tool through which male agents could enact their "larger intentions."

Though a leading actress in Manila's celluloid industry, Lolita Luna, clearly suspecting her circumscribed lot, desires "her own ticket out of the country" (177). This ticket presents itself in two highly suspect forms: Lolita can appeal to her sexual patron, General Ledesma, to secure her a visa to the States; failing his help, Lolita "has one more option"—to accept an offer to star in an "experimental art film" which "would involve lengthy close-ups of Lolita Luna's vagina . . . teased by the gleaming blade of a knife, for example, or perhaps a stubby black pistol" (177). "Beauty" excuses the explosion of bodies on screen as it later justifies the implosion of bodies off screen. That is, this aestheticized violence repeats itself in the form of Imelda Marcos's beautification campaigns designed to make the country more hospitable to tourism and cinematic culture. In her efforts to render Manila a mecca for filmmakers, the First Lady announces the construction of a privately supported thirty-five million dollar cultural center. When the partially erected structure caves in, the Iron Butterfly orders the building to continue: "More cement is poured over dead bodies; they finish exactly three hours before the first foreign film is scheduled to be shown" (130).[14]

Whereas colonialism designates an era of overt violence that ostensibly "ends" with the withdrawal of occupying troops, "imperialism lingers," as Edward Said suggests, in the bodies of formerly occupied peoples:

> Imperialism . . . lingers . . . in a kind of general cultural sphere as well as in specific political, ideological, economic, and social practices. . . . Although that era [of empire] clearly had an identity all its own, the meaning of the imperial past is not totally contained within it, but has entered the reality of hundreds of millions of people, where its existence as shared memory . . . still exercises tremendous force. (Said 1993, 9, 12)

The most obvious aspect in which empire lingers is through neocolonialism, a repetition of imperialist strategies by "native" agents. Thus, violence, economic exploitation, and civil rights abuses, though condemned when perpetuated by foreign powers, become sanctioned as necessary components of a native nationalist program. In the same way in which art-house directors recuperate pornographic violence in the name of "art," neocolonialists reframe violence as necessary to the interests of nativism. These recuperations of violence leave women somewhere in the middle; their bodies become the terrain across which colonizers and neocolonialists alike ruthlessly represent themselves.

Who is the enemy and who the savior, then, between the art-house producer and Lolita's lover, General Ledesma, highest-ranking member of the nation's military cadre? The former wishes to confer her greater currency in the European market, while the latter wishes to confine her to his personal use at home. At the mercy of the cinematic imperialist on the one hand and the nationalist military leader on the other, the *bomba* star bears a striking resemblance to Gayatri Spivak's subaltern woman. Describing the symbolic use of women around the issue of *sati* (widow immolation), Spivak writes "the abolition of this rite by the British has been generally understood as a case of 'White men saving brown women from brown men.' . . . Against this is the Indian nativist argument, a parody for lost origins: 'she wanted to die.' The two sentences go a long way to legitimize each other. One never encounters the testimony of the women's voice-consciousness" (Spivak 1988a, 297).[15] In the imperialist portrait, women are the objects of male protection. In the native nationalist's description, women are indeed the subjects of the sentence but only by virtue of their sacrificial capacities (i.e., they come into subjectivity only by embodying native tradition). In neither discourse are women speaking.

Lolita Luna, by contrast, does speak, and given Spivak's formulation, she is not properly subaltern. However, one might characterize her as sharing the postcolonial female subject's peculiar position—caught between two patriarchal discourses (the imperialist's and the nationalist's). Both narratives take her up as a symbolic banner while depriving her of subjectivity.

When politics is conceived in terms of a struggle between the nation and its imperialist invaders (or its variant, the nation versus transnational corporations), women's issues run the risk of being marginalized as subordinate points, or of being curiously evaporated (only symbolically attended to) through the mechanism above, whereby women are both seemingly present yet apparently absent(ed) from nationalist and imperialist agendas. The problem becomes how to acknowledge that the nation is a suspect category in a transnational age, while not losing sight of issues regarding gender and sexuality.[16] While these imperatives are not inherently incompatible they are often ranked in importance, with gender and sexual oppressions configured as a subset of the more salient and widely appealing subject of postnationality.[17] If one doesn't remain vigilant against this binary framework of nation and empire, then one risks interpreting events that dispute national rhetoric—or that critique the exclusions of women from native, nationalist programs—as efforts to augment a new transnational imperialism. Such vigilance in Hagedorn's case translates into her local practice of constructing narratives of what might seem inconsequential quotidian events (watching movies, having dreams, gossiping, having sex) that are clearly imbedded in national and transnational frameworks and that simultaneously focus upon female and gay subjects.

In the depiction of Lolita Luna's domestic relations (her affairs with General Ledesma and, before him, an Englishman with "colonial obsessions" [170]), the novel further suggests that in the most intimate of spaces and the most mundane of life's events (e.g., who one chooses as a lover), one finds the traces of a political history that is simultaneously gendered and (trans)nationally mediated. Getting the scoop on Lolita's boudoir activities offers anything but a retreat from politics; rather, claims upon her "vagina" by nationalists against imperialists and vice versa show politics writ large on a zone of femininity no longer separate from public power regimes, if it ever was. In focusing on the daily lives of her characters and the arena of gender relations, domestic interactions, and sexual intimacy, Hagedorn's narrative commits itself to topics, spaces, and times conventionally thought to be trivial and shallow—decidedly, outside the realm of grand, "intelektwal" schemes and narratives for either changing or mapping (dialectical) changes in the world. As we have seen in the case of Gish Jen's work, focusing on the daily lives and domestic spaces of her characters corresponds to a blurring or setting out of focus grand historical events, such as "kingdoms [rising] up, kingdoms [collapsing]" (Jen 1991, 22). Hagedorn takes a slightly different tack. Though the preponderance of Hagedorn's narratives are about women as sexual subjects, she also wishes to tie those stories to a particular moment of national crisis, hence the roman-à-clef references to Marcos's regime and the assassination of Benigno Aquino Jr. in 1983. As Casper points out, the novel does not explicitly unfold during the time period of Marcos's rule (both Rio and Pucha set the narrative in the fifties), even as the novel's incorporation of events from that turbulent period of martial law would suggest otherwise. Where Casper finds this a lapse in chronological consistency, I would construe it as a further development of Hagedorn's negotiating with her stories of gendered and sexual subjects at the same time she wishes to highlight how the lives of female and gay characters intersect with "world events" such as decolonization, the siting of international military bases, tourism, and trade agreements. In other words, these chronological slips might be the trace of Hagedorn's choice both to link her stories of female embodiment to national questions (as in the story of Daisy Avila, upon which I will elaborate at length) and yet not to concede all forms of topical legitimacy to questions of nationalism and national allegory. Rather, she also explores as a bona fide political theme in itself the issue of women constrained within wombs/tombs (Dolores Gonzaga) or in country clubs—sites supposedly of protective wealth, revealed as sites of violent homosocial bonding (see my later discussion of Girlie Alacran).

Ultimately adopting a narrative strategy quite different from the one employed in *Typical American*, whereby the chronology of the family overshadows historical time and whereby spaces of politics are quite hidden and separate from domestic spaces of the house and suburbia, Hagedorn's novel continually stresses how politics—the legacies of colonial power relations, machismo, and patriarchal sentiment—impinge upon the intimate venues of sex, seduction, and family, and the narration of those part-public, part-private events over time. For instance, in Joey Sands's narration of the sexual overtures of his American lover, Neil, Hagedorn reveals a thorough embeddedness of sexual relations in global politics and culture:

"Call me Neil," he said. . . .
"NEIL. What kind of name is that?" I loved making fun of him.

"Good sport," he'd laugh with me, jabbing at his own chest with one of his large hands.

I spit on the floor in contempt. "Man, you don't have to talk to me like I don't know anything! *Puwede ba*—good sport," I mimic, rolling my eyes. "What do you think this is? The Lone Ranger and Tonto? . . . Man, I'm no savage." (73)

A simple pick-up line, hallmark of daily life, becomes an occasion mediated by global cinema and marked by a history of American imperial violence. That Joey uses a film reference makes this instance particularly illuminating, not only for Hagedorn's endorsement of politics as inseparable from the erotics of the everyday, but also for those critical concerns over Hagedorn's postmodern, cinematic representational style. That is, Joey throws into the American's face the image of both Neil's and America's colonizing obsession—the Lone Ranger and Tonto. Joey capitalizes on the offensive image to violate Neil's Western superiority, even as he, himself, enters a relationship (most likely one of explicit hustling) that effectively reinscribes him as sexual servant. The filmic allusion thus provides the colonized with a means to signify on and radically reverse the colonizer's position; yet it also dangerously normalizes this imperial relationship for easy (and unconscious) imitation.

This repetition of cinematic references speaks to Hagedorn's own practice. In denouncing their illusions is the author inadvertently reinforcing these movieland tropes? To respond in the affirmative is to ignore the oppositional effects inflecting repetition. While the relationship between the Lone Ranger and Tonto is encoded as a model of race relations to be emulated, Joey decodes and redeploys the couple's iconography to other ends. No longer does Tonto accompany the Ranger because of the latter's beneficence and civilized superiority or because of their interpersonal friendship. Rather, what holds the pair together is a commodified sexual transaction. Colonial ideology has been stripped bare of its lofty trappings to reveal its essence in bodies and trade.

In the foregoing instance, then, Hagedorn illustrates the translation of media images and challenges notions of direct, unmediated communications. As an alternative to the linear model of sender/message/receiver, Stuart Hall describes mass communications as a process "sustained through the articulation of linked but distinctive moments," where the translation of the media image into some form of social practice is necessary to the completion of the communications circuit (Hall 1980, 128). Hall also emphasizes the discontinuities between the moments of "production and reception of the television message [which] are not . . . identical, [even as] they are related. . . . What are called 'distortions' or 'misunderstandings' arise precisely from the *lack of equivalence* between the two sides in the communicative exchange" (Hall 1980, 130–31). In the example above, we can think of Hall's "social practices," then, as Joey's translation of the Tonto image. He reproduces the stock character to remind the American of several fictions, most formidably the fiction of the brown man as savage, as well as the fiction of amicability between colonizer and colonized. Clearly, the Lone Ranger and Tonto hold oppositional possibilities despite their producers' intentions.

Hall's revised notion of mass communications requires our further reassessment of the role of Hollywood iconography in Hagedorn's text. Certainly the pervasiveness of tinseltown images testifies to the United States' cultural dominance in the Philippines. Yet, the fact that Hagedorn exposes cultural imperialism does not then imply that she portrays Filipinos as passive recipients of American artifacts, who, furthermore, lack a culture of their own. In this respect, my argument diverges from Rafael's analysis of spectacle, wherein viewing remains an exercise in passivity. This is indeed the common mistaken perception of Hagedorn's book—that it mutes its revolutionary potential by repeating Western cinematic images. Such an argument both ignores that moment of transformative possibility on the reception side of mass communications and denies the capacity of oppressed peoples to transform the possibilities of their oppression. It also limits the appropriate content of oppositional texts to "pure native" materials. Yet as Hall's analysis suggests, the degree to which a text is resistant is not just a matter of assessing how culturally or politically pure a particular discursive material is, but of seeing that assessment, itself, as moot because the process of reception always already "taints" or transforms the "original" material.[18]

The transformative effects of decoding are redeployed by Hagedorn herself. Not only does she show her characters reworking the intended effects of various exported narratives, but the author herself uses the penetrating force of cinematic gaze to reverse the usual power relationships between spectator and spectacle. I would recall here Laura Mulvey's characterization of classic cinema as the male gaze taking pleasure at the female space of the screen. Out of this conception emerges the "feminist" possibility of only disavowing pleasure, for instance through the filmmaker's use of fragmented narratives and disynchronous sound and visual effects designed to thwart the male gaze. However, critics of Mulvey suggest that cinematic illusion "should not be thought of as the exclusive property of dominant codes, serving solely the purposes of 'oppression' " (De Lauretis, 68). Such critics wish to dislodge illusion and pleasure from their immediate associations with falsehood and to interrogate instead how illusion and pleasure take hold of their spectators.[19] Such a dislodgment, in Rey Chow's formulation, would also lead to a retheorizing of the ethnic spectator; instead of condemning the ethnic, in her case Chinese, spectator for experiencing viewing pleasure at Western, orientalist film images, one would have to examine how such persuasion works, and how cultural artifacts—that may not be pure or that may in fact sustain normative oppressions—are transformed by native agents.[20]

Hagedorn's transformation of Western artifacts, then, are not in the last instance circumscribed by Mulvey's disavowal of pleasure. Instead, the author dissects cinematic seduction by scrutinizing spectacle as a social relationship wherein the spectator's pleasure rests on the disavowal of the commodity transaction. In her narration of two types of live "sex shows," Hagedorn zooms in on this disavowal. Both scenes depict the Westerner's desire to see native "savagery," and the subsequent breakdown of the native as useable, visual object in this setting.

The first episode begins with the German filmmaker, Rainer's, interest in the "shower dancers," which elicits a somewhat exasperated response from Joey, his "native informant" and prostitute for the evening:

> "What are shower dancers?" he wants to know. They all want to know. Then they want to see it for themselves. . . . [I] tell Rainer about Boy-Boy and his job at Studio 54. . . . Hungry young boys crowd the stage, lathering their bodies with soap while an audience watches. . . .
>
> "Are they hungry or greedy?" Rainer asks. I look at him, perplexed by his question. "There's a difference, you know," he adds, gently.
>
> What a pain in the ass. "Hey, man. How should I know? Boys are hungry, so they perform. Audience pays to sit there, greedy to watch—" . . .
>
> "Do they do it slowly? . . . Are they hard? Do they come onstage? . . . What about your friend, Boy-Boy? Does he like it?"
>
> I hope I'm getting paid for this interrogation. (141–42)

The dynamics of spectatorship, in this instance, are displaced. Rainer doesn't actually watch the shower dancers, and Joey mostly recounts this performance through what Boy-Boy "has told [him]" (142). Yet Rainer's questions drive home what is at stake in this exchange: who gets to represent the "native's" desire. Is that desire to be construed as extravagant or as necessary?

Sau-ling Wong's thematic survey of Asian American literature along the paradigm of necessity and extravagance proves instructive here: "The terms *Necessity* and *Extravagance* signify two contrasting modes of existence and operation, one contained, survival-driven and conservation-minded, the other attracted to freedom, excess, emotional expressiveness, and autotelism" (S. Wong 1993, 13). Extravagance remains associated with privilege, yet also with autonomy, agency, and self-determination. Necessity, by contrast, remains the condition of the nonautonomous, the underprivileged, the native rather than the imperialist, the woman and slave rather than the man and master. Returning to Joey's and Rainer's assessment of the shower dancers, then, one sees the double-edged effects of stressing extravagance in the context of neocolonial relations. If the native extravagantly has pleasure, his desire exceeds the framework set up by the gazer. This pleasure, as testament to the native's self-sufficiency, has dual implications with respect to the spectator. First, the onlooker might be relieved at how this pleasure appears to absolve him of guilt. That is, the possibility that the shower dancers enjoy themselves—that is, ejaculate, have pleasure—implies a complicity in their own commodification. Secondly, the spectator may fear the native's pleasure unrelated to his gaze (i.e., the native doesn't need the Western audience to fulfill his desires). These dual implications suggest the perils and liberations of pleasure, not unlike the mixed benefits Hagedorn and the reader get from cinematic images.[21]

Both a titillating fear and a desire for absolution, then, inspire Rainer's question "Are they hungry or greedy?" Joey's perplexed response underscores Rainer's formulation as too simplistic to account for the issues of spectatorship at hand. Even though he counters that the shower boys are hungry and the patrons the ones who are greedy, Joey cannot shake Rainer's verbal voyeurism and more importantly, this verbal voyeurism as a way to deflect Rainer's own guilt at having watched or wanting to have watched. Seeing pleasure absolves the spectator of his pleasure at seeing, which becomes the very means through which the commodification of the native is transacted. Pornographically, then, the represented pleasure cancels the violence of objectification, and the spectator does not have to acknowledge the humiliating effects of his own gaze. By focusing so intently on the native's body (in the questions, Is he hard? Does he come onstage? Does he do it slowly?), Rainer avoids looking at himself. He highlights the content of the spectacle rather than the context of the gazing. He therefore denies the power differentials and sexual exploitation that produce such conditions for gazing.

Significantly, the verbal voyeurism ends when Joey says, "Shit. You wanna go there and see for yourself? I can arrange it" (143), an invitation which Rainer declines. If he hadn't, one could imagine the spectacle playing itself out along the lines of an earlier narrated "live show," where Joey, upon request, takes two American tourists to see a boy and a girl copulate on a dance floor: "When it is over, the young man looks up at the white men while the girl tears off some toilet paper, dabs it in alcohol, and wipes herself off. 'Okay, boss?' the young man asks eagerly, grinning at the stunned Americans. 'You want us to do that again?' " (75). Greedy or hungry? The questions are almost superfluous in this scene, where the commodity relationship between gazer and gazed, Western tourists and sexualized natives, overdetermines the entire encounter. The sex show becomes a representation, not of the pure sexuality of natives, but of what money can't buy—the erasure of the imperial relation.

Hagedorn, then, does not negate pleasure as much as multiply it by reflecting and refracting pleasure back upon itself as in a hall of mirrors. Her feminist practice involves scrutinizing the gaze that is not just male, but imperial. In effect, Mulvey's gaze theory and its progeny are decoded or hybridized by Hagedorn and transformed into a critique of the colonizer-colonized relationship that has taken on a new "spectacular" form in the dynamics of tourism. At the same time, Hagedorn's special attention to specularized bodies allows the author to place at the center of her narrative the predicament of entertainment workers, beauty queens, *bomba* stars, prostitutes, and mistresses—in short, subject positions often, though not exclusively, associated with women. These positions are often silent images, ones looked at rather than looking back. Yet, in *Dogeaters*, these objects of touristic and male gazes take on lives of their own, becoming the privileged perspectives from which multiple stories are narrated.

THE GENDERED AND HETEROSEXIST TRAPS OF NATIONALISM

While the gendered dynamics of looking-relations has emerged as a focal point for much of feminist film theory, the imperial dynamics of looking-relations has had its own elaboration in the field of postcolonial studies.[22] Yet until recently, the temptation in this latter field has been to discard the term "feminist" because it tends to prioritize a collective identity that cuts across the colonizer-colonized divide.[23] Despite the pressure to shy away from the term, I have found it strategically necessary to name Hagedorn's practice as feminist. This naming, while informed by my own commitment to antisexist politics, more importantly identifies the novel's deconstruction of gender oppression made ever more remarkable by the text's simultaneous assertion of a postcolonial *nationalist* agenda.[24] As Cynthia Enloe notes, nationalism—often central to decolonization efforts—rarely takes "women's experiences as a starting point for understanding how a people becomes colonized or how it throws off the shackles of that material and psychological domination. Rather, nationalism typically has sprung from masculinized memory, masculinized humiliation and masculinized hope. Anger at being 'emasculated'—or turned into a 'nation of busboys'—has been presumed to be the natural fuel for igniting a nationalist movement" (Enloe, 44). Though the putative goal of nationalist movements is to recover native manhood, the immediate agenda of such movements often involves policing women's behavior.[25] Thus, Muslim women's wearing the veil or Indian women's practicing *sati* become signs of nationalist devotion to an extent unparalleled by similar male practices.[26]

Clearly, feminism has a stake in exposing the male bias of nationalist agendas. This exposure has often taken the form of condemning nationalism on the assumption that the oppression of women is immanent to nationalism. To a certain extent, *Dogeaters* puts forth such a gendered critique of nationalism, representing neocolonial elite society as offering few choices for Filipinas. Yet, at the same time, Hagedorn takes another route. She also constructs a nationalist, feminist subject-position through her portrait of Daisy Avila, who comes into her nationalism through feminism. This path toward politicization stands in stark contrast to normative notions of postcolonial identity, where one typically subordinates women's issues to the primacy of anti-imperialist causes.[27] Instead, Hagedorn presents a character who first comes into her feminist consciousness, and from this political awakening she proceeds to become a nationalist leader. Moreover, it is under her leadership that Joey, San Juan's nationalist hero, is introduced to the guerrilla brigade camped in the hills.

Daisy represents a feminist alternative within nationalism, which counters not only the obvious military nationalism of General Ledesma but also the implicitly masculine "opposition" of her father, Senator Avila. Whereas Daisy's father attacks the government's collusion with the West, Daisy herself criticizes the Marcoses' leadership from a different perspective. She upbraids the president and his wife, not because of their devotion to American movies and televisual culture, but because of their systematic deracination of women to serve male-agented ends. Moreover, her counterhegemonic practice relies upon the very broadcast media that have sought to treat her as a visual object.

Having won first place in the national beauty contest, Daisy convalesces at home, overcome by a great depression. The postponement of her "whirlwind tour of the provinces" and the canceling of her cameo appearance in a feature film have cost the sponsors of the pageant "millions of pesos" (106). The First Lady responds to this national crisis by appearing on the TV show *Girl Talk*, where she announces that "Daisy Avila has shamed me personally and insulted our beloved country" (107). The telecast media remains crucial to the construction of the national drama: the camera closes in on "the First Lady's anguished face. . . [She] sobs. She blows her nose. The camera discreetly pulls away" (107). Viewing this spectacle, Aurora Avila calls out to her older sister, "Daisy! Come out and see! You're going to hell for sure—you've made the Iron Butterfly break down and cry!" (107). Yet Daisy has only hidden away in her family home, refusing to be seen by reporters.

The media's reaction to Daisy's behavior, while seeming out of proportion to the event, hints at the salience of the beauty queen's actions. Her reclusion becomes a national crisis because it defies the traditional role of the Filipina to serve her country through self-exhibition. The First Lady's actions, by contrast, exemplify this unquestioned tradition. Even as Imelda's dramatic appearance fosters a critique of the beauty queen's behavior, it also puts itself forth as a model for Daisy's future emulation. Through her own televisual display, the president's wife both verbally indicates and visually performs women's "patriotic duty" to be a spectacle for national viewing.

Daisy's "insult to the nation" thus centers upon her *refusing to be seen*. However, this refusal only fuels nationalist fervor: the Iron Butterfly successfully recuperates Daisy's obscene (literally, off-scene) actions into her own visual display of patriotism. Daisy's only choice is to become a spectacle herself, even as she uses the televisual apparatus to subversive ends. On a nationally broadcast talk show, she denounces the beauty contest as "a giant step backward for all women": "She accuses the First Lady of furthering the case of female delusions in the Philippines. The segment is immediately blacked out by waiting censors" (109). Censorship indicates the failure of the First Lady's efforts to win Daisy over to the presidential notion of feminine patriotic duty. The coercive overtones of censorship suggest that the Marcoses govern less through popular consent than through oppressive strategies. Daisy's dissent from the ideology of women's duty, however, requires her strategic consent to be an object for national viewing. Thus, her actions contesting women's oppression also affirms, even exploits, the hegemony of the televisual apparatus and the way in which it exacerbates a hunger for spectacle.

While contesting the national government's collusion with the West, Daisy's father, Senator Avila, fails to oppose as vigorously the state's representation of itself through women's bodies. The narrative underscores this blind spot in the Senator's oppositional stance by decrying the "supreme irony," whereby "an otherwise wise man [such] as the Senator allows his gullible daughter to participate in a government-endorsed beauty contest run by the First Lady" (101). It is as if the beauty contest is too frivolous a matter to demand the senator's attention. Yet the beauty contests, and more importantly, the gendered ideology that relegates women to be objects for display, circumscribes the female subjects of Hagedorn's text; their patriotic function is to serve as symbolic embodiments of the nation or as helpmates to male, nationalist leaders. Instead of recognizing the integral function of beauty pageants in staging national unity, the senator ignores the political stakes of such contests. Thus, in his overall project to undermine the Marcos government's authority, Senator Avila overlooks the importance of framing women's subordinate status as a nationalist issue.

His daughter Daisy, by contrast, who Hagedorn also portrays as a traditional *nationalist* heroine (i.e., preparing for battle in the hills), critiques the underlying logic of these pageants, which relegates women to a symbolic effect. Daisy precipitates a country-wide crisis by exposing a national reliance upon the objectification of women. In doing so, Daisy successfully negotiates between nationalist and feminist agendas and counters the notion that they remain mutually exclusive political commitments. By reasserting a feminist component to nationalist movements, Hagedorn responds to two myths: on the one hand, the fiction that women's concerns are not indigenous to emerging nations (but only an import from the West), and on the other, the myth that Western feminism is the only originator of antisexist theory and practice. As Enloe puts it, "Coming face to face with a Vietnamese feminist of the 1920s not only makes it less possible for British or American women to imagine that their foremothers were the creators of feminist ideas; it also subverts nervous local men's attempts to write off Third World feminists in the 1980s as nothing more than unwitting dupes of foreign imperialism" (Enloe, 61). Hagedorn thus creates nationalist guerrilla characters (Daisy and Clarita) who come into nationalist consciousness through feminist awakening. It is through these characters that Hagedorn crafts an identity that conjoins feminist and nationalist commitments.[28]

At the same time, Hagedorn doesn't render her novel a complete national allegory,[29] where every tale of female embodiment becomes a parallel commentary on national questions. Only in the two instances cited above does Hagedorn make her stories centrally about female embodiment congruent with a postcolonial nationalist narrative of liberation. Hagedorn also depicts women whose preoccupation with their own female embodiment (oftentimes articulated as bodily disgust mixed with bodily vanity) is homologous with a neocolonial nationalist narrative (the First Lady) and with a lesbian/queer liberation narrative that has a tenuous standing in both neocolonial and postcolonial nationalist agendas (Rio Gonzaga).

To illustrate, the First Lady uses her own good looks and the tropes of Western cinema to offer a fatuous proof of her husband's "just" regime:

> "People talk about corruption. . . . Okay, you say. We are a corrupt regime—a *dictatorship. Dios ko!* . . . I wouldn't look like this if I were corrupt, would I? Some ugliness would settle down on my system. You know the common expression—'ugly as sin?' . . . There's a truth in common sayings, *di ba?* If I were corrupt, I would look like that other movie, *Dorian Gray. Di ba*, he got uglier and uglier because of all the ugliness in his life?" (220)

Again, encouraging spectatorial interest in herself, the First Lady asserts the bodily health of women under Marcos—herself as exemplar—and, by extension, the health of the nation. That the First Lady, and not the president, himself, offers such a proof (however unconvincing in its particulars) ought to alert the reader that, though the major players in national politics during this era are men, Hagedorn is committed to exploring how women mediate and yet do not remain the primary beneficiaries of this power.

In addition to this vignette where the First Lady comments expressly on a national question—the ethics of her husband's government—the narrative depicts scenes from the First Lady's imaginative life that are more disconnected from public policy, though still concerned with gendered and sexual embodiment. For example, the chapter entitled "The President's Wife Has a Dream" recounts her pleasurable fantasies about the Pope, her "[opening] her legs" just as the Pope metamorphoses into "her Ilocano husband leering at her with those painted lips she's enraged by his intrusion" (123–24). The unpunctuated narrative, mimicking the sudden mutations in dreams, associatively connects the "intrusion" of the president's gaze with a startling change in the tenor of the entire dream: "[S]omething's wrong. . . . [S]he sits up in terror. . . . [S]he is aware of the weight of her pendulous breasts" (124). The dream ends with the First Lady's unfocused rage at her husband's playing a trick on her (124). The narrative's devotion to depicting such scenes askew from national questions suggests that textual interest in the Iron Butterfly derives, not first and foremost from her position in national politics, but from her role as a gendered social actor whose function is "to be looked at" both by the voting populace and in the not-so-private realm of her bedroom and her dreams. In short, *Dogeaters*'s narratives about gendered subjectivity do not always intersect with nationalist narratives of saving the postcolony.[30]

Those narratives of nationalism, themselves, have undergone much critical scrutiny as to whether they apprehend the global, transnational systems in which nationalist politics are embedded. For instance, Arjun Appadurai urges readers to think "beyond the nation" (Appadurai, 411), while also considering the residual and resilient appeal of the nation as a collective form of postcolonial mobilization. He describes growing up under this persuasion:

> For those of us who grew up male in the elite sectors of the postcolonial world, nationalism was our common sense and the principal justification for our ambitions, our strategies, and our sense of moral well-being. Now, almost half-a-century after independence was achieved for many of the "new" nations, the nation form is under attack, and that too from many points of view. As the ideological alibi of the territorial state, it is the last refuge of ethnic totalitarianism. As important critiques of the postcolony (Mbembe 1992), its discourses have been known to be deeply implicated in the discourses of colonialism itself. It has frequently been a vehicle for the staged self-doubts of the heroes of the new nations—[Sukarno, Kenyatta, Nehru, Nasser]—who fiddled with nationalism while the public spheres of their societies were beginning to burn. So, for postcolonial intellectuals such as myself, the question is, Does patriotism have a future? And to what races and genders shall that future belong? (Appadurai, 412)

Initially conceived as a tool to liberate colonized people from foreign domination, nationalism emerges as an excuse for ethnic-driven violence and lapsed political leadership.[31] Moreover, as Appadurai makes clear in his limning of the personal appeal of nationalism, only a specific gendered class of society primarily benefited from political programs claiming the primacy of the nationalist movement, namely, the male elite sector of the postcolonial world. Though Appadurai queries "to what races and genders shall [a postnational, patriotic] future belong," his focus is less on the ambivalence with which women are ensconced in nationalist movements and more on the prospects for imagining a "language" to encompass nonterritorial, exilic identities (418).

Hagedorn, by contrast, is also concerned with the violence undergirding nationalism, but she focuses on the peculiar predicament of women in the postcolony who have not been the prime beneficiaries of nationalism yet who have nevertheless been implicated in its violence. Particularly, Hagedorn explores how a fiction of autonomy traps women in a prison of neocolonial complicity from which there is no escape (i.e., where escape itself is deemed co-opted or the terms of escape are so self-violating as to be no escape at all). In her portraits of Girlie Alacran, Leonor Bautista, and Rio Gonzaga, Hagedorn questions the presumptions of autonomy underlying these characters' choices, by revealing their constrained roles in a sex/gender system of which they are neither the beneficiaries nor the "partners."

These issues are most overtly taken up in the narration of Girlie Alacran's dream. In this subconscious vision, Girlie imagines an uprising of the serving class (the golf caddies) against their elite Filipino rulers (the golfers):

> When they attack, the caddies are armed with golf clubs. . . . "I GONNA KILL YOU WID YOUR OWN SHIT! . . ." the dark boys roar in unison. The leader grabs Girlie by the hair. . . . "You must be mistaken," she says, meekly. . . . "I don't even like golf!". . . . An even younger caddie . . . threatens her with a set of Ben Hogans. "It's my brother you want!" she cries. "Not me! Not me!" She is a coward and a traitor, she doesn't want to die. In a final pathetic attempt at saving herself, Girlie arches her back and thrusts her hips in the air, offering her body to the surly boys. (180)

The passage highlights the offering of sexual services as a normative survival strategy for women in a sex/gender economy that "trafficks in women," to use Gayle Rubin's phrase. According to Rubin, this traffic in women underpins kinship networks, which are not "list[s] of biological relatives" but are "system[s] of categories and status markers which often contradict actual genetic relationships" (Rubin, 169). Kinship between men, that is, their social organization beyond the family unit, is secured by the exchange of women as gifts. Yet as gifts, women are not partners to the "quasi-mystical . . . social linkage" created by this exchange but only "a conduit" through which men solidify their relations with other men—relations that have as much likelihood of being antagonistic as of being friendly (Rubin, 173–74). Thus Rubin lists as examples of such traffic "women given in marriage" and "[*women*] *taken in battle*" (175; emphasis added). Though the essay focuses more on the reciprocal side of this equation, Rubin's argument might well be extended to account for the position of women in hostile interactions. Just as women are not partners to the social linkage established in friendly trades, they are likewise not the parties uncoupled in a hostile breach, though such a rupture would likely involve unauthorized "takings" of women. Girlie's nightmarish anticipation of rape reminds the reader of her status as a (sexualized) transactor of male relations—the vehicle through which male rivalry or alliance is expressed.[32] Any discussion of complicity, then, must take into account the difference between being a partner in an exclusive club and being impressed into serving as a conduit for the formation of that club.

Despite her graphic powerlessness in this dream sequence, Girlie interprets her actions as treacherous and scandalous: she betrays her brother, naming him as the real golfer, the one who impresses the caddies into service; and she entertains being raped as a means to save her life. Escaping death requires her self-violation, her consent to be a sexual object. Yet Girlie cannot ultimately "escape" in this fashion not only in a literal sense (the caddies "aren't interested") but also in a more critical sense: this escape requires her acceptance of constraints that render her an object; hence it is no escape at all.

Girlie's dream is juxtaposed to a waking nightmare in which she lounges at the country club with four male peers, observes their ogling other women, and hears them telling of their sexual and military exploits. She stands both inside and outside these accounts of appropriation: her "unspoken contempt for what [the men have] said" suggests an observable distance, but her being groped under the table by one of the conversants, Tito Alvarez, insinuates how easily she might slip from being an auditor to being a theme of his tale (182–83). Despite her "disgust" and "fear," Girlie finds it is difficult to "just get up and leave. . . . [I]t is as if her body has grown heavy with fatigue and become part of the chair; she cannot move" (183). As with the earlier image of her bound and blindfolded by the president and his wife, Girlie finds herself stuck, wanting to escape yet knowing that running away will also confirm her male cohorts' power.[33] She is merely a tolerated presence, acceptable in her capacity to register the salience of sexual machismo.

When Girlie finally exits, the golfers must look for another object through which they can bond. Erotic encounters with tortured bodies provide the alternative premise for male collusion:

> Boomboom Alacran is happy, content to listen to his friends brag about real or imagined exploits. He hopes the afternoon goes on forever. The identity of the man who confessed, the confession itself are inconsequential to Boomboom. All

Boomboom craves are the details: the look on the man's face as Pepe's meticulous agents or Pepe himself prodded and probed in their search for answers, the exact number of seconds, minutes, or hours before the man finally succumbed. (185)

The language here mirrors the substance of the men's earlier boasts regarding their speed and frequency in getting women to sexually "succumb." The combination of disgust and fear immobilizing Girlie might be understood, then, as a semiotic sedimentation of a feminized vulnerability to be prodded and probed—to be treated as a carcass or prize trophy.[34] In contrast to the homosocial pact of Bulosan's depiction that is threatened by the presence of sexualized women, the homosociality to which Hagedorn alludes requires sexually violable bodies, both male and female. The elite male bonding of Boomboom and his friends counterpoises itself not solely to sexualized women (who succumb) but to an impoverished class of men and women who contest Marcos's neocolonial rule.

The men's violent partnership depends upon sexualized scenes of objectification, such as the one quoted above, where the smallness (inconsequentiality) of the exchanged woman's and prisoner's worlds wins for the male partners and torturers their "swelling sense of territory" (Scarry, 36). Detailing the structure of torture, Elaine Scarry calls attention to the inverted logic whereby pain becomes power:

Within the physical events of torture, the torturer "has" nothing: he has only an absence, the absence of pain. . . . [T]he absence of pain is a presence of world; the presence of pain is the absence of world. Across this set of inversions pain becomes power. The direct equation, "the larger the prisoner's pain, the larger the torturer's world" is mediated by the middle term, "the prisoner's absence of world": the larger the prisoner's pain (the smaller the prisoner's world and therefore, by comparison) the larger the torturer's world. (Scarry, 36–37)

It is through such inversions, then, that "interrogation is . . . crucial to a regime" (36). Interestingly, it is through a dreamlike sequence that Hagedorn narrates General Ledesma's torture of Daisy Avila, which is both the narration of her gang rape and the spectacle of a previously tortured man (perhaps her husband), whose testicles have been mashed, eyes gouged, and brain replaced with a Styrofoam cup (215). The loss of bodily integrity speaks for the loss of the prisoner's world and self, a loss unquestionably not of the prisoner's making even though the prisoner's "confessions" insinuate his or her self-betrayal (i.e., a mock consent or admission to purported crimes).[35] The extreme deprivation of the situation clarifies how consent, which presumes an autonomous position, cannot make sense (or only perverts the sense) of the prisoner's relation to violence. The tortured person's proclamations are exacted from him or her; codes of necessity rather than extravagance determine the prisoner's "confessions," which cannot be read as autobiography—the assertions of an autonomous self. The confession merely confirms the loss of autonomy that extreme pain (or necessity) induces.

The stickiness of female consent to male violences is amplified in Hagedorn's depiction of the general's wife, Leonor Bautista Ledesma. Her religious piety, expressed through tortuous acts of self-privation, simultaneously blinds her to and relieves her of her spouse's failings:

> A former piano teacher and distant cousin of the General, Leonor Bautista was *forced to marry* Nicasio Ledesma by her elderly parents. After much *initial resistance* and the intervention of her parish priest, Leonor Bautista *succumbed* and married the General. . . .
>
> Every few months, the General's wife retreats to a Carmelite nunnery in Baguio for rigorous silence. The General encourages her spiritual odysseys and asks her to pray for him. "The Lord Listens to you and only you," he tells her. "Beg the Lord's forgiveness on my behalf." (67–68; emphasis added)

When not in Baguio, Leonor locks herself in a narrow room, "fasting on water and praying prostrate on the cold cement floor" (68). Her self-torture would seem a surrogate payment for the tortures conducted by her husband. Not unlike how filmic, feminine beauty "excuses" pornographic violence, Leonor's spiritual asceticism, her prayer and masochism, expiates the General's perversities. In this scenario, where one female bodily violation (Leonor's self-privation) pays for another (Daisy's torture), the general remains the only beneficiary. Both sides of the equation are expendable to the underlying condition that enables and requires this equivalence—a specifically masculine power to violate.[36]

The question of Leonor's complicity in the general's neocolonizing oppressions is further complicated by the fact that she is forced into her marriage. Like Girlie, she is kept in the dark regarding her husband's violent exploits and has no idea who the strangers are that "frequently troo[p] in and out of her house" (68). As the narration of her banns suggests, Leonor has been unable to "just get up and leave," although she has put up "resistance." She therefore gets "as far away from [her husband] as possible," even though she remains within the "fortress" (read *prison*) of married life (68). The only escape for Leonor is death, also construed as heaven—the utopian site of opulence and perhaps feminine self-determination: "[S]he waits for death to claim her every night. This yearning . . . is her most selfish desire, her greatest sin. Father Manuel has warned her about this many times in confession" (70). Female escape emerges as an extravagant "sin" for so much depends on women's remaining in the economy of exchange. As Father Manuel will not let Leonor fulfill her suicidal desires, so General Ledesma will not allow Lolita Luna's "escape" to that imaginary heavenly place, America.

One female protagonist who does escape is Rio Gonzaga, and in this final part of the chapter, I will examine how native nationalist suspicion of the "transnational class" contributes to the construction of this escape as "sinful." My analysis focuses upon Rio's transnationalism (her escape from native nationalist constraints) as the simultaneous realization and suppression of other "sinful," transgressive identities. I have already rehearsed the gendered, nationalist trap whereby women's emigration to Western geographies is seen as a betrayal of nativity and nation. Under this thinking, the alluring "freedom" seemingly open to women in these sites is merely a false temptation—the white man's plastic carrot. The barb of betrayal, then, lies not so much in female election as much as in foreign men's appropriation of native men's possessions. A presumed heterosexuality, it would seem, presides over this "threat" of women's transnational passage.

Dogeaters frustrates the language of women's betrayal, first, by crediting the United States as a place where women can more easily move about, uninhibited by chaperones.[37] Film, once again, mediates this gender-specific notion of American freedom, with Jane Wyman, as cast in Douglas Sirk's *All That Heaven Allows* (1956), seeming to embody such female independence:

> The cashmere scarf is gracefully draped around Jane Wyman's head to keep her warm. In her full-length, mahogany sable coat, she drives her dependable dark green Buick, the color of old money. It is how I remember the movie: a determined woman alone in the winter driving a big green car on a desolate country road, on the way to see her young lover. *Pobre* Rock, indeed. A woman like Jane Wyman baffles Pucha. Why does she choose to drive her own car, when she can obviously afford a chauffeur? Pucha wants to know. (6)

Douglas Sirk's film focuses on the sterility of social conventions that would doom a wealthy widow (played by Wyman) to lifelong celibacy.[38] Interestingly, the part Rio remembers from the movie is the suggestive scene where Wyman escapes her tomblike household for the promise of sexual fulfillment. The young narrator's fascination with this scene expresses not only her desire for Wyman but her desire for sexual control and sexual choice.

In contrast to Wyman's driving alone to meet the lover of her choosing, Rio sits, watching her cousin Pucha being ogled by a gang of teenage boys. One of them, Boomboom Alacran, "starts making kissing sounds with his fat lips. I am disgusted by his obscene display and the giggling reaction of my flustered cousin. . . . His friends are laughing. I am powerless" (5). Rio longs to exit this scene circumscribed by the noises and needs of Boomboom and his cronies. Hagedorn constructs the United States as the site for women's escape from this male authoritative gaze.[39] Jumping ahead in time, the first chapter reveals Rio's mother leaving her husband for North America, as well as Cousin Pucha's pronounced intention to get "a

US divorse" from a husband who "beats her frequently," Boomboom Alacran (6–7).

It is not just the place (geography) and society of America but the very apparatus of Hollywood film that tempts Rio. She aspires to the cam-erawoman's position rather than to that of a desired screen object like La Luna or Wyman. For instance, Rio announces to Tonyboy Sanchez, "When I grow up, I'm moving to Hollywood":

> [Tonyboy replies with sarcasm,] "I can see it now . . . giant billboards in Quiapo advertising INDAY GOES TO HOLLYWOOD, starring Rio Gonzaga. We'll get Tito Severo to produce it as a musical—" We are slow-dragging expertly. . . . Tonyboy makes a clumsy attempt to fondle my nonexistent breasts. I slap his hand. "Stu-pid—you don't believe me? I'm going to make movies, Tonyboy. Not act in them!" I look at him angrily.
>
> "What an imagination!" Tonyboy laughs, sticking his tongue in my ear. (240–41)

Rio differentiates, here, between acting and making—participating in a spectacle whose terms are already set by someone else—that is or possibly changing the terms of spectatorship. Her statement thus underscores the United States as a place where women's desires might exceed the terms set up by male producers and where women can both produce themselves and inappropriately choose their lovers.

The narrative constructs Rio's long history of challenging her proper (hetero)sexual place in the sex/gender system. These challenges are as much about same-sex desire as they are about resisting a sex/gender system where women are exchanged to fortify male alliances. The impropriety of Rio's desires is figured quite early through her "homospectatorial looks" aimed at Hollywood actresses (Fuss 1992).[40] For Rio, the appeal of Jane Wyman and Gloria Talbott remains unquestionable and direct, in contrast to her cousin Pucha's distaste for these female stars as mediated by projec-tions of male (heterosexual) preference:

> [Pucha and I] compare notes after the movie. . . . "I don't like her face," Pucha complains about Jane Wyman, "I hate when Rock starts kissing her!" "What's wrong with it?" I want to know, irritated by my blond cousin's constant criti-cisms. . . .
>
> "What about Gloria Talbott? You liked her, didn't you? She's so . . ."—I search frantically through my limited vocabulary for just the right adjective to describe my feline heroine—"interesting." Pucha rolls her eyes. "*Ay! Puweda ba*, you have weird taste! . . . [I]f you ask me, *prima*, Gloria Talbott looks like a *trapo*. And what's more, Kim Novak should've been in this movie instead of Jane Wyman. Jane's too old, Pucha sighs. "*Pobre* Rock! Everytime he had to kiss her—" Pucha shudders at the thought. (4)

Comparing the cousins' reactions reveals their differences of desire. While Pucha fawns over "*Pobre* Rock" and wants to know what new heartthrob plays Jane Wyman's spoiled son, Rio finds the latter actor "completely forgettable" (6). Instead, her attention is all for the "strange and interesting" feline heroine and the details of Jane Wyman's figure.

The impropriety of Rio's sexuality spills out in other ways. The scene with Tonyboy is narrated with other accounts of "romantic" interludes that, by contrast, culminate in heterosexual validation—marriage. Rio's brother Raul marries his first love, Belen Garcia, and Pucha weds Boomboom in a "storybook" ceremony (241, 243). The absence of such confirmation in Rio's case becomes noticeable. Furthermore, Rio's desire for Wyman and Talbott, her practicing tongue kissing with Pucha (236), her close-cropped haircut that makes her look "like [the cross-dressing] Joan of Arc" (236), and her blushing assertion to Pucha that "[Audrey Hepburn] is beautiful" (237) all hint at this impropriety. Though neither Rio's homo- or heterosexuality is clearly delineated (in contrast to Joey's), one might further read Rio's Western drag (Audrey Hepburn–style haircut) as a Third World lesbian expression of "acting out."[41] Yet the prescriptions of nationalism encourage us to overlook such an interpretation. If Rio remains in the nation, she either risks being complicit in the exploits of her male cohorts or is in danger of being tortured and raped. If she escapes these double binds by subversively "acting up" and "acting out" in Western masculine drag, she betrays her nation, emasculates its men, and commits a "sin." These formulations return one to the dilemma of defining a subversive practice for the Third World woman whose conditions of necessity (her abjectest of abject identities) take her out of "radical" consideration. That is, female subjects moving from necessity to extravagance are not considered to be making a "radical" choice but are considered passive objects moved by constraining circumstances. Extravagant and gendered notions of autonomy that underlie the mechanics of radicalness thus collaborate to produce the co-optation of female pleasure, agency, and desire.[42] And it is precisely because of this dilemma that Hagedorn negotiates with the (nationalist) structures of violence by crafting a *feminist and heterosexual nationalist* protagonist and by displacing "queer" radicalness onto the *gay nationalist* character, Joey, rather than by wholly embodying it in her transnational female subject, Rio. Though queer subjectivity is seemingly allotted a privileged space in Hagedorn's text, I would assert that it is only gay male subjectivity that enjoys this privilege. The language of nationalism cannot brook Rio's lesbian identity but validates Joey's gay identity, and then, only briefly. That is, once Joey becomes a nationalist hero, his homosexuality also goes "underground."[43]

One could also make a similar case that Hagedorn renders the nationalist overtones of the novel compatible not with female identity in general but with heterosexual female identity in particular. Though Daisy and Rio both respond to the strictures of the neocolonial elite society that offers few choices for Filipinas, their pathways toward liberation diverge precisely over the centrality of female embodiment. In becoming a nationalist leader, Daisy appears to transcend her concerns with a specifically feminine vulnerability, attempting to build a nationalist underground movement despite being raped and continuing to receive threats of being raped. Rio, by contrast, renders her gendered and sexually desiring body the very site of her revolution. She refuses to give up her "sinful" bodily inclinations to fight the nationalist cause, since the prospects of her benefiting from the success of that revolution is questionable. Will nationalist revolution allow her to make movies about self-determining women who desire other such women? This is perhaps a question that Hagedorn indirectly poses to her readers who, in their determinations of this novel as a betrayal of Filipino progressive nationalism, only prove that this is not the case. Ultimately, Hagedorn both negotiates with nationalist constructions of hero(ine)ism, through her portrait of Daisy, and exposes the way in which that same nationalism affords limited opportunities for the expression of female sexual desire, through her portrait of Rio.

Thus, even while capitalizing on nationalist narratives and popular American curiosity about Marcos's rule to garner interest in her tales of gendered subjectivity, *Dogeaters* carefully refrains from portraying nationalism as the definitive balm for all Filipinas. The novel's multiple and heterogeneous tales of female embodiment, though individually and sporadically intersecting with nationalist issues, as a whole, exceed those frameworks. This critical insight importantly amends foregoing evaluations of the novel that have dismissed as politically trivial the gender and sexual content of the novel or have taken those matters seriously only when they can be renarrated as a national allegory:

> [O]ne steady inference from *Dogeaters* is that the typical Filipina, well-fed, well-dressed and housed, well-educated, has betrayed Filipinas-the-nation and the pre-Spanish tradition of the *babaylan* priestess, by being so vacuous. Marriages in the novel . . . are rarely durable. Even under colonial rule, Filipino women had more rights, more empowerment, more equality (outside the sexual double standard) than their European and American counterparts. But the descent of conversation . . . into endless *tsismis* [gossip] is indicative of the infertility, the immaculate contraception, among these female characters. . . . Communitarianism is lost to "What will people think of me?" . . . There is little evidence of fulfillment, of health restored, even in [the novel's] several exceptional females; they are escapees, more neutered than counterforceful. (Casper, 156)

Though apprehending the importance of Filipinas to the narrative's plots and themes, Casper gauges these characters by the degree to which they revitalize the nation. Moreover, the implication that Filipinas cannot invigorate the nation except through their fertility and heterosexual attachments to men leaves no way to conceive of either a postcolonial or neocolonial nationalism that would suffer childless women, lesbians, or gay men.[44]

Casper's criticism does capture well the novel's refusal to offer an unambiguous avenue of salvation for either Filipinas or "Filipinas-the-nation." Hagedorn suggests that there is no singular place of "return" to female/national wholeness, assuming that such a utopian site or subjective state existed in the first place. And this may be partly a function of the multiple varieties of Filipinas—some, whose gendered awakening will coincide harmoniously with the role of heterosexual revitalizer of the nation, and others, whose sexual desires and identities will place them out of any such notion of national healing. Moreover, to assert the earlier point, Hagedorn remains less concerned with positing a way for women to mint anew a widely discredited nationalism (to give nationalism a shiny new gloss) than to focus on the peculiar predicament of women in the postcolony.

• • •

Circling back to my initial characterization of *Dogeaters*, then, I would recall the pair of first-person protagonists, Rio Gonzaga and Joey Sands, whose cross-referenced stories provide the scaffolding for the narrative's multiple plots. If one were to schematically summarize "what happens" to Rio and Joey, it would be easy to produce two narratives of liberation, one tailored for Filipinas, the other for Filipinos: Rio, the daughter of an elite, mestizo family escapes to the utopian site of female self-determination, the United States; Joey, a "hungry" male prostitute (also of mixed American ancestry), escapes the hustler's life for the utopian site of male self-determination, nationalist politics. Both plots overlook the narration of these characters' sexual identities and therefore cannot begin to account for the subtleties, whereby queer subjectivity "goes underground" when Joey escapes to the hills and lesbian desire—because it is attached to and allegorized by transnational feminist subjectivity—cannot "out" itself in a nationalist context. Thus the dichotomous frameworks of colonized/colonizer, nation/transnation, and to a certain extent masculine/feminine fail to narrate postcolonial women and gay men as desiring subjects. Yet in that failure to narrate (as elaborated in chapter 2 of this book), one finds the seeds of a differently defined "radical" practice that subscribes, not to a positivist counterhegemonic representational strategy, but to a negative critical practice that clears the space for alternative, as-yet-unrealized identifications to emerge.

By refraining from a style of transparent transmission, Hagedorn's narrative operates on a metacritical level, in which aspects of transmission and communication (the pleasures of watching, the production of movies, the redeployment of film images) are framed and reframed. Instead of seeing and being persuaded of, or won over to, a universalizing hegemony cemented through the dissemination of Western film, the readers witness the differentiated social strata, the "impossible fragment[ation]" of the nation, and the multiple locations (gendered, sexual, economic, racial, national/ transnational) of Asian American postcolonial subjects. In effect, *Dogeaters* points to the ways in which simultaneously operating hegemonies impinge unevenly upon various subjects, requiring an array of counterhegemonic responses that are, likewise, multiple and uneven.

One hegemony in critical practice that this chapter aims to disrupt is that of reducing the gendered and sexual content of the text to a singular national allegory. Hagedorn's novel takes as its primary topic the desires of Filipinas. Its "semblances of plots" do not rotate on the epiphany of nationalist awakening but on the constraints of female embodiment (e.g., Baby's sweating; Lolita's and the First Lady's spectacular bodies "to be looked at"; Girlie's nightmarish rape; Leonor's asceticism; and so forth). At the same time, Hagedorn offers individual hero(ine)s, such as Daisy and Joey, whose political awakening as a function of their gender and sexual identities is portrayed in harmony, rather than at odds with, a Filipino, postcolonial, national, and communitarian mission. Because Hagedorn does not propose one way to save the world, the novel ultimately does not propose female or gay leadership as the only avenues of collective salvation. Rather, the novel highlights that leadership as legitimate as any other, even while never endorsing this leadership as the final word, the one and only path toward liberation. That stance against the final word—assigning a totality of righteousness on behalf of any segment of the population—is the radical revisioning that Hagedorn offers to her readers, as Viet Nguyen has persuasively argued. However, equally important to that ultimate concession to no single vision are the particular counternarratives (or nonhegemonic narratives) that Hagedorn steers her readers toward considering as equally legitimate alternatives to those hegemonic ones of male leadership, Western imperialism, and native purity. That the subject formation of a female rape victim and a gay son of a prostitute can be in harmony with collective anti-imperial struggle is the radical counternarrative that Hagedorn has her audience consider and upon which her ultimate deconstruction of representational truth hinges.

What many critics implicitly seem to desire of Hagedorn's novel is an affirmative ending—either one that poses a revolutionary solution or one that affirms, at the very least, the representational truths of its foregoing narrative. However, *Dogeaters* refuses to offer such realist affirmations, refraining from positing a harmonious collectivism or a reassuring vision of representational and spectatorial capacity. Moreover, it is questionable whether positing such utopian possibilities fosters, rather than quells, social change. Contemporary reevaluations of realism's utopian impulses argue the reverse: "[R]ealistic novels often share an impulse with their utopian counterparts to project into the narrative present a harmonic vision of community that can paradoxically put an end to social change. Realistic novels have utopian moments that imagine resolutions to contemporary social conflicts by reconstructing society as it might be" (Kaplan, 12). Hagedorn's novel resists this utopian impulse, perhaps subscribing to the philosophy that immersing the reader in outrage—in an unfulfilled desire for justice— serves social change to a greater degree than a conflict that has been resolved through fiction. Significantly, *Dogeaters* does not portray either Daisy's successful revolution or Rio's "acting out" abroad. Leaving these as moments of desire, Hagedorn places them outside her audience's (re)- view, thus outside the space of critique. Ultimately resisting the scopic framework of spectatorship, *Dogeaters* encourages our yearning for the revolutionary movements headed by Daisy and Rio—movements to which we can remain enthralled precisely because they have not yet come.

Global-Local Discourse and Gendered Screen Fictions in Karen Tei Yamashita's *Through the Arc of the Rain Forest*

KAREN TEI YAMASHITA'S *Through the Arc of the Rain Forest* (hereafter referred to as *Through the Arc*) is a quasi-magical realist narrative, set in the *next* turn of the century though written and published a decade prior to the millennium. While the United States functions as a major player in this novel (looming large especially in its role as primary agent of "past" ecological disasters), the central setting and focus of the text is the *Matacão*, an imaginary site in Brazil's Amazon Basin. This territory functions similarly to the American western "frontier" of the nineteenth century, with one significant difference: the agents of (neo)colonial expansion derive not only from European stock but also from the Pacific Rim. Brazil, like Hagedorn's Philippines, finds itself infiltrated by a U.S. cultural and economic dominant. A New York firm mines Matacão plastics; American movies provide the mold for the Matacão's theme park; U.S. entertainers and tourists appropriate the Amazon Basin for their Live Aid benefits and tanning sessions. However, the United States is not a singular "foreign" presence in the country. A Japanese immigrant with a peculiar capacity to locate Matacão plastics, journeys across Brazil as a prototypical twenty-first-century mobile laborer; his cousin, also a recent arrival, orchestrates the recycling of global capital into a national charity fund. What is one to make of this peculiar Asian American novel and its focus, not so much on America or Asia, but on a region corresponding roughly to the Pacific Rim and NAFTA zones?

If Bulosan's and Jen's works disclose Asian immigrants' desires for a "door" into America, and if Hagedorn's text alternatively explores Asian postcolonial struggles against the seductions of that "big city across the Pacific," Yamashita's narrative moves Asian American literary criticism toward a more sustained and expansive consideration of "the globe." Yamashita's "parable of ecological devastation" (Campbell, 16) thus does more than highlight the exclusions of U.S. institutions or critique the invasiveness of its popular culture onto other terrains. Its divergence from an East-West emphasis—its diminishment of both Asia and America by the presence of a third location, Brazil—requires a rethinking of the orientalist and counterorientalist dualism undergirding much of Asian American criticism.

The very anomalous character of Yamashita's text thus occasions interrogation and reflection upon key hermeneutical options in Asian American literary and cultural studies.

It is my argument that *Through the Arc*'s very focus on globalization[1]—and its playful, domesticated way of making globalization felt—makes it an uneasy fit with traditional definitions of Asian American literature, which, according to a number of critics, places too much emphasis on U.S. nationalist politics. As recounted in the introduction, these critics have proposed alternate formations of mobile, Asian-infused communities, variously called the "Asia-Pacific," the "Pacific Rim," and the "Asian diaspora," all of which represent a displacement of the American optic. However, where these latter formations reterritorialize their alternative communities in Asia and the Pacific, *Through the Arc* more thoroughly displaces the entire East-West dichotomy by tackling globalization through a local focus on a quasi-fictional site in Brazil. One of the primary purposes of this chapter is to explore the eccentricity of Yamashita's subject matter not only to U.S.-centered definitions of Asian American literature but also to "Asia-Pacific" paradigms that may enshrine a new East-West partnership at the expense of a third party or exploitable territory, in this case, Brazil.[2]

Though *Through the Arc* is technically an Asian-immigrant text, reviewers have largely neglected to characterize it as such, possibly because its environmental focus and quirky, fantastical details appear askew from those earnest themes closely associated with Asian American literature—for example, biculturalism, racial conflict, generational conflict, and resistance to U.S. hegemony.[3] Rather than dismiss the peculiarities of this novel as rendering it irrelevant to Asian American concerns, I argue that these very oddities make it all the more important to read the novel as an Asian American text and to question why its displacement of subject matter into the twenty-first century and onto a Brazilian landscape takes it beyond the pale of Asian American scrutiny. If *Through the Arc* can only be tenuously characterized as Asian American literature, what does this tell us about the latter tradition, specifically its exclusion, not only of certain geographic terrains, but also of the fantastical and the soap operatic? In the first part of this chapter, I situate *Through the Arc* in relation to theories of the "Asia-Pacific," analyzing the way in which the novel's global themes seem to exceed the Pacific boundaries of the latter concept. Then, I examine the shadow presences of Asian American themes in the novel, arguing that Yamashita walks a fine line between decentering the theme of Asian identity and globalizing Asian tropes. The next two parts of this chapter focus on why such characteristics such as the novel's fantastical, playful demeanor are seen as antithetical to the serious work of political critique that Asian American literary texts are expected to perform.[4] In other words, I take issue with the presumption that, since the novel is modeled after a televisual domestic drama, it is too frivolous to shed light on either Asian American or global concerns. Yamashita makes visceral her global thematic by filtering the upheavals of time-space compression through a series of love stories. In doing so, she makes apparent distinct gendered perspectives on the issue of globalization.

DECENTERING AMERICA

As recounted in the introduction, the displacement of an American optic has been urged by a number of critics who suggest its replacement by a host of options, such as a refocused attention on Asian Studies (Mazumdar), a trans-Pacific region (Okihiro), a framework of diaspora inevitably tied to a specific Asian nation (Hu-DeHart), and an Asia-Pacific or Pacific Rim idea (Dirlik 1993; Dirlik and Wilson). Though partly motivated by a desire to enable Asian-Americanists a wider area of study (specifically outside or beyond the United States), these critics, paradoxically, establish new boundaries around their subjects by evoking reformulated regions (Asia, the trans-Pacific, the terrains of Chinese exodus, the Pacific Rim) that might be substituted as the proper domain of Asian American Studies.

In particular, I am interested in the ways in which Yamashita's novel both participates in and resists the centerless quality of the "Asia-Pacific" idea, which focuses attention not so much on a singular nation—the United States or Japan, for example—but on a network of economic zones in a wider "supraregion" tenuously associated with the Pacific.[5] Because there has been considerable dispute over the meanings and uses of the "Pacific Rim" idea, it makes it difficult to speak about "*the* Asia-Pacific" and what this term encapsulates conceptually.[6] However, generally speaking, the Pacific Rim issued forth as one of several ways to represent organizations of capital in the late twentieth century (Connery; Cumings; Nonini).[7] According to Arif Dirlik, the modern incarnation of "the Pacific Rim" began as a parallel initiative to the European economic community and anticipated the formalization of the North American Free Trade Area (Dirlik 1993, 8).[8] From one aspect, the Asia-Pacific idea appears the subset of a particular type of *global* discourse: transnational economism, as distinct from international diplomacy or human rights discourse, for instance.

From another aspect, however, visions of the Pacific Rim have a peculiarly American cast, a means by which U.S. corporations responded to the economic successes of East Asian nations after World War II—Japan, in particular. Posing the United States as part of an Asian-Pacific region or Pacific Rim was to take part in those "miraculous" growth scenarios in the "newly industrialized countries" (NICs) of the East (i.e., Taiwan, South Korea, Hong Kong, and Singapore), even if that meant the ambivalent recognition that capitalism had been de-Westernized (Woodside, 24).[9] To quote Christopher Connery, "[T]he [Pacific Rim] discourse of equality and connectedness reflects, in part, a reaction to East Asian 'success': When Japan is number one, the only way not to be number two is to transcend the nation" (Connery, 6). A primary reason for evoking a postnational community, then, is to deny the waning of U.S. superiority by reincorporating "outsider" threats into a new transnational coalition.

As a preemptory strike at the economic potentiality of Asian-based entrepreneurs, the Asia-Pacific, on the one hand, merely extends the United States' discourse of Manifest Destiny. On the other hand, by evoking a region defined by an economic logic specifically designed to transgress national borders, the Pacific Rim undermines the persuasiveness of territorial nationalism, U.S. or otherwise. A tension, therefore, develops between the general boundaryless capacities of capital flows—which the concept of the Asia-Pacific tries to capture—and the territorial conceptual order suggested in the term "Pacific Rim." To illustrate, Dirlik argues that the relationships comprising the Pacific Rim cannot "be understood without reference to global forces that transcend the Pacific" (4). Claiming that the "Pacific Region idea" is not about spatial fixity, though it is named after a geographical marker, he proposes "that the terms [of the Pacific Rim] represent ideational constructs that, although they refer to a physical location on the globe, are themselves informed by conceptualizations that owe little to geography understood physically or positivistically" (Dirlik, 3).[10] Instead, they are distinguished by human activity and networks that are nonetheless associated with the grand expanse of the Pacific:

> There is indeed a Pacific region in a different (and more meaningful) sense than the physically geographic. Motions of people, commodities, and capital over the last few centuries have created relationships that traverse the Pacific in different directions and have given rise to regional formations with shifting boundaries. . . . Such motions continue to this day and account for the gap between the Pacific area (conceived physically) and a Pacific region conceived in terms of human activity. Emphasis on human activity shifts attention from physical area to the construction of geography through human interactions; it also underlines the historicity of the region's formation(s). (4)

The emphasis on human interactions becomes crucial to Dirlik's argument that the Asia-Pacific, generated by economists and military strategists, might be converted to cultural ends. In other words, what was intended as a trope to catalyze financial partnerships and increase corporate profits might be diverted for other purposes, namely, to describe the human labor, suffering, and ecological fallout blithely covered over by allusions to a co-prosperity sphere. Thus, Asia-Pacific theorists search for cultural forms that might speak to an alternative Asia-Pacific consciousness produced out of the "human networks that endow the region with a social reality" (307).

In his early mapping of the Asia-Pacific, Dirlik turns to the cultural nationalist writings of Frank Chin and Jeffery Paul Chan as possible protoexpressions of the Asia-Pacific ethos: equal partnership in a Pacific region rather than assimilation into an anglicized United States (Dirlik 1993, 320–25, esp. 323). In this way, "claiming America" is rehabilitated under the Asia-Pacific rubric as an effort to claim America for Asia or for the Pacific region. In other words, if America, like China or Japan or Korea is part of a vast Asian-Pacific network, then claiming America is not necessarily a denial of Asia, but rather, a disclaiming of the United States as an Anglo-Saxon preserve. Replacing or vying with the notion of America as an extension of European civilization is the idea of an Asia-Pacific that extends into America.[11]

In a more recent cultural project, Dirlik and coeditor Rob Wilson attempt to rectify the absence of Pacific Basin cultures in definitions of the Asia-Pacific. The editors include creative works by Pacific Islanders and Asian-Pacific Americans in order to highlight "indigenous traditions as alternatives to construct social identity" (Wilson and Dirlik, 13). Orthographically, "Asia-Pacific," with a hyphen, refers to the capitalist utopia, while "Asia/Pacific," with a slash, indicates a "counter-hegemonic 'space of cultural production' " derivative of the local memories of Pacific Basin peoples (Wilson and Dirlik, 6). Interestingly, both of these attempts to refine and develop the Asia-Pacific as a cultural category fail to comprehend a text like *Through the Arc*, which neither claims America for Asia nor represents the local memories of Pacific Basin peoples.

It is my argument, then, that both definitions of the "Asia-/Pacific," as well as the fictional work *Through the Arc*, can all be viewed as responses to the unsettling effects of globalization or time-space compression. To quote Doreen Massey, time-space compression refers to "movement and communication across space, to the geographical stretching-out of social relations, and to our experience of all this" (Massey, 147), in other words, to a spreading out onto a global terrain of the social relations that determine the meanings and specificities of local places. In the same way that theories of the Asia-/Pacific apprehend social identities and cultural artifacts through spatial, regional, and emplaced languages, so does Yamashita's novel provide a new, perhaps provisional, conceptual container for prospective communities. However, the quasi-fictional place that unites the "imagined community" of Yamashita's novel is neither an island in the Pacific nor a nation that rests on its Rim, but the Matacão, "an enormous impenetrable field" located in "the southern region of the Amazon Basin" (16). Though situated outside the "Asia-Pacific," this fictional site conceptually resembles the former geographic zone. As in the case of the Pacific Rim, the Matacão describes not a fixed and singular territory established by political claims but a shape-shifting region (later regions) defined by the presence of a "miracle" substance—in the Matacão's case, a highly mold-able, magnetic plastic. Like the Pacific Rim, the Matacão is a quasi-geo-graphical place name, somewhat contiguous with the Amazon Forest yet also marked by indeterminate boundaries.

Throughout the narrative, Yamashita confronts her reader with both the geographic specificity of the Matacão—its Brazilian distinctiveness—and its formation through global flows that belie such locational limits. The Matacão comes to light as a phenomenon caused by external forces, gar-bage of the most populace and polluting nations sunk down into the Earth's molten layers and redistributed to the "virgin areas of the Earth. The Ama-zon Forest, being one of the last virgin areas on Earth, got plenty" (202). The local specificity of the former Amazon, its "virginal," isolable qualities, paradoxically, contributes to the undoing of its "local" determination. At the same time, the narrative suggests that the notion of place boundaries is, itself, a fiction, yet one necessary to get a handle on the increasing com-pression of the world, signaled in the violation of such boundaries. Limning the effects of global financial flows, media networks, and migration routes requires the construction of a border to trespass, to mark the infiltration of local (native) identities by global (alien) influences, and vice versa.

Whereas theorists of the Asia-Pacific grapple with the effects of global capital by highlighting the trespass of East-West dichotomies, Yamashita's novel highlights globalization as a multinoded cultural intermingling that is not relayed through the merging of two "opposites," Asia and the United States, for example, but through the compilation of heterogeneous na-tional, racial, and cultural components all in one site: the Matacão. Thus, an Amazonian native, a Japanese immigrant, a New York entrepreneur, a São Paulo denizen, and a pilgrim from Ceará all converge at this mystical place. Moreover, several of these characters are themselves embodiments of racial, regional, and cultural cross-fertilization: the narrative attributes Chico Paco's blond hair to "the old Dutch conquerors of [the northeastern] part of the country" (25) and describes the São Paulan protagonist, Batista Djapan, as "a mellow and handsome mixture of African, Indian and Portu-guese" (12).

The novel especially highlights the global constitution of local identities in its portrait of the Amazonian denizen Mané Pena. Even though Mané has never traveled beyond his native stomping grounds, he remains greatly affected by the increased mobility of others: tourists "from every corner of the world" flow into Mané's unbounded locality, a veritable "wonder of the *world*" (16–17; emphasis added). He builds his home, arguably his most localized setting, from the "residue" of hotel construction sites and deco-rates its interior with the remnants of global products (17, 23). When a national network comes to tape a documentary on the altered Amazon, Mané Pena appears contradictorily as "a poor, barefoot regional type" yet dressed in a "faded Hawaiian shirt splattered with Aloha" (18, 23). The revelation toward the end of the novel that the Matacão, itself, is a conglomeration of waste from industrialized, high-polluting countries only confirms the sense of globalized localities and localized globalization (202).

Because Mané lives in a region of particular international interest, the restriction of his life to this singular place actually intensifies his connections to people from other locations and to global culture. In this respect, he seems to exemplify what Doreen Massey describes as those who are affected by "time-space compression" but are not in control of it; in fact, they might be imprisoned in it.

> Different social groups have distinct relationships to . . . mobility: some people are more in charge of it than others; some initiate flows and movement, others don't; some are more on the receiving-end of it than others; some are effectively imprisoned by it. . . .
>
> [T]here are the people who live in the *favelas* of Rio, who know global football like the back of their hand, and have produced some of its players; who have contributed massively to global music, who gave us the samba and produced lambada that everyone was dancing to last year in the clubs of Paris and London; and who have never, or hardly ever, been to downtown Rio. At one level they have been tremendous contributors to what we call time-space compression; and at another level they are imprisoned in it. (149–50)

In drawing out the distinct positions of various peoples with respect to these global flows—what she calls "the power geometry of time-space compression" (149)—Massey importantly distinguishes the jet-setters, media moguls, and organizers of international capital from both the undocumented migrant workers and those who physically do not travel yet whose immobility is greatly affected by the mobility of others.[12] Thus, while relatively immobile with respect to the businessmen, tourists, scientists, and government officials who flock to the Matacão, Mané paradoxically finds himself displaced and transformed by their movements and flows.

Through its portraits of Mané and the Matacão, *Through the Arc* broaches themes of globalization that similarly preoccupy theorists of the Asia-Pacific; however, where these latter critics to a large degree rehabilitate a focus on Asia and the States (though redefined in a relationship of partnership rather than hierarchy), Yamashita's novel attempts to displace both these optics by focusing on the fantastical site of the Matacão and on local native identity, not necessarily derivative of the Pacific Basin, but possibly affected by it (e.g., Mané dressed in an "Aloha" shirt).[13] However, by illustrating globalization as a multiform, rather than East-West, convergence, Yamashita also attenuates her novel's connections to both Asian American and Asian-Pacific critical contexts. In not stressing the East-West cultural distinction (but preferring a North-South distinction), Yamashita defies the methodological convention of both these scholarly fields. The question that immediately arises is whether *Through the Arc* is, indeed, relevant to Asian American literary traditions and an Asian American political project. Is the novel's particular outlook on globalization inherently at odds with an ethnic-specific reading? Does Yamashita's exploration of polyglot cultural influences require a revisioning of an implicit communal structure based on pan-Asian racial identity? These questions hint at a fundamental tension involved in interweaving a global thematic with a specific focus on Asian-Pacific and Asian American political concerns. While theories of the Asia-Pacific attempt to resolve that tension through a heavy reliance on geographic and spatial moorings (in essence, to recontain the spread of border-crossing effects), Yamashita's novel negotiates the disjuncture of her global and specific interests by way of literary allusion, narrative voice, wordplay, and discursive details. In the following section, I trace the Asian American specificity of Yamashita's novel that plays counterpoint to its Brazilian and global focus.

The Karaoke-Singing Railroad Worker: Shattering the Space-Time of Asian American Literature

When reviewers broadly characterize Yamashita's novel, they do not label it Asian American fiction; instead, they describe *Through the Arc* as "a parable of ecological devastation" (*New York Times*), a "wise first novel of global dimension" (*Booklist*), and "a mixture of magic realism, satire, and futuristic fiction" (*San Francisco Chronicle*). Though the novel features a Japanese immigrant protagonist, this character is sufficiently altered from the expected Asian immigrant profile—the plantation worker, the gold miner, the laborer in the guano pits, the war refugee—that his presence does not seem an obvious link to other Asian American literary works. Yet, for readers familiar with Asian American cultural contexts, Yamashita's protagonist, Kazumasa Ishimaru, seems a subtle parody of a familiar archetype, the Chinese American railroad worker.

This historical figure has provided grist for the mill in Asian American Studies for nearly three decades. In the late 1970s and throughout the 1980s, Asian American historians, playwrights, and novelists recalled the labor of Chinese immigrants on the Central Pacific to make a case for national belonging (see Takaki 1990a and 1990b; Kingston; Chin; Hwang 1982; see also S. Wong 1993, 124–25). The grandfather in Maxine Hong Kingston's best-selling novel *China Men* (1980) exemplifies the type of heroic portraiture surrounding the Chinese coolie: "[Grandfather] spent the rest of his time on the railroad laying and bending and hammering the ties and rails [until] the engine from the West and the one from the East rolled toward one another and touched. The transcontinental railroad was finished. . . . 'Only Americans could have done it,' they said. . . . [Ah Goong] was an American for having built the railroad" (145). Kingston portrays her forebear, not as part of an *international* work force, but as an "American" by virtue of his toil on the rails. Great national works such as the Central Pacific thus attest to both the part of America that is the inheritance of the Chinese and their remembered labor in the United States that made these immigrants "American."

Playfully riffing on this archetype of Asian American history, Yamashita anticipates those critics who comment on the pressing need for Asian American Studies to go "beyond railroads and internment," which for so long have been the focal points of scholarship (Kim 1993, 12–13).[14] Yamashita both resuscitates this familiar communal "hero" and brings him "beyond" his original meanings by updating him for her twenty-first-century setting. Rather than building a national infrastructure, Kazumasa is a maintenance worker on a fully developed system that is breaking down, both literally and financially, into privatized subunits. After being downsized out of his job, this Japanese, rather than Chinese, worker travels from Sado Island, via Tokyo, to Brazil to find work as a highly specialized technician on the railways.[15] Instead of doing backbreaking work laying rails, Kazumasa—by virtue of his technical gifts (his having a supernatural ball that can sense railway deterioration)—renders travel more efficient by proleptically remedying breakdowns before they occur.[16] Because he is technologically advanced, he has an easy time relocating to South America rather than North America,[17] where his job consists of his riding the rails and waiting for his ball to jerk uncontrollably (8–9).

By evoking this icon of Asian American heroism, Yamashita invites comparisons, not only between the lives of her protagonist and an earlier generation of pioneers, but also between the function that these icons may perform in their respective interpretive contexts. When Elaine Kim urges other scholars to go "beyond railroads and the internment," she may be more importantly urging them to reconsider the nationalist basis of these topics. If the Chinese railroad worker (and for that matter the interned Japanese family) represents an ideal symbol to press Asian American claims upon a national legacy—a move that tacitly accepts myths of American exceptionalism even as the larger project may be to question the "whites-only" basis of that exceptionalism—then Yamashita redeploys that archetype for postnational purposes. Kazumasa, although called upon by "[Japan's] national headquarters [to inspect] the entire national system" (7), finds his past service for the country no match for the corporate bottom line that now favors an "electronic gadget" to take over his functions at reduced cost (8). Precisely by resuscitating this familiar figure whom Asian American scholars are conditioned to admire as a hardworking contributor to the American nation, Yamashita underscores the limitations of this type of centering move. In other words, it is not the case that Kazumasa doesn't have the makings of a national hero; he clearly does. It is rather that in a time when national utilities are fragmenting into competing capitalist units, when building infrastructure is less important than downsizing to maximize profits, when railways signify less as patriotic achievements and more as "a lucrative travel business," then to craft a national hero is to create a deliberate anachronism—a figure who, despite having saved "hundreds, perhaps thousands, of lives" (10)—is outplaced.[18]

By calling the construction of this national hero a deliberate anachronism, I want to stress that Yamashita is temporally relativizing this archetype of Asian American identity respective of other possible hero(ine)s and their chronotopes (space-times), and not necessarily arguing for the transcendence of his significance. In other words, Yamashita redesigns rather than abandons this archetype of Asian American cultural nationalism and, in doing so, does not so much urge an end to the romance with the "railroads and the internment"[19] as much as she encourages a reasoned exploration of what connections could be made between these traditional topics (and the terms of nationalism upon which they presume) and her global thematic concerns, development in the South and time-space compression. Thus, while acknowledging the railroad worker's importance to twentieth-century Asian American politics, the narrative proposes that his twenty-first-century counterpart may be less heroically and singularly imagined in the future. In addition to an Asian immigrant protagonist, then, the novel features five other main characters.

Yamashita negotiates the tension between keeping focused on her Asian immigrant character and diminishing his importance respective of other racial, gendered, and classed subjects by constructing a first-person narrator that has both a localized perspective and yet can panoramically detail five other "lives" set in disparate regions. This narrator, a baseball-sized globe hovering inches from Kazumasa's forehead, at first identifies closely with the Japanese protagonist: "Of me you will learn by and by. First I must tell you of a certain Kazumasa Ishimaru to whom I was attached for many years. It might be said that we were friends, but . . . we were much closer. . ." (3). The initial chapter of the book concentrates solely on Kazumasa's life in Japan. Once "the ball" travels to Brazil, however, s/he becomes a fully omniscient voice:

> While I could not, of course, control the events that were to come, I could see all the innocent people we would eventually meet. . . . There was old Mané Pena, the feather guru, and the American, Jonathan B. Tweep. There was the man they called the angel, Chico Paco, and there was the pigeon couple, Batista and Tania Aparecida. . . .
>
> . . . These things I knew with simple clairvoyance. I also knew that strange events far to our north and deep in the Amazon Basin, events as insignificant as those in a tiny northeastern coastal town wedged tightly between multicolored

dunes, and events as prestigious as those of the great economic capital of the world, New York, would each cast forth an invisible line, shall I say, leading us to a place they would all call the Matacão. (8–9, 15)

It is as if, in choosing to limn a specific globalized locale in the twenty-first century, Yamashita cannot keep her focus solely on the Japanese but must spatially displace the point of view from an individual body to a number of scattered, multiethnic, multinational, and multiregional perspectives.

By crafting five non-Asian protagonists, the author somewhat disarticulates narrative focus from Asian or Asian American identity. In this respect, *Through the Arc* once again strays from the cultural nationalist project of searching for the origins of an Asian American collective identity through rehearsals of the past labors, migration patterns, conditions of colonization, and cultural artifacts of Asians in the United States. Rather, Yamashita's text grapples with both new and old imaginative formations of community and coalition enabled and transformed by spatial convergences particular to postmodernity or late capitalism.[20] These alternative communities are composed of nationally and racially heterogeneous social actors who are globally interrelated by virtue of worldwide media links, touristic travel across borders, international financial networks, transnational trade, and a shared ecology. Yet significantly, in the novel, they are also connected via a satellite who is associated, at least initially, with an Asian immigrant character.

Another means by which the author balances her global thematic and ethnic-local preoccupations is to make the two projects homologous by giving globalization an Asian cast. Whereas many theorists who explore the spread of social relations across space tend to equate globalization with the dissemination of Western culture,[21] Yamashita makes clear that the widening of Japan's influence is also her concern. The North American and later multinational firm GGG incorporates "old courses in Japanese corporate business sense" into its operating model (53). Likewise, the three-armed New Yorker, J. B. Tweep, describes himself as an East-West hybrid, a man who has "the security of a Japanese businessman" but the mobility and instability of "an American worker" (125). Playing with signs and acronyms, Yamashita colors her narrative with other references to Japan, for instance, in J. B.'s initials which might stand for "Japanese Brazilian," and in Batista and Tania's last name, a homonym for "Japan." Such wordplay, along with other overt references, build to a cumulative effect hinting at the Japanification of Brazil and the United States.

I have characterized such references as part of the author's attempt to resolve the tension between her global and ethnic-specific interests, by making globalization a synonym, not for Americanization, but for the spread of Japanese culture. Yet, some perhaps unintended consequences

result from this particular type of negotiation. Firstly, in a somewhat utopian vein, Yamashita imagines an Asiatic globalization that occurs seemingly without violence. For instance, in her chapter entitled "Karaoke," the
author details the expansion of this "style of nightclub invented by the
Japanese" until "almost every town in South America had one" (88). The
narrative portrays both the immigrant Kazumasa "singing with abandon in
his specially built karaoke shower at home" and the local São Paulan, Batista Djapan, expressing all of his pent-up *saudades* (a particular form of
Brazilian longing) at Hiro's Karaoke on the Matacão (149, 128). Here,
Japanification is envisioned as a relatively harmless cultural invasion, by
which a local Brazilian's expression is mediated, perhaps even facilitated,
but certainly not quashed by Japanese technology. In other words, the author seems to suggest that Japanese inflows ought not to be viewed with
orientalist anxieties about another "yellow peril."[22] Such perceptions can
catalyze a racist and institutionally sanctioned backlash that affects all Asian
Americans, as the Vincent Chin case well illustrates.[23] By the same token,
by portraying these Japanese influences as detached from a worldwide complex of uneven development, Yamashita understates the power asymmetries
between Japan, an economic superpower, and Brazil, a country in virtual
bondage to the International Monetary Fund and to "First World" lender
nations. According to Swasti Mitter, this debt crisis has led to "20 million
abandoned and undernourished children in Brazil, a country that has the
resources to feed not only all its own children but also millions in other
countries" (Mitter, 73). Though the novel does not comment on Japan's
role in Brazil's debt crisis, it does underscore the extraction of Brazil's
wealth to enrich the coffers of other nations.[24] The fictional run on Brazil's
newest "miracle" resource, the Matacão, mimics past expropriations of the
country's assets: "Brazil had once before emptied its wealthy gold mines
into the coffers of the Portuguese Crown and consequently financed the
Industrial Revolution in England. This time, if there was any wealth to be
had, it had better remain in Brazil. Some scoffed . . . saying that the treasure
of the Matacão might, at best, make a small dent in their continuing interest
payments to the International Monetary Fund" (96). Japan's cultural infusions in Brazil are merely one among many cultural "invasions" and exchanges involving Portugal, Britain, the Netherlands, Africa, and the
United States. Whereas, for critics of *Dogeaters*, international influences
were signs of an insidious Americanization and Hispanicization, in Yamashita's novel globalization has a much wider scope.

Secondly, Yamashita suggests that as the configuration of world power
shifts in the late-twentieth and early-twenty-first centuries,[25] it may be impossible or only nostalgic for Asian Americans to see themselves innocently
as part of the Third World oppressed—the ones being invaded by cultural
influences from elsewhere. Setting her tale in "the future," Yamashita, like

Jen, focuses on a world where Asian immigrants to the Americas are just as likely to be the owners of capital and the exploiters of labor as to be the persecuted migrant worker memorialized by Bulosan or Kingston. No longer does the Asian immigrant's critique of America—like that of Bulosan's protagonist, Carlos—unambiguously indict capital and, in particular, the instrumentality of Third World labor and racial stratification to capitalist processes. Instead, Yamashita challenges the assumption that Asian American cultural texts offer testament to a strictly downtrodden racial-economic subject largely defined by his or her victimization in the West. *Through the Arc*'s Asian immigrant protagonist, Kazumasa, remains an elite transnational who benefits from the services of a Brazilian maid.

At the same time, the novel refrains from triumphally hailing Asian (American) capitalist ownership as the natural and just ending to prior narratives of toiling, dispossessed Asian labor. Kazumasa hardly resembles the up-by-the-bootstraps individualist made memorable by Gish Jen, the immigrant who deliberately chooses acquisitive formulas of self-making as his pathway toward national belonging. Rather, this Asian transplant to Brazil hardly knows himself an agent of capitalist development. Instead, his cousin, Hiroshi, "an entrepreneur and investor par excellence" (81), invests Kazumasa's windfall fortune without his knowledge:

> No matter how much money Kazumasa gave away and despite Hiroshi's harangues about Kazumasa's giving, Hiroshi was able to triple whatever remained, so there was virtually no end of it. Many people . . . began calling [Kazumasa] the Japanese Robin Hood. It was . . . just a more modern way of stealing from the rich and giving to the poor. Hiroshi himself explained the phenomenon to the press as "recycling capital." Kazumasa would not have thought of any of this. He was simply listening to people's stories and their desires, trying to figure out what it was that people wanted or should want out of life. (81)

The narrator, here, draws a sharp distinction between the capitalist processes of accumulation, pursued by Hiroshi, and the social mechanisms of distribution and community building that preoccupy Kazumasa. Though both Hiroshi and Kazumasa, by virtue of their assets, fit the profile of the new Asian transnational (im)migrant, only Hiroshi, like Ralph Chang in Jen's novel, pays attention to accumulating wealth. Kazumasa "instinctively [gives] his money away" (61). Significantly, then, Kazumasa, rather than Hiroshi, wins the heart of the maid, Lourdes, a plot point that symbolically endorses the virtues of charity and wealth distribution over accumulation and extracting surplus. The trope of marriage, thus, solidifies Kazumasa's symbolic role as a bridge figure who not only links Asian American temporalities but also enters into a family relationship with a person from a different race, culture, and class to form a further border-crossing social formation.

The futuristic portrait of *Through the Arc* fictionally suggests that rather than identifying first and foremost with the nineteenth-century railroad worker and rallying behind his exclusion from national belonging, Asian Americans might widen the scope of their struggles and de-ethnicize their communal fidelities in order to fight for the poor and oppressed regardless of national origins.[26] At the same time, *Through the Arc* stresses the unevenness of Asian-Pacific nationalities and regions, as suggested by the different meanings attached to the spread of karaoke and the global travel of "Aloha" T-shirts. In effect, Yamashita underscores the need not for a complacent reiteration of Asian America's past or for an uninformed reorientation toward Asian America's vexing and prospective subjects, but rather, for a stereoscopic view of both, incarnate in her railroad worker who sings karaoke.

Moreover in Kazumasa's marriage to Lourdes, Yamashita suggests a bridge figure between, on the one hand, Asian capital and labor (the karaoke-singing railroad worker) and, on the other, the Asian professional-managerial class and contemporary Latina figures of labor—the Brazilian domestic, for instance. In other words, when Asians become associated less with the laboring bodies of historical memory—nineteenth-century coolies, plantation workers, migrant field laborers, cannery workers—and more with the ownership of capital and professional occupations (e.g., engineering, nursing, teaching, law, accounting, journalism)—Asian American writers may negotiate that financial-economic ascendancy by (re)-claiming proletarian solidarity through the symbolism of marriage. This technique operates conversely, in substance, but with logic identical to that of the much-discussed outmarriage rates of Asians in the United States who have been theorized as shedding a minoritized identity by evidence of their incorporation—through marriage and kinship—into the white, economically privileged mainstream.[27]

The aligning of professional Asian immigrants with the Latin American working class through the plot development of heterosexual marriage is not without its problems. Marriage, itself a social contract fraught with power inequities, ought not be mistaken for a social panacea, magically resolving incommensurabilities of class, politics, and culture. Moreover, couching Kazumasa and Lourdes's employer-employee relationship in terms of a burgeoning romance obscures the economic exploitation of Latinas by men from the Asian NICs. In this respect, Yamashita follows the example of soap operas that have been critiqued as politically retrograde in their emphasis on class stratification simply overcome through love and marriage (Modleski, 113; Mumford 10, 91, 93). Yamashita's emphasis on sites of romance and domesticity, from one aspect, can appear as a trivializing of the entire work, distracting readers from the novel's more serious work of critiquing global phenomena. However, it is precisely through the narration of Kazumasa's domestic life that the novel broaches the position and agency of Asian migrants in a transnationally defined society. Put simply, Kazumasa gets the girl where Hiroshi doesn't. Notably, then, the locus of domestic relations, romance and family—the arena, in fact, of *telenovelas* (Brazilian soap operas)—provides the ground for the narrative to register sympathy for one type of Asian transnational, the traveler seeking love, friendship and kinship, over his cousin configuration, the entrepreneur-investor.

It seems imperative, therefore, to examine exactly what purchase Yamashita more broadly gets from placing sites of domesticity, love, marriage, and kinship in the novel's foreground. *Through the Arc*'s emphasis on domestic spaces and activities done at home—as opposed to grand feats accomplished on the national terrain—once again places the novel at odds with Asian American cultural nationalist paradigms and to a certain degree with Asia-Pacific formulations as well. (Analyses of the Asia-Pacific tend to focus on the large-scale border-crossing phenomenon of media links, transnational cultural flows, and labor migrations.) However, it is my argument that Yamashita renders domestic narratives instrumental to the novel's global themes, and thereby revises her audience's perspective on globalization (showing hegemonic narrations of globalization as gendered).

THE INTIMACY OF GLOBAL OPPRESSION

In her author's note at the beginning of the book, Yamashita introduces her narrative as "a kind of *novela*, a Brazilian soap opera [in which the] story is completely changeable according to the whims of public psyche . . . although most likely, the unhappy find happiness; the bad are punished; true love reigns; a popular actor is saved from death."[28] The admission of melodramatic indebtedness has not endeared the book to critics who lambaste the conventions of melodrama and, by extension, Yamashita's work (Pfeil; Harris).[29] Rather than ignoring the novel's reliance on the telenovela formula, I wish to place this stylistic issue in the foreground, as does the author herself, to analyze the reasons behind Yamashita's modeling her narrative on this slightly-regarded specimen of popular entertainment. How does this stylistic choice augment or detract from the narrative's global themes? What are the gendered implications of the novel's reliance on a "Brazilian soap opera,"[30] especially in relation to this text's place in the evolving canons of Asian American and Asian-Pacific literatures?

In tackling these questions, I would first contextualize Yamashita's work in terms of a concurrent anthropological project she was conducting in Brazil.[31] This project would later yield the historical novel *Brazil-Maru*, which excavates Japanese immigrant history in South America. The utility and function of this type of work to Asian American Studies is obvious: the novel memorializes ethnic community, builds transcontinental links, and broadens definitions of Asian America to include Asian diasporas to Latin America. Yamashita's personal reasons for writing *Through the Arc*, as a creative release from this other sort of labor, are worth noting here.[32] Her ethnographic research began as a series of oral histories of Japanese Brazilian women from the period 1908 to 1924. However, Yamashita soon became convinced that her female informants could not answer "all of the big questions" she was interested in, regarding "land, settlement, immigration, community, society, and Japanese culture" (Murashige 1993, 23); in short, that she "couldn't do little oral histories of women between 1908 and 1924" if she wanted to get the "larger picture" (Murashige 1993, 23, 22).[33] After two to three years of research, Yamashita wrote three entirely new manuscripts before even submitting what became *Brazil-Maru*, the gendered contents of which deserves an essay in its own right. It was during the arduous drafting and redrafting of this work that Yamashita, on the fly and in collaboration with her husband, Ronaldo, improvised the multiple tales she later interwove into her fantastical novel *Through the Arc*.

The overlap in time periods in which the two books were constructed is not the only point worth noting. Premised upon a prime-time melodrama, *Through the Arc* is comprised of a series of love triangles: lovers separate, missed communication prevails, exaggerated domestic situations provide the filter through which the audience perceives the novel's global themes— for example, destruction of the environment and "First World" overdevelopment as the active underdevelopment of the "Third World." In comparison to *Brazil-Maru*, which details the founding of a unique artistic and spiritual Japanese settlement in Brazil (c.f. Tsuchida), the romantic emphasis of *Through the Arc* might seem trivial.[34] In fact, one might argue that for the author, herself, the license to be playful with the minutiae of everyday life was in fact a primary reason for its being written; its express purpose was not to render history or to comment on the sociology of Asian Americans. Despite the author's separation of her two writing processes into one that was work, and correlatively did work for community building, and one that was more like play, and whose utility to Asian America is therefore less clear, I would argue that *Through the Arc* does accomplish a type of work in relation to Asian American literary criticism.

I have already outlined a number of ways in which this novel forces its readers to come to grips with several changing parameters of minority discourse. To reiterate, *Through the Arc* shatters the space-time of Asian America through its choice of a fantastical projection of a twenty-first-century world without boundaries, thereby urging Asian Americanists to frame their analyses not only in terms of national politics but in terms of transnational or global conditions. Moreover, it is under the generic constraints of a form that emphasizes "personal feelings," the small acts of everyday life, and women's sphere that *Through the Arc* comments upon "the global condition" (Vink, 187). This task is no small feat when one considers that the most common languages to conceptualize globalization remain highly theoretical and detached from the life-worlds of those they are intended to describe. For instance, a preferred means of mapping globalization since the late 1960s[35] has been to point to changes in the organization of capital (see Harvey; Jameson; Rouse; Massey; Miyoshi). In the postwar period, multinational and transnational corporations have become increasingly powerful and wily in their capacities to make profits by spreading out operations across multiple national terrains, thereby obtaining raw materials on the cheap, getting around trade restrictions, and taking advantage of nonunionized labor sectors (usually women) in Latin America and Asia.[36] According to Doreen Massey, "regional and local economies are increasingly locked in, not so much to national economies, but directly to the world economy. . . . Each geographical 'place' in the world is being realigned in relation to the new globalities. . . . [T]heir boundaries dissolve as they are increasingly crossed by everything from investments flows, to cultural influences, to satellite TV networks" (161). It is through that sense of porous boundaries, of hyperlinks to a global rather than national economy, that Yamashita makes her global preoccupations felt. However, Yamashita does not directly condemn the economic base driving the spread of social relations across national boundaries; rather, she ties her playful critique of "development" to several romantic story lines. One laments, not the impoverishment of toiling laborers by the greed of the transnational bourgeoisie, but the spreading out of social relations across space that thwarts the intimacy between lovers.

Therefore, though Yamashita's novel may be responding to the new world (dis)order brought on by the spread of capitalism, her critique of globalization exceeds, or is not confined to, a critique of global capital. She also scrutinizes the forms of life and social relations that are altered by global communications networks, technologies of high-speed travel, world cultural organizations, and ecological movements that are not reducible to capital's effects. As Roland Robertson points out, many discussions of globalization have focused on the causes or driving forces behind globalization—the spread of Western capitalism and the role of imperialism, for example. Few commentators have essayed a "cultural focus," by which he means an analysis of the ways in which people have made sense of "the compression of the world" and have articulated an "intensification of consciousness of the world as a whole" (Robertson, 28–29, 8).

Within the fictional landscape of Yamashita's novel, soap operas provide one means of "mapping the global condition"—to borrow the title of one of Robertson's chapters. For example, while the drastic changes in Mané Pena's life have clearly resulted from both national and international development plans, the former rubber tapper uses the formal structure of soap opera to make sense of the upheaval in his daily routine: "To have one's life changed forever, three times, amounted in Mané's mind to being like one of those actors on TV who slipped from soap opera to soap opera and channel to channel, being reincarnated into some new character each time. One story had nothing to do with the other except that the actor was the same" (18). Soap operas, rather than the discourses of cybernetic management or cultural imperialism, provide Mané a means of making sense of his rapid transformation and coexistence in several space-times. One can, of course, point out that the telenovela is an internationally broadcast media, hardly a cultural artifact derivative of a local or native understanding. However, these romantic serials are also a means of familiarizing or domesticating public issues through narratives of love and friendship, a point to which I will return shortly.[37] Yamashita's readers find themselves in a position similar to Mané's, comprehending the "global condition" through the domestic tropes, thematic emphases, and cyclical structure of soaps. Rather than handicapping her audience, however, this reconstruction of soap opera deepens the reader's sense of globalization by privileging, what Donald Nonini in another context calls the "human scale" of globalization (Nonini, 162–63), or the perspective of people caught up in time-space compression but not necessarily in control of it.

Soap operas prove apt vehicles for the delineation of experiences on a human scale because of their emphasis on "life in its everyday realisation through personal relationships" (Brunsdon 1981, 34). That this emphasis on personal life is also a particularly gendered mode of presentation becomes clear upon critic Charlotte Brunsdon's further claim:

> [Personal life] can be understood to be constituted primarily through the [soap-opera's] representation of romances, families and attendant rituals—births, engagements, marriages, divorces and deaths. In marxist terms this is the sphere of the individual outside of labour. In feminist terms, it is the sphere of women's 'intimate oppression.' Ideologically constructed as the feminine sphere, it is within this realm of the domestic, the personal, the private, that feminine competence is recognised. (34)

Though there is no inherent association of women with "personal life," Brunsdon suggests that material and ideological constraints imposed upon women have resulted in their exclusion from public life and their accountability first and foremost to the household, often under patriarchal rule.[38] The ability to manage feelings and emotions, to sustain a nurturing atmosphere at home, is an invisible and unpaid labor that many women perform and that both soap operas and telenovelas implicitly recognize. Also in the spirit of telenovelas, *Through the Arc* does not restrict its narrative scope solely to the domestic realm but represents the arena of commercial affairs through a quotidian perspective. For instance, in Yamashita's portrait of the multinational corporation GGG, the author stresses workplace minutiae, such as the secretaries' squabbles at the Xerox machine (19), that coexist alongside the company's balance sheets and diversified holdings. What happens at the commissary gets equal time as the profiles of GGG's international buyers (20).

By intertwining the personal, quotidian aspects of everyday life with the public, historical significance of these same acts, Yamashita, like Hagedorn, emphasizes their mutual constitution. For example, the Matacão stages such global spectacles as the World Hockey play-offs or the Pope meeting his South American flock alongside events of "less than international significance": "Candomblé affairs . . . weddings, folk-dancing, operas, stand-up comedy, scenes provided for daily television soap operas. . . . Many couples claimed that they had experienced love at first sight on the Matacão. One mother and father decided to have their baby born there, while an old woman insisted on fasting there to complete the cycle of her life" (102). Through such juxtaposition, the author at once filters the grandiose term "globalization" through the perspective of an old woman dying, and renders this small act an "internationally significant" event. In contrast to Jen's inverse manipulations of familial and historical chronologies, Yamashita does not so much privilege domestic events, such as births, weddings, and funerals, over and above global happenings. Instead, she stages them in the same space, relying upon the telenovela's ability to blur the hierarchical distinction between highly publicized acts and the personal, familial cycles of the everyday.[39]

Yamashita, thus, highlights other discursive structures that commingle the public realm of finance with the private arena of domestic emotions. For instance, a love letter from Tania Djapan to her husband, Batista, mixes expressions of tenderness with news of her recent business escapades:

> "Batista, honey, how I miss you. Mother and I have been very busy. You can check your release times but Gugu came in at 2:30 PM on Tuesday the 4th, and Kaka came in at 6:00 AM the next day. Well, to get to the point, I met Sr. Carlos Rodrigues, who owns the Pomba Soap Company. What a cute old man!" (Batista cringed.) "Well, he really liked the idea. . . . Imagine people all over Brazil will get the message about Pomba Soap. We got a very nice commission, you know, and a year's worth of Pomba soap. What do you think? Kisses and hugs, your Tania Cidinha." (94)

Like the melodramatic radio serials that later evolved into televisual programs, Tania's "pigeon advertising" business begins as a vehicle for selling soap. Fittingly, news of her joint venture into the public world of finance and corporate dealing is conveyed in the cooing tones of a love letter. Interestingly, the narrative highlights, not Batista's delight in his wife's business acumen, but his jealous flinching over Tania's flirtation with the "cute old man" Sr. Carlos Rodrigues. Thus, even while presenting aspects of high finance and passionate turmoil in the same breath, Yamashita suggests that the requirements and effects of global travel may attenuate romantic links, alter the gendered roles necessary to domestic harmony, and fundamentally transform the structures of emotional attachment and desire.

Somewhat paradoxically, then, Yamashita's reconstruction of soap opera at once deepens the reader's sense of globalization—presenting it from a local, quotidian perspective—and also challenges the primacy of globalization (read: global capital, transnational technologies, earth-wide ecology) as a commonplace, shared discourse speaking to the material realities of her readers. Rather Yamashita's novel presumes upon other fundamental reference points—domestic strife, kin and community relationships, romantic and erotic desires—and forms of discourse, such as love letters and gossip, that circulate in everyday life. In her incorporation of these informal categories of speech, Yamashita adopts a style similar to that of Hagedorn, who reproduces radio melodramas, love letters, and *tsismis* (gossip), all unofficial sources of oftentimes gendered information. Yet, distinct from Hagedorn's project, Yamashita's work does not underscore women as a separate class, a group situated differently with respect to imperialism, postcolonial nationalism, or Third World development schemes. Instead, while using a narrative mode focused on domesticity, Yamashita challenges the gendered ideology of the domestic realm as the exclusive province of women.

For example, in her portrait of the gay couple Chico Paco and Gilberto Yamashita presents two men who each take on tasks traditionally reserved for women, cooking and lace making, in effect challenging gendered social conventions of labor. When Chico Paco helps Dona Angustia in the kitchen, she comments

> "My menfolk won't do any cooking. . . . Who taught you to cook?"
> "My father died when I was little. I always helped my mother out. . . . Some cilantro and green onions would give the fish flavor," he added.
> Dona Angustia nodded, avoiding Chico Paco's glistening green eyes. Those people who lived near the ocean were different she had decided. (48)[40]

Despite Dona Angustia's assessment that Chico Paco is "different" because he flouts gender norms, the narrative helps the reader to recognize gender conventions of housework by placing him in a familiar "hetero" configuration. That is, Chico Paco's defying gender conventions can be ascertained by the presence of Dona Angustia, who does the work that "menfolk" refuse. In a same-sex (e.g., gay male) household, by contrast, Chico Paco's labor in the kitchen, and the division of household tasks more generally, would be difficult to read in gender-stratified terms.

According to recent scholarship on the gendering of labor in the household, the conceptualization of domestic labor as gendered feminine, itself presumes heterosexual couples as a reference (Oerton, 424–25). Hence, researchers of domestic labor in lesbian and gay households, attempting to rectify this bias, account for inequities in the parceling out of housework through factors other than gender (e.g., parity of income, length of cohabitation, skills and abilities, time schedules) (Oerton, 423–24). Surveying both types of "gender-empty" and "gender-full" scholarship, Sarah Oerton proposes that gendering processes informing housework—though not strictly born out in same-sex households—might still inform the latter's dynamics: "Gender power relations may be inextricably linked with heterosexual, couple-based households, as research has suggested, but it would be surprising if lesbian and gay relationships did not also reflect some of the ways in which gender is deeply implicated in power relations, albeit in complex and contradictory ways" (426). Moreover, to entertain gender-full analyses in examining lesbian and gay households also expands our notions of "new forms of masculinities and feminities" (428). Such new masculinities are embodied in Chico Paco's and Gilberto's taking on domestic tasks that other Brazilians assign strictly to women.

In the figure of Chico Paco, then, Yamashita offers her readers a model of a "new masculinity" that values domestic relations and domestic work rather than equating them with emasculation and disempowerment. As mentioned in chapter 3, the adoption of household work by men, or being turned into a "nation of busboys," has often been a rallying point for collective revolution and stands as an exemplary instance of domestic work's association with nationally construed impotency. Under this persuasion, Chico Paco's willingness to cook and maintain the household testifies to his—and by extension other Third World men's—subordinate, because effeminate, role. Yet I would propose that Chico Paco's domesticity intervenes into nationalism's emphasis on women's subordinate status, simply by refusing the equation of domestic labor and housewifery with an abject identity. The narrative contests gender conventions from a perspective that values "women's work." At the same time, Yamashita deconstructs any natural association of domestic labor with women. Chico Paco's "special attentions" toward Gilberto and his culinary talents—in sum, his engaging in tasks traditionally reserved for women—implicitly call into question the presumption that social roles of caregiving, nurturing, running the household, and other forms of "women's labor," proceed from biological sex differences.

Following the example of telenovelas, *Through the Arc* magnifies the importance of the domestic realm by depicting how much effort is required in negotiating its demands. However, this magnification of the domestic does not necessarily translate into an exclusive focus on women or a feminist emphasis on their gendered difference. Rather, Yamashita takes aim at gendered institutions, such as the apportioning of certain tasks based on biological sex differences and constructing an ideology of specific work as "natural" to a particular sex, precisely by depicting two male characters who take on domestic work that, by Brazilian convention, are restricted to women. However, the genre of telenovelas accommodates defiance of gender and sexuality norms quite distinctly. That is, even as Yamashita simply posits a gay household as as legitimate a formation as any other, her narrative only accommodates Chico Paco and Gilberto's homosexuality to a certain degree. The two men's homoeroticism is visible only to the extent that it can be ascertained through tropes of domesticity, and, even more specifically, domesticity at a crisis due to globalization and technologies of travel.

Yamashita narrates the crisis to Chico Paco and Gilberto's home life once the latter—a former invalid—regains his mobile capacities. At first the two are separated when Chico Paco undergoes his first pilgrimage to the Matacão to give thanks for the miracle of Gilberto's legs. Yet even after Gilberto joins Chico Paco at the Matacão, the crisis of spatial displacement continues as Gilberto learns to walk, then run, becoming enamored of "movement and speed" (166). The narrator details the stress suffered by Chico Paco due to his domestic partner's accelerating experiments: "Inevitably, Gilberto would crash or tumble in his escapades . . . [getting out of] most of these episodes with only bumps and bruises, but to Chico Paco's dismay, even a broken bone did not slow his friend down much at all. What had happened to the invalid quietly weaving lace in the shade of a coconut tree? thought Chico Paco, gripping his heart and wondering whether he could live through another one of Gilberto's crazy episodes" (166, 170). Gilberto's desire for spatial displacement eventually persuades Chico Paco to construct for his lover a global fantasy world or theme park, called Chicolándia, that literalizes the annihilation of time and space:

> Everything in Chicolándia was being made of Matacão plastic, from the roller coasters to the [interiors] designed to imitate scenes from Gilberto's favorite movies—*Cabaret*; *Heidi*; *Cleopatra*; *Snow White*; *Spartacus*; *Hello, Dolly*; *Cat Ballou*; *Raiders of the Lost Ark*; *The King and I*; *Star Trek IV*— . . . [arranged in a] maze of magnificent scenes: Babylonian towers on a desert oasis, the Taj Mahal, the docks of Amsterdam, Times Square in New York City, the Miami International Airport, the French Riviera . . . ancient Rome, mythical Greece, and the moon. . . . [T]he former invalid, who had never known any place other than his birthplace . . . could soon be suddenly anywhere in both time and space. (168)

Built with the financial backing of the multinational corporation GGG and concocted from a global (here, U.S.) imaginary of popular movies, Chicolándia literalizes a centrifuge of disjunctive geographies. Yet even as the amusement park presents in microcosm a spatially compressed and temporally displaced world, it functions within the unfolding narrative as an elaborate love token from Chico Paco to Gilberto.

Though Gilberto's fantasy land clearly symbolizes the realization of global consciousness, it is equally important to the narrative's illustration of the domestic tensions and pressing desires developing between the childhood companions once Gilberto regains his mobility. When he is a childlike invalid sewing lace under a coconut tree, the relationship between the two men is suggested to be a close, brotherly friendship—homosocial but not necessarily homoerotic. However, once Gilberto moves to the city, begins roaming and testing his desires, the narrative makes explicit the men's romantic, sexual relationship, portraying them sleeping "snugly in each other arms" (189) and later naming them expressly as "gay" (191). On an allegorical level, Chicolándia becomes the ground upon which the narrative stages the two men's different abandonments to homoerotic desire. Chico Paco initially conceives of the amusement park as something to "placate" yet contain Gilberto's passion for speed, a way of letting his desires run amuck but in a controlled setting under "twenty-four-hour guard" (169). Though the park's surveillance cameras are designed to lessen the effects of Gilberto's transgressive desires, they inadvertently offer new opportunities for staging flamboyant fantasies. Gilberto mugs to the cameras, costuming himself elaborately, and flouts all attempts to settle him down (169). Similarly, when Yamashita reveals Gilberto's and Chico Paco's homosexual desires, she underscores the heterosexual mandates that attempt to contain their love in homosocial, brotherly, or parental terms, also to no avail: "Some pilgrims were secretly envious of Gilberto and the special attentions Chico Paco, they said, showered on that frivolous child. . . . Perhaps Chico Paco needed to be saved from Gilberto. For the moment, the gossip was fettered by an undercurrent of guilt. Chico Paco was a sort of saint, an angel, was he not? He was the very salvation of thousands of believers. So what if he were gay. So what if he *were* gay?" (191). Chicolándia, in sum, allegorically functions as a regulating structure that, in its policing or restricting of "normal" behavior, enables, even as it suppresses, transgressive desire.

Therefore, homosexual desire—hesitantly expressed both through Gilberto's mobile desires and in Chico Paco's "special attentions" toward Gilberto (191)—is not completely accommodated in Yamashita's text. The author only allegorizes Gilberto's awakened erotic passions in his "love of movement and speed."[41] In effect, the narrative highlights Gilberto and Chico Paco's relationship primarily as a gay version of domesticity rather than as a homoerotic tale of passion. Yet, encouraging the examination of the two men's sexualized, domestic relation in the first place is the narrative's reliance upon the "personal" problematic of the telenovela.[42] Rather than interpreting Chico Paco's significance to the novel solely in terms of his spearheading a potentially global evangelical movement, one must also take account those primary concerns of the televisual melodrama, "gender, love, marriage and family" (Vink, 181).

In similar fashion, it would be a mistake to read Yamashita's portrait of Tania and Batista Djapan strictly in terms of their entrepreneurial part in enhancing transnational communications networks. Though, from one perspective, Tania's activities promoting pigeon advertising might be viewed as a catalyst to time-space compression, this economist interpretation risks missing the gendered connotations of Tania's wanderlust. Though her globe-trotting clearly participates in a broad phenomenon of time-space compression, it also proceeds from and contributes toward the reformulation of domestic relations.

The narrative introduces the pigeon business not as a master plan of global unification but as part of a long-standing conflict between Tania and her husband Batista over the appropriate duties of a wife: "When [Tania] did not live with Batista, she lived with her mother a few tenements down the street. Her coming and going, however, did not please Batista, who could be seen dragging his wife home at some odd hour of the night or prodding her toward her kitchen with the end of a baguette at dinnertime. 'When a man comes home at night, he should have a supper waiting! I'm nearly dead from hunger' " (12). Though Batista himself tarries at the bar after work, he cannot countenance Tania's splitting her time between taking care of her mother, living away from him, and tending to his needs at home. Her limited wanderings thus become connected in his mind to her lack of family ways: "They had no children, and Batista continually accused Tania Aparecida of never being home long enough to have children in the first place" (12). By living with her mother, thereby having multiple homes, and by not having children either willingly or unwillingly, Tania both displaces and undermines the stability of "home."[43] Significantly, Tania's mobility—her actions outside the house—stands in stark contrast to the type of wifely duty embodied in *Typical American*'s Helen Chang; however, in both cases the stability or instability of home rests on the presumption that home work is women's work. Thus, the attributing of instability of home to Tania alone rests on the questionable naturalization of a gendered division of household labor.

Batista's desire for his wife to be always at home—in fact, to act as a marker of home and locational stability—is fraught with anxiety over patrilineage, not only that Tania might not bear him children but that even if she did, they might not be his.[44] Hence Batista's fascination with other men as potential seducers of his wife: "[Batista] imagined Tania Aparecida in every sort of situation of infidelity. He tossed in his bed at night with visions of Tania Aparecida in the arms of another man, or even several men. . . . He imagined the men of every race, creed, religion and color running their foreign tongues up and down the curve of her neck and touching all those secret places only he was supposed to know" (171). Anxieties over nativity become staged around the mobile, female body. To protect his wife from "foreign" invasion is also to protect his own patriline from clandestine infusions.

Tania's peripatetic desire, perceived as adulterous intent, is significantly mediated by Batista's other paramours, his pigeons: "Tania Aparecida looked at the map to see where the Djapan pigeons were flying, and she compared this with so many other exotic places in the world. . . . After all, one had reached New York. . . . Somehow, she would find a way to get to New York" (137). Whereas the pigeons' movements are unrestricted—without passports and without cultural constraints on what types of travel are legal or appropriate—Tania's mobility, by contrast, is gender-restrictive.[45] In trying to get to those "exotic places" Tania must dream up a type of travel that extends domestic values:

> Her marketing approach was to sell pigeons as monogamous, familial, dependable and loving creatures, the perfect messenger to send one's love, best wishes or condolences. . . . It was an immediate success. . . . In no time at all, Tania Aparecida was opening new homing posts in towns everywhere. . . . Soon she found herself as far from her home as Rio Grande do Sul. . . . From there, it was a short hop to Buenos Aires in Argentina. Djapan Pigeon Communications went international. (137)

Further displacing the idea of home, Tania's "greeting-pigeon business" promotes the strengthening yet also the attenuation of kinship, as family values are sent through the airwaves. Though making clear that Tania, as she haggles over the price of bird seed, "[begins] to see pigeons as a profitable source of income" (92), the narrative simultaneously constructs Tania's business sense as an alternative to her domestic labor: "Tania Aparecida discovered that she liked to haggle over prices, to make deals and even to watch the inflation index. Compared to washing clothing, cooking and sewing, this was so much better" (92). The generation of income is part and parcel of Tania's more pressing motive: to escape the realm of unwaged domestic work.

Yet, at the same time, Tania's access to international mobility does not so much indicate a liberation from familial constraints as much as it reconfigures female domestic duties under transnational modes of capital accumulation. As revealed in Tania's sales pitch, the pigeon franchise is an income-producing structure aimed at women who can run the business out of their homes: "We work with a lot of mothers who are busy at home with their children and who can make a little extra money on the side. I know one woman, Dona Clara in Campo Verde, who buys all her groceries from her profits in the network." (172–73). Tania's pigeon franchise both relies upon and extends an ideology of women's primary responsibilities to the household. In framing her franchise as a way for mothers to make "a little extra money on the side," Tania abets the misconception of women's work as supplementary income. According to Mies, when women are "defined as 'housewives,' not as workers," their "productive work under capital accumulation is *obscured*" (123); their toil "does not appear as 'free wage-labour' [but] as an 'income-generating *activity*,' and can hence be bought at a much cheaper price than male labour" (Mies, 116). Contrary to Tania's description, then, Dona Clara is not so much making "a little extra money on the side" as she is doing double duty as a homeworker, contributing to the subsistence of labor, and as a supplier of commodities and services to the world market, providing for capital's surplus. Yet, both of these labors are casualized—unrecognized as a primary support and devalued under the logic of capitalist patriarchy.

Tweaking the gender-specific meanings of Tania's business, the narrator remarks on Batista's puzzlement over the squab recipes that Tania includes in her international newsletter: "He got the newsletter [and] wondered why Tania Aparecida insisted on putting a new squab recipe in the cooking column every week. He had seen the network map grow into a mass of posts over the globe. He knew that their operation was big, but *he had no real sense of it*" (173; emphasis added). Clearly, Tania places the squab recipes in the newsletter to acknowledge the domestic chores women carry out in addition to their waged work, a gesture that Batista simply does not understand. Though Batista comprehends the business's global expanse, he has no sense of its gendered terms.

In interpreting Yamashita's novel, one runs a similar risk of accounting for the novel's global themes and effects without a sense of its gendered meanings. One sense of the novel's gendered meanings is that, in addition to commenting on globalization, the narrative portrays domestic relationships that bear upon gay and lesbian campaigns against heterosexual mandates and on gendered struggles against male domination. Another sense of its gendered meaning is to be found in an understanding of the way in which global economics is articulated alongside gender hierarchy. Swasti Mitter explores the way in which women—and more importantly, gender ideology about women—remain fundamental to the globalization of capital. Transnational corporations are not only shifting labor-intensive aspects of production to the "low-wage, newly industrializing countries of Asia and Latin America" (Mitter, 8) but also to a largely female work force. Mitter makes clear that "it is not the genetic characteristics of women workers that make them the preferred labour force" (13), but rather, a gendered ideology that has constructed them as supplemental, casual workers: "These workers are precisely the ones who have so far been marginalized in the mainstream labour movement. Their very vulnerability has made them a preferred labour force in an evolving pattern of business organization that tends to rely on flexible and disposable workers" (6). Thus the "restructuring of capital"—its increasing profits by lowering wages (i.e., turning to women workers)—"is fundamentally based on the accepted division of work in the domestic sphere. As it is the women who are deemed responsible for housework and childcare, it is considered normal for them to be satisfied with ill-paid and insecure jobs" (14–17).[46] Gendering processes constitutive of and constituted by domestic work become instrumental to capital's flexible accumulation strategies that take place across borders precisely to take advantage of various, localized gender inequities in what counts as labor.

Yamashita's novel destabilizes, to a certain degree, the ideology of household work as women's work that, as Mitter notes, extends transnational capital's accumulative capacities. However, her narration, on the whole, avoids focusing on the gendered ways in which developing countries are portioning the brunt of labor within their own populations. Instead, the narrative depicts men and women together (in heterosexual and homosexual couples) suffering some measure of upheaval, namely, a disruption to their domestic bliss, as in the cases of Baptista-Tania and Chico Paco-Gilberto. The zone of familial, sexual intimacy suffers, but women as a group and men as a group are not engaged or only sporadically engaged as to their different interpellations in capitalist ideology, extraction economics, and transnational strategies of accumulation. Moreover, in the case of Kazumasa and Lourdes, the emphasis on their romantic domestic relation, because it is couched as love rather than labor, tends to obscure the power geometries still operative in a compressed world of transgressed borders and mixed cultures. Put simply, though the two lovers live in the same household, there is still a big difference between being the patron and being the maid. The narrative focus on domesticity thus yields contradictory results, on the one hand, apologizing obliquely for the transnational class, hiding their exploitative potential beneath the mask of romantic lover, and, on the other, affording Yamashita the opportunity to do a certain type of radical gendered work: highlighting the quotidian actions of those in "less than masterful" positions—oftentimes Third World women but here also Third World men—and reconstructing the gendered realm of the domestic, usually hinging upon heteronormative notions of the public/ private realms, as also the province of gay men.

Feminine Pleasure As Asian American Work

Through the Arc's accomplishment thus lies, not only in its mapping the deformations of global capital, but also in its gendered presentation of time-space compression. That gendered presentation takes on many forms, such as the novel's focus on the quotidian, personal aspects of high finance, and its granting a privileged stature to domestic relationships as arenas for renegotiating gender roles and sexual identities. It also comes to light in the narrative's soap opera–like structure, which, in its continual deferral of resolutions, might be said to afford a particular kind of feminine narrative pleasure. Speaking about such narrative deferrals, Modleski contrasts the "antiprogressive" diegetic structure of soap operas with the plot-driven linearity of classic "male" films: "Soap opera is . . . antiprogressive. . . . [It] is opposed to the classic (male) film narrative, which, with maximum action and minimum, always pertinent dialogue, speeds its way to the restoration of order." (Modleski, 106). Drawing upon the work of Luce Irigaray, Modleski further claims that soap operas are in keeping with "an already developing, though still embryonic, feminist aesthetics. . . . [S]oap operas suggest an alternate kind of narrative pleasure experienced by women" (105, 108).[47] The telenovela upon which Yamashita premises her novel has an internal antiprogressive diegetic structure but differs from American soap opera in its eventual conclusion (Lopez 1985, 8). Thus, where Modleski links American soap opera's antiprogressive structure to a "feminist aesthetics," I would emphasize Yamashita's use of telenovelas to forward her critique of development. Thematically, *Through the Arc* takes up the issues of the limits of the world's resources, of environmental degradation, and of the havoc wreaked by consumerism and transnational finance; formally, the novel accentuates these themes through a disruptive narrative structure that emphasizes, in parallel fashion, the limits of discursive and cybernetic efficiency.[48]

I would recall, here, that *Through the Arc* began as a series of playfully improvised episodes that the author subsequently structured into a unified story line.[49] The resulting linear design—punctuated by part titles that stress the sequence, Beginning, Development, Loss, and Return—overlays but does not eclipse the random, improvisational events told in the various episodes. This throughline, like the soap opera's promise of romantic fulfillment, keeps the viewer coming back for more, first acclimating the audience to the interruption of the story line and then releasing them to it. Randomness, disorder, missed opportunities, missed connections—the telenovela enlists all these to prolong viewing pleasure.[50] Similar to what happens in a soap opera, the characters' pathways in *Through the Arc* cross over and abut, oftentimes without purpose. Not every meeting can be traced back to a specific intent. The disruption of the throughline produces an erotics of suspense, an affective and participatory design rather than a neat display of straightforward flows.

This tension between communicational efficiency and emotional dalliance is dramatized in New York magnate J. B. Tweep's first impressions of Brazil. Embodying cybernetic efficiency, the three-armed Tweep finds his own "overdeveloped" capacities directly challenged by the specific tempo and conditions of the Matacão: "[J. B.] thought his third arm might be atrophying in this hot tropical weather. And it exasperated him that things did not seem to work in this country. There was no organization. . . . J. B. was beginning to have serious doubts about his effectiveness in the Third World" (75). Doubt is an affective sensation hitherto unknown to J. B. who has always regarded himself as "a better model, the wave of the future" (30). Try as he might to eliminate the emotional quotient so as to be supremely "effective," J. B. finds his own "exasperation" mirrored in the emotional breakdown of his employees:

> [J. B.] had the Human Resources Department [of GGG] re-cloned and flown in. Except for the fact that power failures were frequent and caused chaos close to hysteria (Human Resources had several ongoing seminars to help shocked employees: "Working in the Third World," "Controlling Emotions in Dysfunctional Elevators and/or Dark Copy Rooms," "What to Do When the Air Conditioning Fails" and "Sexism in a Friendly Country"), everything seemed to fall into place. (76)

The author hides with one hand what she reveals with the other, with the assertion, "everything seemed to fall into place," literally disrupted by the long section in parentheses describing mass hysteria. The exaggerated corporate jargon also reflects upon the indivisibility of language with culture. The tortuous phrase, "Controlling Emotions in Dysfunctional Elevators and/or Dark Copy Rooms," suggests that J. B. and GGG have an extravagant need for control over the unfamiliar terrain of the "Third World." That desire for control and "order" produces its own excesses (the crazily proposed seminars).

Throughout the novel, Yamashita both stylistically and thematically highlights what some might identify as unproductive communication and what others might call embellishment or artistry—using language and communicative devices against their express denotative purposes. If, in the above passage, one pays attention only to the primary clause, "everything seemed to fall into place," in essence eliminating the wasteful energies of the parenthetical, one overlooks the other meanings to be had in the very tension between an economy of prose—and, correlatively, of business management—and the pleasurable, affective meanderings of storytelling, and of people's emotions. That tension becomes explicit in Yamashita's portrait of J. B.'s and Mané's differing approaches to work. J. B. gives Mané an electronic beeper ostensibly so that he can keep tabs on "the father of featherology" at all times. However, Mané gives the beeper over to his cronies at the local pub who use it as a form of entertainment: "If J. B. wanted to talk to Mané, he had to go down to that oudoor bar. J. B. tried to make Mané wear a pager or a mobile phone, but these things invariably got lost or broken. For a while, Mané's cronies in the bar put money in a jar and passed around the pager everyday, wearing it conspicuously on the belts of their pants. If the pager went off while a crony was wearing it, he got the winnings in the jar" (77). By (mis)using this device, the bar cronies radically alter its significance, transforming an instrument of speedy work-related communication into a fanciful toy, an object suited to their unemployed hours. Originally intended to make J. B.'s and Mané's time more productive, the pager becomes redirected toward playful, unproductive ends. Similarly, Yamashita transforms efficient, streamlined syntax—for example, "everything seemed to fall into place"—into an extravagant display of contradictory clauses and double meanings that are linguistic correlatives to the culture clashes resulting from the compression of the world.

Yamashita thus imitates Mané's work with the beeper, filling her soap opera with an extravagance of wandering prose. In the same way that the author questions the merits of a strictly purposive and productive use of language, she throws into doubt the supposed beneficence of "progress," especially when it is equated with overdevelopment and with the colonizing of all time to the "public" realm of work. The narrative pursues this critique of "productivity" through the personal travails of Mané Pena who finds his life completely altered by his involvement in GGG:

> Mané Pena rarely saw any of his family anymore. He missed the little ones . . . and all the grandchildren who once drifted in and out of his house. He missed talking to the youngsters. . . . Even Chico Paco . . . did not come around after Angustia and the family had left. It was not the same, not the same full house of poor but generous people who shared everything they had. . . . This, he was told, was the price one paid for progress. . . . [It was] as if his TV were suddenly made to pick up signals from some foreign country like the United States. All the old shows he loved so well, all the old soap operas, everything had suddenly been made to come out somehow differently. Everything was much finer; nobody picked their teeth or squatted at crossroads to contemplate the right way. Everything seemed to work; all time was taken up with a purpose. (151–52)

The narrative leaves open whether this productive ethos of "all time . . . taken up with a purpose" is of unquestionable benefit. In contrast to such productive time is the languorous pace of "the old soap operas," where characters have "time . . . to speak and to listen lavishly" to dwell on romantic preoccupations, and to worry over the children (Modleski, 106). Thus, *Through the Arc* stresses the visceral pleasure in time *not* taken up with an (implicitly economic) purpose. If the reader assesses Mané's life in terms of his career and global renown, then certainly he appears to have followed a path of continuous, upward "progress." Yet, Yamashita includes this account of Mané's "success" in a section entitled, "More Loss," suggesting that a strictly economic gauge might not be the most suitable measure of life.

In its portrait of Mané, *Through the Arc* promotes sympathy for "less than masterful" positions often associated with women under patriarchy but also pertinent to the formerly colonized and enslaved, and to the subaltern classes of the Third World.[51] Thus, Yamashita redeploys what American feminists have called the "gendered screen fiction" of soap opera to validate the perspectives not only of female protagonists but also of characters such as Mané Pena, Chico Paco, and Gilberto (Nochimson, 4): all are subjects affected by time-space compression and transnational capital but not necessarily in control of their effects. Yamashita's novel expands the gendered terrain of domestically oriented melodramas to consider the subaltern classes of the Third World, thus answering the call of Asian American feminist critics, such as King-Kok Cheung, who urge a transformed feminist studies sympathetic to the experiences of "men of color" (Cheung 1990, 245–46).[52]

Somewhat paradoxically, Yamashita's mode of narrating global issues from the perspective of "less than masterful" positions—her playing havoc with cybernetic and communicational mastery—does not guarantee the novel's endearment to Asian American social agendas. I earlier mentioned the narrative's privileging of "nonproductive" (domestic) issues such as love, longing, and desire. On a discursive level, this ethos of nonproductivity is accentuated by Yamashita's penchant for nonpurposive prose, where extended playfulness and mixed meanings, rather than communicational efficiency, are primary. For champions of a "feminist aesthetics" such antiprogressive, nonteleological structures offer potential liberatory pleasures. By contrast, this championing of unpurposive language, semantic ambiguity, and inconclusive narratives is likely to be viewed with suspicion by Asian American critics who desire realist idioms—as evident in critiques of *Dogeaters*—and, more generally, a language that conveys sociological and historical truths. As Sau-ling Wong points out, Asian American writers have largely approached themes of play and artistry quite gingerly, given a communal context that devalues such activities as wasteful expenditures of energy. Claiming that some Asian American authors associate (stylistic) extravagance, play, and art with whiteness, while others view it as a "natural human desideratum" (S. Wong 1993, 180), Wong argues that, for both groups, the temptations of extravagance are contrasted with the economics of necessity—the pressure of placing one's energy in the service of some immediately perceived economic gain for one's family or ethnic community. For those overwhelmingly driven by the codes of necessity and survival, play and art seem self-indulgent efforts producing hardly any material benefit, and because Asian Americans, for the greater part of their history, have labored under severe constraints (e.g., miner's taxes, laundry taxes, exclusion laws, confiscation of property and imprisonment during internment, alien land laws, hate crimes), they remain particularly ambivalent about the value of playful, artistic endeavors.[53] Indulging in soap operas and opaque prose, given this context, is to risk communal opprobrium.[54]

However, Wong speculates on a possible work that assertions of play and artistry may serve in this current historical moment:

> At this juncture in history, the seemingly apolitical advancement of play by Asian American artists serves a political function: it subverts white society's expectations on the Asian American's proper place. . . . From the "coolies" of the nineteenth century to today's technicians and nonmanagerial professionals, the historical role of Asian Americans has been to serve the interests of the dominant society as "good workers": industrious, focused, dependable, accommodating, serious-minded, eminently useful. (210)

The novel's cumulative gendered effects—the personal emphasis, the focus on women's emotional life and homosexual domesticity, the antiprogressive structure—all make the novel suspect in Asian American studies, where mimetic, straightforward declarations or grand narratives against oppression are prized over and against the dilettantism of artistry. However, as Wong suggests, being playful—ignoring the codes of productivity—when enacted by Third World subjects may be a subversive act. Rather than not accomplishing any "work," *Through the Arc* precisely questions the valuation of all activities and artifacts on a scale of both capitalist and masculine productivity.[55]

Wong's analysis, in suggesting a possible rehabilitative function to playful, "nonproductive" themes and cultural artifacts, also clears the way for a fuller analysis of *Through the Arc*'s gendered and sexualized "domestic focus" that might otherwise be neglected as less important or even distracting to community issues. Thus, contrary to Yamashita's claim that she couldn't write about public, historically interesting issues while maintaining a focus on women, in *Through the Arc* the author in fact writes about Brazil's history, as an extraction zone for "First World" nations, through the erotic aesthetic of the telenovela structure, making the small details of familial life have the bigness of world events. In allowing herself the space to improvise and focus on domestic concerns, Yamashita, moreover, questions the gendered presumptions underlying assessments of global import or what counts as a relevant analysis of globalization.

• • •

Even though *Through the Arc* does not fit into traditional Asian American literary paradigms, I would caution against its neglect as an Asian American text. In fact, Yamashita's global emphasis might be of particular interest to critics of Asian American literature precisely because it encourages a greater scrutiny of the underlying presumptions of their interpretive contexts. In this respect, *Through the Arc* appears well suited to the current scholarly critical climate in Asian American Studies, which has seen a great deal of speculation over the viability of cultural nationalism and American-based paradigms of collective identity. The novel's focus on globalization and its decentering of the theme of Asian American identity[56] might be more appropriately viewed as anticipatory of a wider trend in Asia-Pacific theorizing that emphasizes border-crossing, trans-Pacific social networks. At the same time, Yamashita does not urge an abandonment of Asian America's older concerns, but alludes to them, transforming the terrain upon which such past articulations might be reinterpreted for contemporary relevance.

In her allusions to and updating of the Asian American railroad worker, for instance, Yamashita suggests that the past does not retain a fixed, singular significance but is reinterpretable and made useful in accordance with present and prospective social concerns. I have argued implicitly that one of the more pressing social concerns informing Asian American cultural critique is that of globalization and the prospects of Asian/Pacific community amidst increasing transnational traffic. Another pressing concern needing Asian American critical review, yet one often ignored or devalued, is that of gender and sexual identity; more specifically, the struggle against gender- and sexual-based oppressions. The novel's decentering of "America"—and for that matter "Asia" or the "Asia-Pacific"—and its focus on domesticity, emotional life, and gender and sexual identity results in the novel's double marginalization. I have attempted, therefore, to reconstruct *Through the Arc*'s relevance to Asian American cultural critique on the basis, not only of its commentary on the transnational, global economic and cultural terrain in which Asian American institutions are embedded, but also of its distinct gendered mode of broaching these issues. In other words, I believe it is possible and valuable to analyze the novel's revisions to Asian American literary traditions and political agendas without leaving gender behind or intentionally obscuring a "feminine perspective," even though, in the conventional terms of "public" discourse, this feminine perspective might be considered a diminishment of the "broader" ways in which *Through the Arc* intervenes in discussions of Asian American themes and the field's theoretical and methodological options. Rather, I view the novel's generic indebtedness to the soap opera as enhancing the appeal of this novel as an object of analysis and as an object that tells us something about, not only the past national and prospective transnational terrains of Asian American critique, but also the gendered terrains of those possibilities.

Asian American Feminist Literary Criticism on Multiple Terrains

As NANCY ARMSTRONG SUGGESTED over a decade ago, political power does not reside solely within "official institutions of state"; rather, one must recognize the "political history of the whole domain over which our culture grants women authority: the use of leisure time, the ordinary care of the body, courtship practices, the operations of desire, the forms of pleasure, gender differences, and family relations" (Amstrong, 26–27). Armstrong's crisp assessment of the gendered and sexual domain as also political, while clearly affirmed by much of Asian American literary criticism thus far (Cheung 1990; Kim 1990; Lim 1993), has yet to filter into the "new" mainstream of Asian American critical reading practices, those that shift Asian America's terrain to postnational, global frameworks. As part of the effort to make gender central to these newer terrains, my study has underscored the ways in which Asian American writers, through their border-crossing fictions, reveal the exercise of political power, not only on the level of national and international policy, but simultaneously (and sometimes more forcefully) through the structuring of sexual desire, the gendering of identities and domestic labors, and the disciplining of family formations. Moreover, my reading of these particular Asian American fictions has afforded a more expansive scrutiny of the dominant frameworks—the political hermeneutics or "ways of knowing"—that traditionally determine the meaning of these and other such texts in a unidirectional fashion: as relevant to a (trans)national critique or a critique of gender relations but not as a simultaneous articulation of both.

Jane Desmond, in puzzling over analagous parlayings of national group agendas against gendered group agendas, notes that the

> problem lies precisely in overlooking the relationship among these categories of difference and their ... underwriting of each other in various discursive realms. ... Not only do these categories of difference intersect, they do so differentially at different times. The discursive activation of one category at a particular time [and in opposition to another] ... is something we can take as an object of analysis itself. For example, under what conditions and for what stakes do discourses of race supersede discourses of gender [and vice versa]? (Desmond, 94, 105)

Each of the foregoing chapters takes as its very object the activation of a broad discourse (for instance, that of globalized labor or postcolonial nationalism) to the neglect of an alternative discourse of gender. In composite, then, these chapters address the narrowness of our interpretive grids and, in particular, the mistaken assumption that a focus on women, sexism, and heterosexism is, first of all, antithetical to an antiracist, postcolonial project, and, therefore, counter to the larger political interests of Asians and Asian Americans. Too often, concern over narratives of gender and sexual awakening are accused of undermining the "serious" work that Asian American texts are expected to perform: to expose anti-Asian sentiment in the United States, to limn the trauma inflicted upon Asians by Western imperialism, to envision better worlds where Asians and Asian Americans will not be construed as foreigners in their own homes, to create a common cultural ground for pan-Asian unity, and (more recently) to apprehend Asian Americans' larger global-economic agendas and cross-border alliances.[1] Each of these social agendas comprises a supportable priority. However, it would be a mistake to interpret the pursuit of these goals as anomalous or more important than the exposure of tyrannies within the household, or the envisioning of a future where sexism and homophobia are not givens.

Throughout this study, my larger concern has been about how political power and contests over political power occur within and beside gendered and sexual processes usually thought separate from and of lesser importance than the state and the global economy. My method has been to examine gender, not detached from, but in relation to what America the nation, America the imperialist invader, and America the capitalist developer means in these Asian American novels. For to extract the gender and sexual content from the historicity of these broader developments and social forces seems to me as much a distortion of an Asian American feminist criticism as would be the ignoring of the gendered contents of these works altogether. In other words, the contribution of these literary texts to an Asian American gendered political criticism also lies in their critiques of America's myths of abundance, how they are not open to everyone (as suggested by Bulosan and Jen), and how that very dream of a national, limitless wealth relies upon the gendered racialization and exploitation of minorities and Third World denizens both within and outside America's borders (as revealed in Hagedorn's and Yamashita's works). Moreover, in contemplating the newer images of the Asian financier and the Asian transnational migrant, these authors further propose that the "Americas" to which Asians gravitate are themselves variegated, with Asians' historical and imaginary relation to South America requiring Asian Americans' self-critical review of their own privileged impositions and colonizing effects.

In delineating how Asians as a group find themselves in changing locations and class positions respective of North and South Americans, the four texts examined in this book help to disentangle a central discussion in Asian American cultural studies over appropriate paradigms, epistemologies, and methods for comprehending the changing demographics of Asian immigration (alternatively Asian diaspora) since 1965.[2] It has been my argument that Asian American cultural criticism's emphasis on its enlarging (or contracting) terrains ought to occur in relation to interrogations of gender and sexuality, for instance by probing how configurations of masculinity, femininity, and eroticism help Asian American authors narrate (and possibly critique) an expanding political-economic vision. As revealed in the foregoing chapters, gendered formations—such as the household, the fraternity, the gay, lesbian, and heterosexual couple—as well as gendered and sexual awakening itself, are engaged by Asian American authors to remark upon and frequently contest the historical, contemporary, and prospective locations of Asians in nation-states and global-economic institutions. It would be a mistake, however, to assume that identifying the gendered contours of these particular formations yields a uniform radical critique. For instance, one such formation, the homosocial collective made memorable in *America Is in the Heart*, has been engaged by one author (Bulosan) to contest capitalism and by another (Jen) to show the abetting of the same. That Bulosan poses a gender-exclusive imagined community as an alternative to America's capitalist-driven violences, and that Jen instead conflates the two (depicting this gender-exclusive imagined community as part and parcel of America's capitalist logic), reveals the variable and shifting political meanings of these gendered representations in each of their historical contexts.

On the whole, however, I have been less interested in tracking how a singular gendered formation, such as the fraternity, evolves over several authorial representations,[3] and more concerned over the diverse gendered, genealogical, and sexual tropes through which these authors clarify the changing temporal and spatial dimensions of the economies and social-political milieus in which their individual narratives are set and which, in composite, represents the changing terrains of Asian American literary tradition and prospective community. That these terrains are changing and, to a certain extent, "new" does not necessarily mean, however, that their gendered approaches will present a radical break with the past. Hence, Yamashita's using the heterosexual romance to register modernity's developmental upheavals is similar to Bulosan's use of brotherhood to remark on America's non-egalitarian economic and class structures. Both these authors, in contesting official institutions of the state and of the economy, implicitly abide by the logic whereby the health or pathology of the domestic arena indicates the moral righteousness, or lack thereof, of (trans)national leaders and their socioeconomic systems. In this respect, Bulosan and Yamashita extend representational practices found in African American literature, by forging what Claudia Tate calls "domestic allegories of political desire" in which the blissfulness or dysfunction of the household or the kinship group provides commentary on the political and economic structure of the wider world (Tate, 8–9, 14–20).

Hagedorn, by contrast, finds it more difficult to forge an allegorical relation between her narratives of gendered desire, on the one hand, and of national and global critique, on the other. In her text, there appears more of a disjunction between the postcolonial nationalist plot and her plots of romantic seduction and female desire. Through that schism, the author forwards a critique aimed, not solely at History (the narration of imperialism and capitalist exploitation), but also at the very disjunction between History and the range of activities and spaces in which women are traditionally engaged. Following in the mode of past "women's revolutionary fiction" as outlined by Paula Rabinowitz, Hagedorn's novel shows "two . . . discourses [in] combat: the dual narratives of desire (of the gendered body) and history (of class and anti-imperialist politics). . . . [Representing] both narratives in one classed [also colonized] and gendered body connects them to each other, breaking the conventional plot patterns of each" and challenging the critical assessment that the combination is "incommensurable" (Rabinowitz, 10–11). As American women writing under the persuasion of 1930s literary radicalism had to grapple with the overwhelming pressure to subdue their gendered stories in order to narrate the implicitly male proletarian subject, so too does Hagedorn struggle to write the stories of women's and gay men's particularities in the postcolony. Sometimes working through the false separation between desire and history, and at other times simply forging narratives of female embodiment that do not appear commensurate with nationalist liberation, Hagedorn employs a gendered strategy quite distinct from rendering the zone of desire, domesticity, and kinship an allegory of historical, economic relations.

Interestingly, a text like Jen's partakes of both gendered strategies; on the one hand, commenting allegorically on wider socioeconomic structures through metaphors of household peril, and, on the other hand, underscoring the disjunction and relation of hierarchy between zones of the erotic and the political-historical, in part by disallowing specific forms of eroticism and sexual identity to be neatly incorporated into the wider nationalist or antiracist critique she also forges. Thus, Jen's story of suppressed lesbian desire, as is the case with Hagedorn's story of the same, cannot be used allegorically to comment on the health of the nation as can the stories of the nuclear family, the homosocial collective, the heterosexual couple, and the feminist individual. The question of why and how such specific genders and sexualities become more troubling to national and transnational allegories (and their counternarratives) points to future avenues of inquiry for which this work acts as a starting point. Clearly, my study is intended as an initial opening up of feminist and gender-specific questions in relation to Asian America's paradigmatic shifts, rather than as the definitive word. Thus, while my study restricts itself to four Asian American texts, an analysis of the two strategies of gendered allegory and disjunction, as well as the relation between the two, might be usefully pursued in a much wider array of minority and Third World literature.

In opening up or, more precisely, widening the way in which we frame our feminist and gender-specific questions, this study moves the interrogation of Asian American cultural production beyond, but also in reference to, the emasculation debates of yore. As several of these texts demonstrate, America cannot be reduced to late nineteenth- and early-twentieth-century immigration policies that imperiled heterosexual family formation for Asian male laborers. Though it is tempting to narrate Asian American literature as a product of changing immigrant patterns to America and the gendered subtexts of U.S. immigration laws, such an analysis only takes the critic so far, by presuming that gendering processes begin and end on American shores. As this study suggests, we might do well to think of Asian American literature as a product, not merely of Asian in-migration to the United States, but also of America's expansion eastward and of Asia's spreading influence in Latin America. When the terrains of Asian American literary study shift in such a way, what types of gendered methodologies accommodate these transitions? Clearly, gendered analyses of Asian American literature must take into account, but not restrict themselves, to looking at the gendered subtexts of U.S. cultural scripts. We must also pay attention to the ways in which Asian women—and the positions that women hold within postcolonial and Third World societies—become symbolic of the righteousness of oppositional nationalisms and developmental programs to save the world. Furthermore, we might examine in detail the way in which Asian American authors pursue their critiques of masculinist ideologies that subordinate women through narrative forms that allow for a focus on domestic spaces, the zone of the everyday, the realm of what is missed in more typical narratives of male heroism, nationalist awakening, and First World industrialization schemes.

In their depiction of the various nationalist and transnationalist discourses with which their gendered narratives compete (and sometimes mediate), several of these authors additionally scrutinize the very claim to verifiable, objective reporting that would mask how "History," "modern progress," or "the march of civilization" are themselves stories that abet certain racial, gendered, and sexual groups' control over resources, the production process, the shape of domestic spaces, and the expression and pursuit of erotic desires. We might dwell, then, on the implications for studies of gender and sexuality of these and other Asian American writers' use of parodic and postmodern modes of breaking up the narrative, not for the mere sake of promoting fragmentation, but rather, to frustrate and thereby bring to an affective level the reader's consciousness of his or her desire for Truth—for a universal and singular perspective that, though promising to transcend foregoing (racially and gender-) biased histories, in actuality only repeats the false claims to a totality of knowledge, as have other past accounts of the material world. The critical awareness that no singular narrative will settle the "truth . . . once and for all" (Flax, 48) does not mean that one no longer seeks better, alternative representations—that the production of, for instance, feminist or Asian American counternarratives stops; rather that critical awareness supposes that the reader, critic, or author pauses to reflect upon how even the corrective histories and cultural myths one offers to ameliorate past exclusions also leave out others (those who are then identified as doubly, triply, or exponentially excluded). We must pause to reflect, not only on those exponentially excluded others, but also on this very compulsion to seek out a total knowledge, method, or liberation narrative that can rescue everyone, that can somehow avoid missing some crucial component of a fully liberatory program. As Gayatri Spivak and Robyn Wiegman, among others, have pointed out, such compulsions toward a total vision are deeply implicated in structures of Western modernity, its disciplining of the material world to its singular ethos and method of progress, through rationality, universal subjectivity, and objective truth. Without this critical pause, we risk marching dogmatically in paths of "progress," "liberation," and "development" that future counterhistories may reveal also to be paths of native dispossession and ecological devastation. His-story, in short, may repeat itself.

Even though the narratives examined in this book do caution their readers away from singular programs to save the world, they are not free, ultimately, from the more narrow scope of our interpretive grids, which habitually determine the meaning of texts in a unidirectional fashion: as relevant to a (trans)national critique or a critique of gender relations but not as a simultaneous articulation of both. My study thus intervenes into this contemporary critical milieu which still regards the feminist analysis of gender and sexuality as extraneous or diversionary to the real work of critiquing state power and the political economy. In doing so, the foregoing chapters participate in a larger feminist project, one that has not always been embraced by Asian American critics interested in demystifying the operations of gender and desire, precisely because feminism has seemed to offer its own kind of dogmatic, exclusionary script.[4] Under this persuasion, feminism is charged with focusing too closely on gender to the exclusion of other axes of group subordination (such as race, sexuality, class, religion, and age) to be of use to more broadly defined (e.g., postcolonial nationalist, antiracist, anticapitalist) projects and their analyses of power (Espiritu 1997; Radhakrishnan). Yet the best of feminist inquiry in the last decade or so has recognized these limits and taken steps to ameliorate a prior narrow focus. To proceed, then, as if feminism cannot be situated in anything but a relation of ambivalence or hostility toward women of color or race studies only "fixes" feminism in a past formation and impoverishes both Asian American Studies and feminism's potential alliances. In other words, feminism, itself an evolving methodology and political practice, demonstrates, through its self-critical revisions, that it can be as large and capacious as the macropolitical frameworks with which it competes, so as to be persuasive to a progressive project like Asian American Studies.

However, the very will to reproduce or revise feminism as a macropolitical discourse that will encompass everyone and that will address each terrain of political struggle misses the particular strength of poststructural feminist analyses that link feminist inquiry with an ethos of intervention and tactics (Chow 1993), that acknowledge their own limitations, emphasizing "marked" speech, positionality, situated knowledges, and critical, rather than dogmatic, practices (Haraway; Spivak 1993; Wiegman; Flax). These several critics have proposed the very eschewing of macropolitical positions as feminism's strength as a theory, and this is how feminist inquiry has inspired my own analyses. Jockeying with a lot of different commitments, rather than making one's gendered commitment a global discourse, may be the preferred practice of women—particularly women of color— due to their occupying scattered sites of privilege and oppression rather than their trying to lobby for a territory/field all their own.

I believe that this alternative strain of feminist inquiry, one that does not aspire to be the sole or ascendant macropolitical framework, has the most to offer to an Asian American feminism and gender studies. Robyn Wiegman, drawing upon Jane Flax's work, refers to this feminism as one that is "disloyal" to itself by recognizing that it cannot "innocently" guarantee political liberation (that in its liberatory efforts, there will be inevitable exclusions, people overlooked or "left out" of the progressive vision it proposes) (180): " 'The end of innocence' . . . points to the recognition that feminism itself is not outside power or hierarchy, is not the truth to which power and domination must reconfigure themselves. Its innocence lost, its loyalty unassured, feminism faces a future unwritten by a methodological guarantee" (Wiegman, 187). This feminism, always alert to what it has excluded, feels uncomfortable posing itself as the definitive counternarrative to broad (yet implicitly male) "collective" narratives to save the world. Such a feminism past "innocence" remains useful to Asian American critics of gender and sexuality, even as it is oftentimes invisible to them, precisely because of this feminism's refusal to be assuring of its programmatic vision of progress.[5]

Somewhat paradoxically, then, a feminism past innocence, the feminism that I have characterized as most persuasive to Asian American gender and sexuality critics, is one that both acknowledges that it is not outside power (that it cannot disavow how it works through dominance and exclusions) and yet still forwards its tactics and interventions—its alternative epistemologies—as necessary, even while not definitive, correctives to the History of Universal Man. This contradictory notion of forging a better way of knowing, while also recognizing the entrance into power that accompanies that will to know, has implications, of course, for this very project. In the foregoing chapters, I have pointed out the significant ways in which gender mediates visions of America and visions of political change both within the U.S. nation-state and against it. Clearly these observations have been partially motivated by the belief that this apprehension of gendered processes has been missed, unremarked upon, trivialized, or framed as distracting to broader economic and social movements and the liberation narratives that Asian American Studies has conventionally adopted. My hope is that the analyses that I have provided will lend greater insight into the operations of gender in relation to nationalism, postcoloniality, transnationalism, and globalization, even as I abide by the crucial feminist tenet that knowledges are partial, situated, and therefore that every attempt to see better, to map and interpret better (to forge new ways of knowing in juxtaposition to older and concurrent ways of knowing) extends or is complicit in the modernist project of seeking a total vision. If every attempt at filling in what has been previously missed is complicit in Western modernity's quest to discover an all-encompassing Truth, then my project is no more able to transcend that seduction and extension of truth-claims (to be "pure" of Western influence) than is any other scholarly project historically situated in America's institutions of learning—even those that expressly acknowledge their partiality and limitations. As Jane Flax writes with regard to feminists, "[W]e cannot simultaneously claim (1) that the mind, the self, and knowledge are socially constituted and that what we can know depends upon our social practices and contexts and (2) that feminist theory can uncover the truth of the whole once and for all" (48). My readings of gender and sexuality in the foregoing chapters, informed as they are by feminist theories, are offered with the knowledge that they do not "uncover the truth of the whole once and for all" and, also, in the hope that extending that self-critical lens to Asian American criticism will help fuel Asian American Studies' desire—always exceeding its present achievements—to envision and effect a better world.

Number of Plots in *Dogeaters*

Character/Perspective	*Full-Length Chapters*
1. Rio Gonzaga	"Love Letters," "Tsismis," "Sprikitik," "Her Mother Rita Hayworth," "High Society," "Luna Moth"
2. Severo Alacran	"The King of the Coconuts"
3. Baby Alacran	"The White Bouquet," "The Weeping Bride"
4. Joey Sands	"Mister Heartbreak," "His Mother the Whore," "Heroin," "Paradise," "Hunger," "Redemption," "Terrain"
5. Romeo Rosales	"Serenade," "Romeo Rosales," "Last Chance"
6. Trinidad Gamboa	"Serenade," "Last Chance"
7. Leonor Ledesma	"Her Eminent Ascent into Heaven"
8. Dolores Gonzaga	"Her Mother, Rita Hayworth"
9. Lolita Luna	"Surrender," "Movie Star"
10. Daisy Avila	"Sleeping Beauty," "Epiphany," "Breaking Spells," "In the Artist's House," "The Famine of Dreams"
11. Clarita Avila	"Excerpt from the Only Letter Ever Written by Clarita Avila"
12. The First Lady	"The President's Wife Has a Dream," "Bananas and the Republic"
13. Girlie Alacran	"Golf"
14. Puncha Gonzaga	"Pucha Gonzaga"
15. all of the above	"Kundiman"

Epigraphs and Other Quoted Material in *Dogeaters*

Epigraphs, Newspaper Clippings, etc.	*Subject(s); Principal Actors*
"Coconut Place" (excerpt from Jean Mallat's *The Philippines*)	sleeping persons (metaphorically Filipinos)
"Jungle Chronicle" (excerpt from Jean Mallat's *The Philippines*)	Negritos
"Floating Bodies" (fictional news item)	three headless bodies, General Ledesma, Major Rivera (police commander)
"President William McKinley Addresses a Delegation of Methodist Churchmen, 1898"	Filipinos, McKinley, the United States
"Avila Arrested in Human Rights Rally Dispute" (fictional news item)	Baptista Magalona, Roman and Baltazar Montano, Senator Avila, Sister Immaculada Panganiban, Lt. Col. Carreon, Professor Maria Avila, Clarita Avila, Father Igarta, Police Chief Reyes
"One Christmas in a Mountain Lodge up in Baguio, Date Unknown"	Senator Avila, General Avila, Nicasio Ledesma
"Jungle Chronicle" (excerpt from Jean Mallat's *The Philippines*)	Filipinos
"The Song of Bullets" (epigraph from Jose Rizal)	Filipinos awakening to consciousness
"Man with a Mission" (fictional news item)	General Ledesma, rebels in the Mindanao region, Lt. Col. Carreon, Senator Avila, the President and First Lady, Lolita Luna, George Hamilton, Van Cliburn

"Dateline Manila" (fictional news item)

actors and movie moguls: Lolita Luna, Bootsy Pimentel, Patsy Pimentel, Tito Alvarez, Max Rodriguez, Tirso Velasco, Severo Alacran, Nestor Noralez

"Insect Bounty" (actual news item)

residents of Manila, Lt. Col. Romeo Maganto

"Jungle Chronicle" (excerpt from Jean Mallat's *The Philippines*)

Filipino children who die young

Notes

1. In his study on the pastoral and heroic traditions of Hawaii, Stephen Sumida implies a dialectic of interanimating influence running from context to text and back again (ix–x). He suggests that the rich interpretive schemes gleaned from the broad view of an ethnic literary tradition help make sense of the statistical data and historical documents compiled on a particular ethnic group. Framing the literary critical project in less hermeneutic and more political terms, Sau-ling Wong argues that establishing intertextual links among Asian American prose works helps build a cultural base for the political interest group of Asian Americans (S. Wong 1993, 9). Finally, Shirley Geok-lin Lim and Amy Ling take an entirely different approach, simply presuming that the rich and growing reserve of Asian American poems, prose works, and drama deserves critical scrutiny. They do not address the significance of literary criticism to political activism or social change but focus instead on the belatedness of Asian American literary criticism compared to that devoted to Euro-American texts.

INTRODUCTION

1. R. Radhakrishnan insists that looking at women's politics remains at odds with looking at national politics. In a series of questions more rhetorical than probing, he queries, "Why is it that nationalism achieves the ideological effect of an inclusive and putatively macropolitical discourse, whereas the women's question—unable to achieve its own autonomous macropolitical identity—remains ghettoized within its specific and regional space?" (78). He advocates gender becoming a macropolitical framework by way of its going beyond "its originary commitment to merely one special or specific constituency" (79–80). Thus he misses the particular strength of poststructuralist feminist analyses that link feminist inquiry with an ethos of intervention and tactics (Chow 1993) and that acknowledge their own limitations. Perhaps the very refusal of macropolitical positions is feminism's strength as a theory.

2. See Kolodny's *The Lay of the Land* and Rogin's *Ronald Reagan, the Movie.*

3. Exemplary of this narrow nationalist vision was the myth-symbol school, which stressed the United States as a "world elsewhere," divorced from politics (see Pease 1990 and 1993) and from a global ecumenism that took into account the continuity between America's domestic self-definition and its encroachments onto "foreign" realms. According to Amy Kaplan, American Studies stemming from Perry Miller's work to the present has turned away from the international scene, drawing hard lines between domestic and foreign realms so that "America—once cut off from Europe—can be understood as a domestic question, left alone, unique, divorced from the international conflicts—whether the slave trade or the Mexican

War—in which that national identity takes shape" (Kaplan 1993, 7). What Kaplan argues with respect to the United States may be symptomatic of nationalisms more generally. Thus Paul Gilroy uses the optic of transnationalism to challenge the rigorous efforts by nation-states to define themselves insularly. By proposing a "transatlantic" region (distant relative of the "Pacific Rim" region), Gilroy underscores how nation-states like Great Britain have defined themselves against migrations and cultural influences from outside their borders and how territorial lines and the geopolitical structures following upon them are established through this work of disavowal. See also Rogin's (1987 and 1993) deconstruction of the United States' "cultural structure of motivated disavowal" that willfully forgets the history of U.S. imperialism.

4. Briefly remarking on Asian American Studies's "uneasy alliance with scholars of American history and civilization," Mazumdar soon glosses over the conflicts and differences between Asian Americanists and practitioners of American Studies. Instead, Asian American Studies is made to stand in for American studies so that the nationalist focus of the latter is now the nationalist focus of the former (30). This ghostly presence/absence of American studies in her article leads to further mystifications: while Asian American Studies and Asian studies can change their focus (to become more aware of each other strengths, to wed their scholarly emphases), American studies is not to be a site of transformation. For rhetorical purposes, then, Mazumdar reifies American studies as a narrowly nationalist field of inquiry. Yet, American studies scholars of late have been challenging that very nationalist focus by emphasizing the international dimensions of U.S. studies, the hemispheric implications of the term "America," and the local and global political and economic frameworks that have been formative of both "American civilization" and the study as well as critique of its favorite myths and self-definitions (see Kaplan; Pease; Saldívar; Buell). If Asian Americanists are to be urged into a conversation with Asianists who have had particular faults (like the tendency to avoid race and politics, and/or to be economically conservative, according to Mazumdar), then certainly they might be willing to share insights with Americanists who have not only exhibited a blindness to American empire and ignored a global framework, but have recently recognized these ideological investments (see Kaplan and Pease).

5. See Chan et al. (1991), preface to *Aiiieeeee!*, xii; also, in the 1972 essay "Racist Love," Chin and Chan dwell at considerable length on pitfalls of the "dual personality" (72–73, and 76).

6. Citing material reasons, Wong also argues that claiming America remains an important task in Asian American cultural politics:

> By "claiming America," I refer to establishing the Asian American presence in the context of the United States' national cultural legacy and contemporary cultural production. . . . [I]f claiming America becomes a minor task for Asian American cultural criticism and espousal of denationalization becomes wholesale, certain segments of the Asian American population may be left without a viable discursive space. . . . [I]ndividual Asian Americans— even first-generation ones, and especially youngsters who have to go through the American educational system—often recapitulate the "old" struggles. These are "old" in the sense of being familiar to Asian Americanists or having been superseded by concerns more amenable to the lexicon of poststructuralism and postmodernity. But they are far from "old" for

the subject contending with diverse interpolations, of which the injunction to "Americanize" (often delivered with threats of physical violence) may at times be most clamorous. (S. Wong 1995, 16–17)

7. In her introduction to *Cultures of United States Imperialism*, Amy Kaplan locates the genesis of American Studies on the shores of Africa. In boldly stating that "the field of American studies was conceived on the banks of the Congo," Kaplan rejects the national parameters Americanists have created for themselves, claiming instead that U.S. domestic and foreign policies are inseparable, that U.S. "imperialism is also about consolidating domestic cultures and negotiating intranational relations" (14). Reading "westward expansion" as territorial colonization of "foreign" peoples that later took the form of incursions into the Philippines, Cuba, Panama, Vietnam, Hawaii, and Guam, Kaplan asserts a continuity between racial politics formerly configured as "domestic" affairs and the racial domination at the heart of American empire (see also Rogin on this point).

8. Chin and Chan's metaphors for "racist hate" and "racist love" are deeply gendered. They depict a hostile "racist hate" embodied by male figures that fosters a certain adult male integrity in those it would repress: "White racism has failed with the blacks, the chicanos, the American Indians. Night riders, soldier boys on horseback, fat sheriffs, and all them goons and clowns of racism did destroy a lot of bodies. . . . But they did not stamp out the consciousness of a people, destroy their cultural integrity and literary sensibility" (Chin and Chan, 66). By contrast, they portray "racist love" as a suffocating maternal figure who thoroughly "stunts" her victims: "In terms of . . . the destruction of an organic sense of identity, the complete psychological and cultural subjugation of a race or people, the people of Chinese and Japanese ancestry stand out as white racism's only success. . . . They loved us, protected us. Love conquered. It's well-known that the cloying overwhelming love of a protective, coddling mother produces an emotionally stunted dependent child" (66, 69).

9. See both *Aiiieeeee!* introductions, "Racist Love" and "An Introduction to Chinese-American and Japanese-American Literatures."

10. Many of the passages in "Racist Love," which first appeared in Chin and Chan (1972), are rehabilitated, verbatim, in the introduction to *Aiiieeeee!* and in "An Introduction to Chinese-American and Japanese-American Literatures," which was reprinted in a volume edited by Houston Baker. For instance, the passage on Asian Americans' "deprivation of language" appears in all of these essays. In "Racist Love," the authors link this denial of language to their refutation of the "dual concept personality," which requires that the Chinese-American speak in the native tongues of Chinese or English and not in his own Chinese-American brand of English (76). In *Aiiieeeee!*, by contrast, the editors lay the denial of language at the feet of American institutions that demand standardized English and specifically at those critics who fault Asian Americans writers' language and punctuation (23–25).

11. The prose of Chin and Chan is both tendentious and rhetorically savvy. Though they never outright state that the cultural project of Asian American writing is to reinstall male privilege, they do render a series of claims that in effect make this argument. As they construct it, the cultural integrity of the Asian American community is measured by the degree to which Asian American men dominate

their literary tradition (Chan et al. 1991a, 14–15). Moreover, if the function of Asian American literature is to promote or recover the community's cultural integrity, then the main preoccupation of Asian American writing must be to express a "recognized style of Asian-American manhood" (24).

12. The assumption that Asian American culture is more properly the domain of male writers—or writers who express a worldview that doesn't threaten Asian American male leadership—contributes to the need for specialized spaces devoted to Asian American women's culture. Hence, anthologies like *Making Waves, The Forbidden Stitch, Home to Stay, Unbroken Thread, Our Feet Walk the Sky, A Lotus of Another Color,* and *The Very Inside*--as well as the critical and creative collection, *Asian American Sexualities,* and the more recent *Making More Waves* and *Dragon Ladies: Asian American Feminists Breathe Fire*--clear spaces for Asian American women to contemplate the intersecting oppressions of sexism, heteronormativity, racism, and capitalist patriarchy.

13. Centering women and focusing on "America" seem at odds to Okihiro partly because of the equation of America with the immobile land mass lying east of Asia, west of Europe, north of Mexico, and south of Canada. If one construes Asian American historical action to occur only within these boundaries, then Asian American history will certainly marginalize women, placing them in a second wave of immigration following the predominantly male migrations of the nineteenth century. However, in his rationale behind this focus on Asian women, Okihiro acknowledges—perhaps inadvertently—another conception of "America" beyond that of a fixed land mass, portraying it as a global cultural agent.

14. In Okihiro's analysis, the subject of women leads him to reframe Asian American history within the context and hermeneutic of what others have identified as the Asia-Pacific region (see Dirlik 1993). My project takes somewhat the reverse course. Focusing on literary representations that clearly exceed the national boundaries of the United States, I ask whether the thematic concerns and discursive strategies appropriate to their transnational foci enable a better view of women—as argued by Okihiro—or whether the alternative (postcolonial and transnational) Asian American political readings available in their new vistas merely require ever more scrupulous gendered methodologies.

15. More concerned with such transnational kinship networks in our current historical moment, Aihwa Ong interrogates Asian women's negotiations of a patriarchy transformed by the flexible (transnational) modes of accumulation (1993). Other examples of feminist works attending to the gendered terms of transpacific culture include Tadiar (1993 and 1995), S. Wong (forthcoming), Lowe (1996), Grewal, and Santiago, to cite only a few.

16. One should note that American patriotism was not necessarily the animus behind this emphasis on Asian American labor and settlement in the United States. Rather, Asian American writers, historians, and social theorists stressed these feats in order to claim for Asian Americans the full rights and privileges accruing to citizens regardless of race (see Takaki 1994, 1990a, and 1990b; Omi and Winant; Espiritu; Wei; and Kingston).

17. As the hegemony of an U.S. optic has waned, Asian American critics now find themselves in an apparent condition of what might be called "postconsensus" regarding the political and cultural terrains of Asian American critique. In this post-

consensus period, Asian Americanist critics have not abandoned their commitments to effecting social change, though they have broadened the scope of what counts as the social: some see it in terms of contesting U.S.-based racial discrimination; others see it in terms of dismantling U.S. imperialism and Western colonial discourse; and still others tie Asian American communal politics to tackling the deformations and oppressions of late capitalism. This postconsensus moment, then, is marked not so much by a unified political agenda but by a shared discursive/theoretical commitment to deconstruct the older, more restrictive ways of framing Asian American identity as "non-Christian, nonfeminine, nonimmigrant" and limited to "three subgroups—Chinese, Japanese, and Filipino" (S. Wong 1993, 8).

18. In their introduction to the volume, "Thinking Theory in Asian American Studies," Michael Omi and Dana Takagi characterize Asian American Studies as undergoing a period of "anxiety and change": "Shifts in racialization fueled by global and national economic restructuring and the rise of conservative political movements, far-reaching demographic changes in the Asian American population over the past twenty-five years, and the shifting terrain of academic disciplinary boundaries have precipitated a dramatic rethinking of the field's founding paradigmatic assumptions" (xi). Though the editors later comment on feminist theory as a source of theoretical inspiration for Asian American Studies, the theoretical shift that they focus their attention on primarily occurs with poststructuralism. Contributors to the volume were asked to comment on the theoretical crossroads they perceived. What I find interesting is the way gender is contained in these essays: it figures strangely as a minor integrated part of these analyses that are mainly focused elsewhere—on other issues, the effects of poststructuralism, theories of globalization, the promise of Marxism, and so forth.

19. The merits of this essay are manifold, not least of which is Wong's warning that this reorientation in Asian American Studies from a nation-based to an international border-crossing politics not be viewed as a progress narrative. She warns against overlaying a developmental narrative over this changed emphasis from cultural nationalism—with its emphasis on U.S. territorial borders, indigenization through American labor, and East Asian ethnic groups—toward diasporic and Asian-based perspectives: "It would be far more useful to conceive of modes rather than phases of Asian American subjectivity: an indigenizing mode can coexist and alternate with a diasporic or a transational mode, but the latter is not to be lauded as a culmination of the former, a stage more advanced or more capacious. In short, there should be no teleology informing our account of the transformations in the world and in the field of Asian American studies" (17). Nevertheless, her own account cannot help but posit cultural nationalism as a more or less "consensual theoretical basis of the Asian American movement" whose time is now past (5). That is, the moment in which Wong herself writes is one wherein that hegemony has already been disrupted—a moment occurring *after* the full force of cultural nationalism held sway. I would name this moment a "postconsensus" condition where, indeed, the endpoint or telos of Asian American Studies may be up for grabs; nevertheless the departure from cultural nationalism from a feminist perspective does appear on the surface as a worthy progression.

20. Quite tellingly, Robertson's book-length survey of globalization theories devotes less than four pages to "a note on women and gender" (105–108), in which

he cites very few sources on feminist analyses that address international issues and the topic of globalization.

21. Nonini gives this definition of the Asia-Pacific region: "the 'Asia-Pacific' or 'Pacific Rim' can best be understood as the trope for a set of economic, political, and cultural processes creating relationships within a supraregion of Asian and the United States that have been under way since approximately the mid-1970s—processes arising from what the Marxist geographer David Harvey has called the 'spatial displacements' or 'spatial fixes' of contemporary capitalism (Harvey 1985, 1989)" (163). See also Dirlik's reinterpretation of Asian American studies in accordance with the Asia-Pacific idea (Dirlik 1993, 305–29).

22. However, the Pacific Rim idea also can represent "an effort to define and control one area of the world as a preserve of economic powers of world scope (such as the United States and Japan)" (Dirlik, 10). See also Woodside's claim that "The real key to much of the economic success of the Asian side of the Pacific Rim is the repression of the consumption rates of subaltern social groups and classes. . . . In its present form, the Asia-Pacific myth mobilizes the poor of the region for economic production without representing or encouraging their political and social claims" (22, 24).

23. Positing a cultural base for the Asia-Pacific idea may potentially naturalize the hierarchy between nations and peoples in the region into a myth of equal partnership; eclipse factors of gender, race, and ethnicity by interpolating all subjects to economic standing/function; and enhance a futurological discourse of utopianism combined with Darwinism.

CHAPTER ONE
FRATERNAL DEVOTIONS

1. Exemplary of this approach to Bulosan's text is Ronald Takaki's *Strangers from a Different Shore*. See also San Juan 1972; Kim 1982; Alquizola; S. Wong 1993; Mostern; and Gier. Wong claims that the text's "not-so-subtle indictments of racism . . . make the book a favorite choice in Asian American studies and ethnic studies curricula" (S. Wong 1993, 136), and Gier's argues that Bulosan's "commitment to a collectivist and proletarian politics" has made his novel especially compelling to a younger generation of Flip (American-born Filipino) writers concerned with the relationship of labor and social movements in the United States and the colonial/neocolonial experience (Gier, 14).

2. An exception to this silence is Elaine Kim's observation, made over a decade ago, that "with the exception of the mother in the Philippines, Bulosan's women are mostly either prostitutes or idealized white women who symbolize the America to which the narrator so ardently seeks to belong" (Kim 1984, 63). Whereas Kim formulates a descriptive characterization of women's stature in the novel, this essay analyzes more precisely the function of gender and sexuality in mediating the narrator's vision of competing collective identifications, of which "America" is just one.

3. In an oft-quoted passage, Bulosan talks about the "mockery" whereby "Filipinos are taught to regard Americans as our equals. . . . The terrible truth of America shatters the Filipino's dream of fraternity" (quoted by San Juan 1978, 43; McWilliams, xiii; Melendy, 35; and S. Wong 1993, 135). Anticipating more famous postco-

lonial critiques of Western Enlightenment philosophy, Bulosan portrays the political awakening of colonial subjects who can more keenly feel and denounce Western society's betrayal of its own purported principles. See Fanon's characterization of the psychical structures of the colonized (*Black Skin, White Masks*) and Aimé Césaire's claim that "colonization works to *decivilize* the colonizer" (Williams and Chrisman, 173).

4. Upon coming to America, the narrator Allos realizes that his name is being changed by those around him to Carlos. To avoid confusion, I will refer to the narrator as Carlos to emphasize this narrative as a retrospective account produced in light of the narrator's exile in America as well as his childhood in the Philippines. Tomas Santos has also remarked on this nominal division of the character into "Allos the peasant boy . . . [and] Carl, the educated and class conscious voice" (408).

5. Of Chinese mestizo origin, this ruling class, with the backing of American and British trading houses, established vast farming and milling businesses in the archipelago's countryside during the mid-nineteenth century. The sons of these same hacendados traveled to Europe for education, returned as *ilustrados* (enlightened ones), and took over the originally peasant leadership of the mass revolution against Spanish colonialism in 1896. See Anderson 1988, which traces the rise of "cacique democracy" in the Philippines—that is, the bicameral, elected government that is today dominated by members of the hacendado, mestizo class. Anderson underscores the role of American colonization (1898–1934) in increasing this mestizo class' landholdings and in consolidating these *nouveaux riches* as a ruling class (11).

6. Katipunan insurrectionist Andrés Bonifacio launched an insurrection against Spanish authorities in 1896 that initiated the revolution. He was executed in 1897 by General Emilio Aguinaldo, who later headed the republic of the Philippines during its brief tenure from 1898 to 1902. See also Luzviminda Francisco's account of "The Philippine-American War 1899–1902," which details the bloody campaigns of the United States Army. Following on the heels of that bloodshed were American colonial administrators and educators who effectively recast the war and the subsequent U.S. occupation of the islands as "benevolent assimilation" (see Miller; Constantino, 45–49; and Takaki 1990b, 57–58).

7. See Ileto for a history of the *Kataastaasan Kagalanggalang Katipunan ng mga Anak ng Bayan*, or The Highest and Most Respectable Society of Sons of the Country (Ileto's translation, 75). Offering an overview of peasant revolutionary societies in the Philippines from 1840 to 1910, Ileto revises the dominant view in scholarship that stresses the rise of nationalism through a mestizo, "Westerniz[ed]" leadership—a trickle-down theory of enlightenment. He essays a "history from below," documenting a popular "peasant tradition of unrest" that has been historiographically marginalized by accounts presupposing an "elite-led movement for independence" (Ileto, 6).

8. According to Lilia Quindoza Santiago, women's role in national liberation has been eclipsed by male-centered accounts of the Katipunan. To rectify this view, Santiago contests the dominant historical view that Bonifacio initiated the formation of the woman's chapter of the Katipunan and that membership in this chapter was limited to the wives, daughters, and sisters of the male members (116–17). While I agree with the overall thrust of Santiago's argument that women's efforts

were instrumental to the founding of the Filipino nation and not merely derivative of the men's efforts, I would caution against her overemphasis on the gender neutrality of Bonifacio's revolutionary society. Despite the gender-equivocal title of Bonafacio's organization, *Kataastaasang Kagalanggalang na Katipunan ng mga Anak ng Bayan* (The Most Supreme, Most Esteemed Society of the Children of the People), the very existence of a separate women's chapter indicates the gendering of its boundaries, rendering the common mistranslating of *Anak ng Bayan* as "Sons of the People" ironically telling.

9. In this "dramatic event," one remains unsure whether the nameless woman is a virgin. One only knows that smoke has failed to appear—implying that she has failed the test. Virginity, it would seem, must be indicated by the husband who presumably lights the fire in the hearth. The man's failure or refusal to perform this act signals the wife's impurity, which then becomes "justification" for the mob's marking of her body as sexually abject. The crowd beats Leon's wife, imprinting her body with signs of illicit identity. Yet, even as these events seem to confirm Leon's bride as impure, the narrative reveals her sexualized status, not as a prior material fact, but as a series of performances that reiterate her scandalousness. Thus, woman is distinctly not author to her body's virginity; rather the groom's and crowd's actions around her body establishes and regulates her identity as sexually impure.

10. According to Sucheng Chan, the sex ratio of Filipinos on the mainland of America in 1930 was roughly nineteen to one (Chan, 109); Ronald Takaki reports that in 1930 only 2,941 of 45,208 Filipinos (6.5 percent) were women (Takaki 1990b, 58); however, Fred Cordova offers slightly different figures from the 1930 census: 2,500 women amongst the 45,200 Filipinos counted (Cordova, 152).

11. San Juan gives this account of push-pull factors encouraging massive Filipino immigration to the United States from the turn of the century to World War II: "semi-feudal exploitation of the peasant majority and the intensified underdevelopment of an agrarian economy" encouraged peasants in the Philippines to seek opportunities abroad, while "the accelerating demand of California and Hawaii growers for cheap labor" resulted in the large-scale recruitment of Filipino laborers by American farming companies (San Juan 1978, 44).

12. In one of his correspondences, Bulosan explicitly links the exposure of grievances to the forging of a "higher dream of human perfection": "I only want to expose what terror and ugliness I have seen . . . so that . . . others will find a reason for a deeper grievance against social injustice and a higher dream of human perfection. . . . Beneath the ugliness is a stream of beauty that never dies" (Bulosan 1995, 177).

13. Precisely because these moments of intra-ethnic violence are less explicable in terms of capital and labor, they go ignored by E. San Juan Jr. in his book-length study on Carlos Bulosan (1972). Yet these vexing sites reiterate the thematic of brotherly dispersion established in the novel's first part. Accounting for this continuity remains crucial to any reading of Bulosan's narrative.

14. The narrator further establishes Myra's "fault" by admitting his own "distract[ion] by Myra" who "was careless with herself, in a house where she was the only girl" (150–51). Moreover, the text glosses over the complicated effects of spousal abuse by suggesting Myra's complicity. "I won't do it again, honey. . . . I love you

darling. . . . I love you! I love you!" says Myra after being battered (151). Classically blaming the victim, the narrator wonders "[W]hat kind of girl was she?" (151).

15. It may be the case that this textual suppression of woman as a laboring subject enables the textual promotion of her as a principle of social connection—the brotherly bond—rather than as a subject who has the privilege of connecting. In other words, she symbolizes the principle that allows men to bond and strangely remains necessary to that connecting dynamic even as she is thoroughly marginalized by it.

16. The narrative describes this "bestial" eroticism in Carlos's first glimpse of Macario's living quarters, wherein he observes "three American girls [and] ten Filipinos" laid out improperly: "One of the girls was in the bed with two men. The other girl was on the couch with two other men. They were all nude" (132). The narrator calls the sleeping arrangement a "debased" and "desperate" rebellion—one that proceeds not from hope for a prospective brotherly society but from cynicism engendered by its current absence.

17. In its critique of capital, Bulosan's text also exposes the limits of Marx's analysis of capital. As Lisa Lowe puts it,

> [T]o the extent that Marx adopts the abstract and universalist propositions of the economic and political spheres, his classic critique of citizenship cannot account for the particular racialized relations of production on which this nation has been founded. Despite its trenchant indictment of liberal democracy as the protector of capitalist relations, Marx's theory cannot account for the historical conditions through which U.S. capital profited precisely from racializing Chinese, Japanese, and Filipino immigrant labor in distinction to white labor and excluding those racialized laborers from citizenship. . . . [I]n the history of the United States, capital has maximized its profits not through rendering labor "abstract" but precisely through the social productions of "difference," of restrictive particularity and illegitimacy marked by race, nation, geographical origins, and gender.' (Lowe 1996, 25, 28)

18. Cynthia Enloe, Floya Anthias, Nira Yuval-Davis, and Jan Jindy Pettman all comment on the specific ways in which nations regulate women's behavior with more intensity than men's behavior, especially with regard to their sexual and reproductive choices. See Cynthia Enloe, *Bananas, Beaches and Bases*, 54; Floya Anthias and Nira Yuval-Davis, introduction to *Woman-Nation-State*, 9; and Jan Jindy Pettman's "Border Crossings/Shifting Identities: Minorities, Gender, and the State in International Perspective."

19. See also the full text of Goldberg's essay "Bradford's 'Ancient Members' and 'A Case of Buggery . . . Amongst Them.' "

20. I am not suggesting that forging interracial tolerance is antithetical to feminist work, but rather that even within antiracist movements gender oppression occurs, often by way of an elision of gender-specific issues.

21. I would recall, here, Gayle Rubin's essay "The Traffic in Women," in which she demonstrates kinship as a communal mode of power that rests upon the exchange of women as gifts. As Rubin points out, though women are the vehicles across which men bond, women are neither the partners of the exchange nor the recipients of the greater power afforded by these male networks. See my later discussion of Rubin in chapter 3.

22. E. San Juan Jr. notes that Salvador Lopez was still alive in 1972, three decades after the writing of this "Letter" (San Juan 1972, 89).

23. See Rabinowitz for a reading of the gendered dynamics of the 1930s literary radicalism movement, wherein the very priority of history, the economy, and politics over the realm of literature appeared gendered: "[I]t is easy to see that this model of analysis [adopted by the literary radicals] is profoundly gendered even as it erases gender as a salient category for organizing thought. Power flows from the public spheres of history (controlled and determined by men) to the private spheres of literature (produced and consumed by women)" (Rabinowitz, 20).

24. San Juan's analysis of Bulosan's unflattering portrait of the narrator's patronage of a prostitute offers an interesting sidelight on this issue. The novel depicts both Carlos's involuntary participation in the encounter—"the men pinned me down to the cot, face upward, while Benigno hurried fumbled for my belt" (159)—and the narrator's overwhelming repulsion upon copulation—"I plunged through the wall of sheets and started running between the cots to the door" (160). Yet San Juan recuperates the scenario as a demonstration of erotic fortitude: "[The narrator's] reaction to sexual intercourse with a Mexican woman in Guadalupe, part of an initiation rite, suggests not his ambivalence but the potency of the erotic force in man, its capacity to abolish a class-conditioned 'shame' " (San Juan 1972, 100).

25. I am grateful to Alycee Lane for the phrasing, "joint ownership in whiteness."

26. Cheryl Harris also notes the role of whiteness and its privileged status in consolidating a national identity. She paraphrases Andrew Hacker's observation that "white became a 'common front' established across ethnic origins, social class, and language" (Harris, 1743); this common front facilitated the "amalgamation of various European strains into an American identity" which contrasted itself to the de-privileged identities of blacks and—I would add—of various-colored and "foreign" bodies.

27. Marilyn Alquizola has analyzed opposing interpretations of Bulosan's novel as a function of the historical context both of the novel's writing as well as of its readings. She compares the 1946 reception of the text, which emphasized its pro-American sentiments, to the critical response to the text after its 1973 republication, which emphasized the novel's ending as an ironic and strategic concession to American publishing interests. See also Kenneth Mostern, who argues that "America is the privileged location of socialist struggle" and that America represents a spiritual renewal for the narrator (Mostern, 36); and Elaine Kim, who characterizes Carlos Bulosan's writing as a "testament of one who longed to become part of America" (Kim 1982, 57).

28. Sau-ling Wong's links this term, "extravagance," to utopian, imagined impulses. See my later discussion in chapter 3.

CHAPTER TWO
GISH JEN AND THE GENDERED CODES OF AMERICANNESS

1. Jen leaves equivocal the "national" roots of this vertical family structure, leaving ambiguous whether patriarchal hierarchies, as Ralph tries to enact them, derive from Confucianism or from American configurations of normative families such as those detailed in the infamous 1965 Moynihan report. In Shanghai, where the novel begins, Ralph is situated in a household where his father is the clear authority;

however, his older sister Theresa also enjoys a degree of authority over Ralph that suggests a kinship structure not wholly conforming to a sexist valuing of sons over daughters. It is in America that Ralph embraces the idea of his natural position as head of the household, simply because he is the man in the family. However, Jen leaves ambiguous whether these acts of male dominance are part of Ralph's acculturation to the United States (and that nation's disciplining of family life in the fifties) or residual effects of his notion of Asian family tradition carried over from Shanghai. Significantly, the American character who clearly encourages Ralph to a patriarchal and homosocial view is Grover Ding, an *Asian American* (second generation or more), with Jen making it impossible to determine whether these views are traditionally Asian or traditionally American.

2. According to Bill Ong Hing, this legislative appeal was enacted not so much because Americans felt less prejudicial toward Chinese but because of their need to court China as a war ally against the Japanese (Hing, 36).

3. The gendered effects of these changes have been astounding with respect to Chinese immigration: "women were almost 90 percent of Chinese immigrants from 1946 to 1953" and the pattern of women outnumbering men among Chinese immigrants has continued up to the present (Hing, 48, 82–83).

4. With regard to the above passage, one should also note the text's typographical conventions. Wherever dialogue is rendered, italics signal words spoken in Chinese. This print style implicitly performs American phrases as "public" and "shared"—the familiar or natural typeface that goes unnoticed. Yet at the same time, Jen's italicized sections privilege Chinese expressions as "interior" and "private"—as foreign perhaps to the reader, but natural to her speakers. Oddly then, in making italic typeface a convention within her own novel, Jen draws attention to the nonitalicized segments of the text as performances—by both the Changs and the author herself—of conventional linguistic scripts. Thus, the italicized "Chinese" phrases create the illusion of an interior identity that paradoxically highlights the exterior, public, and performative aspects of "typical American" habits and speech-acts.

5. The proposition that Asians can only act American rather than be American would seem to perpetuate the politically retrograde designation of them as unassimilable aliens. However, I would propose that through the Changs' imitative and performative excesses, Jen not only questions the criteria of belonging that continually keeps Asians on the margins of American society but also deconstructs several planks of the American Dream that the Changs pursue. As Frederick Buell argues, the Asian American "who realizes that ethnicity is an American act can, perhaps, more radically deconstruct and decenter American culture than someone from a position of revolutionary separatism" (Buell, 188). Through the Changs' representation of "typical American" narratives, Jen becomes a "deconstructionist master of the American system" (Buell, 188).

6. Among the many specious justifications of anti-Chinese sentiment was the notion that the Chinese were unassimilable, an "unchangeable alien element" who "showed no inclination to make this country their permanent home." From there rose nativist notions that America should not be home to the Chinese (Sandmeyer, 25, 38, and 60).

7. Moreover, these actions of women, according to Maria Mies, ought not to be viewed as natural extensions of women's nature or caring duties. As I elaborate in

chapter 4, the defining of women's work as "love, care, emotionality, motherhood and wifehood" tends to obscure women's contribution to productivity (Mies, 31). Jen's approach to showing the labor of women is a bit different from Mies's materialist feminist explanations; Jen emphasizes precisely the love, care, and emotionality of her female characters but also grants narrative value to these practices. Her audience is to measure the Changs' "progress" not only in terms of their changing national identities but also in terms of changes to their household and family dynamics.

8. According to Stephanie Coontz, the model of the "true American" family ("a restricted, exclusive nuclear unit in which women and children were divorced from the world of work") was very much a work of social engineering imposed upon "working-class and immigrant populations," especially at the turn of the century (Coontz, 13, 139).

9. As Biddy Martin and Chandra Mohanty have argued, there are two modalities of "being home" and "not being home": " 'Being home' refers to the place where one lies within familiar, safe, protected boundaries; 'not being home' is a matter of realizing that home was an illusion of coherence and safety based on the exclusion of specific histories of oppression and resistance, the repression of differences even within oneself" (Martin and Mohanty, 195). The security of the home derives from an illusion of homogeneity that willfully blinds itself to the presence of others. Stephanie Coontz remarks on the similar homogeneity of a symbol related to the American home, the iconic American family of the fifties, also a whites-only preserve: Puerto Ricans, Mexican Americans and African Americans were "almost entirely excluded from the gains and privileges accorded white middle-class families during the fifties. . . . [African Americans] were excluded by restrictive convenants and redlining from many benefits of economic expansion that their labor helped sustain. Whites resisted, with harassment and violence, the attempt of blacks to participate in the American family dream" (Coontz, 30).

10. That correspondence of "home" and international politics became explicit in the famous 1959 "kitchen debate," wherein President Nixon "asserted [to Kruschchev that] the superiority of capitalism over communism [was evident] not in ideology of military might but in the comforts of the suburban home, 'designed to make things easier for our women' " (Coontz, 28). See also Elaine May (1988), who details "Cold War ideology and the domestic revival as two sides of the same coin" (May, 10).

11. The connection between home ownership and American, capitalist patriotism was made by William Levitt during the Cold War: this builder of suburban homes declared that "No man who owns his own house and lot can be a communist. He has too much to do" (Halberstam, 132).

12. Thoreau called upon men to be more than good citizens who follow the letter of the law. Instead, he advocated respect, not for the law, but for "the right. The only obligation which I have a right to assume is to do at any time what I think is right" (Thoreau, 236). Occasioning this writing was Thoreau's arrest in 1846 for refusing to pay his poll tax.

13. "Whoso would be a man, must be a nonconformist," says Emerson in "Self-Reliance" (Emerson, 149). However, preventing man from living as a nonconformist is his lack of self-trust (i.e., his doubt over his own divinity): "For nonconformity

the world whips you with its displeasure. And therefore a man . . . needs the habit of magnanimity and religion to treat [the world's displeasure] *godlike* as a trifle of no concernment" (Emerson, 152; emphasis added). Jen later mocks Emersonian self-divinity in her portrait of Ralph's (Chang, not Emerson, but the nominal confusion *is* interesting) desire to be "a man-god."

14. Kaledin notes that by 1955 Norman Vincent Peale's *The Power of Positive Thinking* sold over two million copies. According to Will Herberg, the popularity of this book, rather than attesting to America's new religious fervor, represented a new " 'religiousness without religion' . . . [not a] 're-orienting life to God,' but rather as 'a way of sociability or belonging' " (Kaledin, 13, quoting Herberg).

15. In a recent interview, Jen herself alluded to Americans' conformity in non-conformity: "It's very 'in' to be an independent thinker—never mind that you're being an independent thinker in a very fashionable way" (Jen 1993).

16. The Asian American success story—a.k.a. the model minority syndrome—might be fruitfully read in this context. I would also pose here a series of questions of which the scope of this essay precludes a full analysis. As an intervention into future policy making, I pose these questions for discussion: Does the heterogeneity of America relegate "the poor [and] nonwhites" to an undignified position of difference and handicap? Are assessments of heterogeneity always intertwined with assessments of inequality, and if so, how can a multicultural America that subscribes to a policy of coalitions respective of difference preserve a politics of equality?

17. Such homosocial bonding as Ralph and Grover undertake, on the one hand, remains part of a well-established American narrative that equates rejection of political dependency with a rejection of genealogy (descent) and inherited hierarchy, in preference for a democratically-elected social and political body (forged by consent). In miniature, Ralph exercises an "American" or national sense of social partnership in choosing to affiliate with a non–blood relation, Grover, while rejecting his old-world ties to his biological sister Theresa. On the other hand, Ralph chooses Grover over Theresa and Helen because of the gendered subtexts of national identity and community that an association with Grover affords.

18. Analyzing Leslie Fiedler's reading of *The Scarlet Letter*, Baym suggests that the American novel itself, as Fiedler constructs it, acts as a site of readerly homosocial bonding (Baym, 134). Thus, the male communion already inscribed as an American practice par excellence becomes reenacted through the reading experience of a presumed all-male audience.

19. More recently, David Leverenz has interrogated nineteenth-century canonical American texts for their portraits of men pressured by traditional notions of masculinity. See his *Manhood and the American Renaissance*.

20. While Ralph "[sleeps] on the couch like an oversized pillow," Theresa studies for her medical school entrance boards (77). When cooking, Helen teasingly calls Ralph "fan tong" (literally, "rice barrel," someone who just eats), resulting in Ralph's wondering how he could be "so powerless in his power. . . , yelling 'I'm the father of this family! Do you hear me? The father, not the son!' " (74).

21. In this way, Jen couples the Changs' burlesque of the middle-class American Dream with a narrative of manhood beset (unmanned) and reasserted within the family, a narrative that exposes the male-headed nuclear household, not as a natural structure, but as a formation produced through repression. As Coontz makes clear,

the "happy, homogenous" families of the fifties were themselves "products of . . . direct repression" (33). Some women were institutionalized, coerced into "electric shock treatments . . . to force [them] to accept their domestic roles and their husbands' dictates," while bachelors were "categorized as 'immature,' 'infantile,' 'narcissistic,' 'deviant,' or even 'pathological' " (32–33). Even successful families were won "at enormous cost to the wife, who was expected to subordinate her own needs and aspirations to those of both her husband and her children" (36).

22. I have used "tactic" and "strategy" interchangeably here. However, Rey Chow's distinction between the two terms remains useful in evaluating the interventionist thrust of "not continuing" in terms other than its immediate effects: "A strategy has the ability to transform the uncertainties of history into readable spaces. . . . Strategy therefore belongs to . . . those who are committed to the building, growth, and fortification of a 'field.' . . . A tactic, by contrast, is 'a calculated action determined by the absence of a proper locus' " (Chow 1993, 16). In other words, strategies are invested in building a field, in making themselves "proper" and hegemonic. Tactics, on the other hand, are practices which intervene but do not build their own proprietary field, however oppositional. Put simply, the counterhegemonic becomes hegemonic when tactics turn to strategies. Thus, Chow asks the question, "How do we prevent what begin as tactics . . . from turning into a solidly fenced-off field, in the military no less than in the academic sense?" (Chow 1993, 17). Jen's passage reveals the seeming lack of efficacy in Mona and Callie's "not continuing" when they are with their American peers, in contrast to its felt force within the house. Thus even though "not to continue" does not register within the realm outside the house, this does not mean that what one wants is its hegemonic recognition (i.e., the way it is practiced within the house). Rather, "not to continue" within a Western scheme in which "we cannot but narrate" (Spivak 1990, 19) emerges as a nonoppressive tactical strategy enacted in Jen's novel both by the two girls at school and by the two women's actions to halt temporarily the narratives of male self-making and entrepreneurship.

One might further argue that there is little value in remaining nonoppressive (in remaining tactical). This is, in fact, what Spivak suggests when she talks about negotiating with the structures of violence (Spivak 1990, 101). Jen, however, does not decide to war with narratives on their terms (redeploying violence through Asian American female agents—for instance as enshrined in Bharati Mukherjee's *Jasmine* or Wendy Law-Yone's *Irrawaddy Tango*). Instead, she tactically exposes the violences these narratives keep hidden; yet in doing so, her efforts (in not continuing) run the risk of not registering to her Western audience (those primed to the narratives of speaking as a sign of success and silence as a sign of failure).

23. Here, as in other essays, Spivak warns against the mistaking of a critical for a dogmatic philosophy. In particular, she speaks of the application of Marx's *critical* philosophy to what has become known as international communism (what Spivak would identify as a dogmatic philosophy).

24. Deconstruction thus works as "a corrective" to politics, even as Spivak encourages a break with deconstructive theories such as high feminism in order to engage in politics (antisexist work). See Spivak 1990, 12 and 47.

25. My counterpoising feminist and Asian American scripts does not suggest that these two frameworks are inherently in opposition but rather that they do—

in our contemporary milieu—pose distinct agendas that can be antagonistic as well as complementary to each other. The tensions between nationally defined and gender-related agendas have been well documented. See, for instance, R. Radhakrishnan (1992), Grewal and Kaplan (1994), Liu (1994), and Cheung (1990), and Kim (1990).

26. Said calls the "essence of Orientalism" the "ineradicable distinction between Western superiority and Oriental inferiority" (Said 1979, 42). In other words, the Orient becomes subjugated by Western knowledge through great "anatomical and enumerative" efforts (72). The purpose of this subjugation is to lend the Orient an ontological stability (32) that limns a similar, yet superior, ontological stability for its opposite, the West.

27. See Spivak's account of the postcolonial group with whom she worked in 1987 and who were seeking to privilege "indigenous theory" (Spivak 1990, 69). Positivist counternarratives also abound among literary revisionists, voiced for instance by the editors of the *Aiiieeeee!* and *Big Aiiieeeee!* anthologies. Rey Chow also gives an account of counternarrative strategies to recuperate an untainted native Asia in her critique of East Asian Studies (see Chow 1991 and 1993).

28. This poststructuralist methodology also transmutes the kinds of questions asked with regard to "ethnicity." In his essay on "New Ethnicities," Hall traces the displacement of a politics of access by a "new politics of representation" in black cultural production. The politics of access is dominated by two large goals: the establishment of more black cultural producers and the amassing of "positive" black images to counter stereotypes. Poststructuralism shifts the arena of cultural resistance from a battle over who represents and whether those representations are positive, to an exploration of "the regimes of representation" themselves—to questions regarding what other texts mediate the production of "resistant" works (Hall 1988, 27 and 30).

29. Even though Jen does not write sexual intimacy explicitly into her novel, I describe Theresa's and Helen's relationship as suppressed romantic love to assert the continuum between female homosociality and homosexuality. At the same time, I have refrained from identifying Ralph and Grover's relationship as gay, choosing instead to call their interactions homosocial. The reasoning behind this choice proceeds in part from Eve Sedgwick's observation that the intuitive continuum between "women loving women" and "women promoting the interests of women" has been disrupted in the case of men (Sedgwick 1985, 3). In fact, arenas epitomizing "men promoting the interests of men"—for instance, the patriarchal networks of the corporate boardroom—often foster hostility toward the notion of "men loving men" (hence the homophobia that plagues patriarchal settings). Given Sedgwick's observation, I see my own characterization of Helen and Theresa's relationship as lesbian and Ralph and Grover's relationship as homosocial rather than gay not necessarily as a "radical" reading against the grain. However, given the heterosexual panic that often greets readings that emphasize closeted lesbian or gay relations, my own reading may appear both subversive and illegitimate. Yet, my stressing the sexual component of the two women's intercourse emerges from my commitment to antisexist and antihomophobic work. In essence, I am arguing against those strategies that disable and decenter readings of lesbian and gay relations by way of asserting that sexuality is not central to the narratives in question.

30. Jen likens Helen's marriage string, tying her to Ralph, to the leash her husband attaches to his dog, Grover: "Grover's leash was red—she thought, *the red string*, then she saw herself, being taught to play dead. To heel" (258–59).

31. Jen makes overt the self-parodic character of her own stories by calling Ralph's first story (homologous to Part 1 of the novel) a "scale model" for the later version of this tale, which begins at Part 4.

32. In light of the intentional fallacy, these considerations of Jen's conscious choices may seem beside the point. However, in the same way that Ralph, Theresa, and Helen both follow and depart from a "typical American" script, the author herself makes limited choices within the national and narrative codes that have inscribed her. Furthermore, the intentional fallacy has little purchase with non-poststructuralists, for instance political activists who organize around a belief in individual and collective agency. Thus, even if Jen does subscribe to a poststructuralist ethic, our viewing her novel through a lens of political agency helps illuminate the blindspots of her narrative (its noncommittal antisexism and antihomophobia). In turn, the poststructuralist lens that underscores the way in which national/narrative scripts write the author as well as her characters highlights the utopian foundations of a politics based on individual agency.

33. Walter Benn Michaels attributes a similar excessive capacity or surplus value to language and literature. He further construes literary language's excessive non-correspondence to materiality—its "infinite" capacities—as analogous to the powerful excess promised by and structuring capitalist processes: "[T]he infinite power of . . . language [is] not . . . a threat to capitalism but . . . an essential part of its technology" (Michaels, 55).

CHAPTER THREE
TRANSVERSING NATIONALISM, GENDER, AND SEXUALITY

1. Alluding to the general tenor of this criticism, Nerissa Balce-Cortes writes, "[Dogeaters] has also been criticized by some Filipino critics in Manila as a racist and fetishistic project of a Filipino-born writer claiming exoticism for her acceptance into the U.S. literary mainstream" (Balce-Cortes, 102). Balce-Cortes further attributes these critiques to the high representational demands made of Filipino American literature: "[T]he burden on these breakthrough novels to be 'perfect' or 'authentic' vehicles of Filipino ethnicity and culture will continue to be great as long as there are so few of them" (Balce-Cortes, 102). As for charges that Hagedorn's novel does not represent a postcolonial counterculture adequately, I would point out that the novel does in fact portray nationalist guerrilla characters, and one might argue, moreover, that they are the heroes and heroines of the novel. Acknowledging their presence, E. San Juan Jr. directs his critique of *Dogeaters* at its "capitalist principle of repetition" (which he equates with postmodernist aesthetics) that effectively "neutralize[s]" the novel's subversive "storytelling" (i.e., the representation of revolutionary forces) (San Juan 1992, 125).

2. I am thinking here specifically of Fanon's characterization of radio in Algiers—its first being rejected as an instrument of the oppressor and its later crucial function in forging and mobilizing a native nationalist movement. (See Fanon's *A*

Dying Colonialism, originally published in 1959—the fifth year of Algerian revolution, two years before liberation.)

3. In a moment of self-characterization, the author states, "[I]dentity for me is not only racial, but sexual. I cannot think of myself as addressing the multicultural issue without including gender culture within the framework" (Hagedorn 1994, 178).

4. Another Manila resident, Girlie Garcia, expresses similar views on the influence of American pop culture; she claims that "because of the mass-media, because of the foreign things coming in to the Philippines, the youths, they're very inclined to go American, you know. . . . You look around you and you have Madonnas and Cindy Laupers walking around on the streets. And I think every Filipino's dream is to go to America and just to see the place because we've heard so much about it" (Denton and Villena-Denton, 180).

5. Hagedorn has made clear her intentions to avoid any overtly didactic content: "What is literature for? . . . You don't go to literature and say I need to feel good about my race, so let me read a novel." She adds, "I hate preaching. It puts me to sleep." (Sengupta, C1).

6. Lowe underscores the complex racial and national sedimentation of Filipino society that renders questions of purity and authenticity virtually unresolvable: "In a country with seventy-one hundred known islands and eighty dialects and languages spoken, as well as a cultural and racial hybridity that has mixed Spanish, Malayan, Chinese, Arab, Hindu, North American, and others with 'native' groups over the course of four centuries, the distinction between the 'authentic' and the 'inauthentic' may be less salient than the turn around different kinds of 'seeming,' the cultural, racial, and linguistic admixtures that are the contemporary expression of a history of colonial and commercial encounter in the Philippines" (Lowe 1996, 118).

7. Hagedorn herself has commented on the controversy her novel inspired (Sengupta). See also Casper, San Juan (1992), and Gonzalez for critical views of *Dogeaters*'s social-political practice and aesthetic accomplishment.

8. Realism has so many charged meanings, as Amy Kaplan points out, that it is imperative to note that Casper never explicitly uses the term. However, Casper does express his desire for *Dogeaters* to cleave more to qualities of narration that the realist narrative enshrines, such as an emphasis on character, on social relations, and on a utopian resolution wherein some common ground between divided classes is posited (see A. Kaplan 1988).

9. Casper never definitely states, but does suggest, that *Dogeaters* cannot be "written off as a negligible scrapbook of colorful eccentricities and absurdities" (Casper, 155).

10. Realism, however, has had a changing fate in literary criticism, as to determinations of the degree of its resistance or collusion with capitalist forces: "Changes in the historical understanding of realism have accompanied the reevaluation of realism's political stance, from a progressive force exposing social conditions to a conservative force complicit with capitalist relations" (7). Realism might "[express] consumer culture" and be a "form of social incorporation" rather than a call to arms (Kaplan 1988, 7).

11. For instance, Casper finds fault with Rio as a narrator, calling her teenage perspective "defective"; moreover, he finds her later mature recollections also lack-

ing: "[H]er capacity for critical understanding has not grown" (154). Casper finds fundamentally flawed Hagedorn's lack of adult narrators with intellectual capacities for "critical understanding"; adolescents and street persons and other nonintellectual types, in this estimation, cannot narrate to either aesthetic or political effect.

12. The review of *Dogeaters* appears in the second half of San Juan's essay entitled "Beyond Identity Politics," which has divisions "A" and "B," the latter subtitled "Toward the Production of a Filipino Racial Discourse in the Metropolis." Because the notes for Part A appear at the end of that part, and not after the conclusion of both parts, one might be encouraged to view "Beyond Identity Politics" as two distinct essays, rendering Part B more of a review essay than a contemplation of Filipino racial discourse in the United States. However, because San Juan links the two "halves" under a single title, it becomes impossible to read his review of *Dogeaters* without contemplating Part A's account of a symposium where Asian American writers and critics came head-to-head over who could speak of and for Asian American collective identity. By San Juan's account, writers "found themselves privileged . . . as the fountainhead of answers to questions of Asian American person/collective identity," while critics were eschewed for using theory and for being ensconced in elite institutions (San Juan 1992, 104–105). San Juan laments the event's missed opportunity to scrutinize problems of racial representativeness in preference for "a theater of naive and pathetic self-congratulation . . . another day swallowed up in the *mise en abime* of ghetto marginality and ethnic vainglory. Liberalism and identity politics have conquered again" (San Juan 1992, 109).

13. Out of fourteen story lines in *Dogeaters*, three feature male protagonists and eleven feature female protagonists. I have distinguished story lines based on the number of first-person and third-person over-the-shoulder perspectives through which Hagedorn narrates events. See appendixes.

14. There is a factual testament to this aestheticized violence: as part of her beautification campaign, the First Lady hosts "an International Film Festival for which the Folk Arts Theater was hastily built at the cost of many workers' lives" (Evangelista 1993, 52).

15. For further discussions of *sati*, see Lati Mani (1990a and 1990b) and Rajan.

16. Both Masao Miyoshi (1990) and Arjun Appadurai (1990 and 1993) delineate the limited usefulness of "nation" as a category of analysis, proposing transnational and postnational frameworks in its stead.

17. See the introduction for a more detailed account of the ways in which issues of gender and sexuality take a backseat to debates over the nexus of nationalism-transnationalism in Asian American cultural critique.

18. Along similar lines, Hagedorn critiques narratives of "pure" identity by depicting Rio's father's rejection of his mestizo ancestry. Freddie Gonzaga, to the chagrin of his wife, Dolores, decodes his bloodline as Spanish rather than Filipino: "I don't understand," she exclaims. "You are definitely Filipino! A mestizo, yes— but definitely Filipino" (8). How Freddie's genetic material is encoded remains decidedly less important than how he "feels" (8) (i.e., how he narrates his ancestry). Moreover, that decoding—however false or contested—has more influence on the way in which Freddie lives his life than does the supposed genetic codes he inherits. The transformative effects of decoding, then, can be subversive (as in Joey's reversal

of the Tonto stereotype) as well as nonsubversive (as in Freddie's translation of his bloodline into pure Spanish stock).

19. According to Gaylyn Studlar, Mulvey's theory of spectatorship and much of feminist film theory that follows in its wake are based on male psychic mechanisms "which inscribe pleasurable (and power-laden) patterns of looking between spectator and screen" (Studlar, 2–3). As an alternative to this model, based on the psychodynamics of the castration complex, Studlar investigates "pleasures of male spectatorship that are beyond mastery," that are based on the psychodynamics of the oral (mother-centered) phase where pleasure is associated with submission, passivity, and dependence—with masochism, in short. Studlar goes on to define a "masochistic aesthetic," based on suspended desire and linked to strategies of concealment, that remains the hallmark of film: "Masochism obsessively recreates the movement between concealment and revelation . . . , seduction and rejection, in emulation of the ambivalent response to the mother who may either abandon or overwhelm the child. In masochistic fantasy, seduction offers the promise—and the danger—of symbiosis" (Studlar, 21).

20. See chapter 1 of Chow's *Woman and Chinese Modernity*, especially pp. 19–25.

21. I will return to this discussion of necessity (dependence) and extravagance (autonomy) in the final part of this chapter. For more on the politics of pleasure, see the volume edited by Jameson, *Formations of Pleasure*.

22. To cite but a few such studies, I would refer the reader to Said (1979); Alloula; Li; and Moy.

23. Feminist interventions into postcolonial studies owe a great debt to the work of Gayatri Spivak who critiqued the shunting of women aside in subaltern revisionist histories (see Spivak 1988b). Other critics interrogating the masculine bias of postcolonial nationalism and the Western bias of feminist studies include Chandra Mohanty, Jenny Sharpe, Trinh Minh-ha, Deniz Kandiyoti, Sara Suleri, Inderpal Grewal and Caren Kaplan.

24. This is not to suggest that feminism and nationalism are inherently at odds. Rather, it is to acknowledge the way in which "national identity [has] serve[d] the interests of patriarchies in multiple locations" (Grewal and Kaplan, 22).

25. The manhood to be "recovered" by nationalist leaders is thus a specific brand of masculinity premised upon phallocentric notions of male dominance over women.

26. Enloe finds the issue of Muslim women's wearing the veil remarkable precisely because of the importance men in these communities assign to it: "One is hard pressed to think of an equally heated debate in any national community about men's attire—or diet or linguistic style—in which women have had so predominant a role to play. Sikh men's wearing of customary turban is important to Sikh communal solidarity. . . . Yet one doesn't see Sikh women acting as the chief proponents or enforcers of this male ethnic practice" (Enloe, 53–54).

27. See Enloe (60) for a deconstruction of this "not now, later" tabling of women's issues by nationalist leaders.

28. There are several Filipina nationalist political groups that precisely work to dismantle both the obvious neocolonial structures (military bases, transnational corporations, single-crop plantations) and the less obvious oppression of women upon which such foreign exploitation rests (as witnessed in the prostitution around

military bases, the cheap female labor servicing transnational industries, and the gendered division of labor and wages in farm work). See Brenda Stoltzfus on GABRIELA, a Filipina organization that joins "the struggle for justice as Filipino people with their struggle for justice as women" (Stoltzfus, 310). See also Lilia Santiago, for a history of the women's movement in the Philippines since the Spanish colonial era.

29. In 1986, Frederic Jameson coins the term "national allegory" to describe Third World texts, those emanating from countries that "have suffered colonialism and imperialism": "[T]hird-world texts . . . necessarily project a political dimension in the form of a national allegory: *the story of the private individual destiny is always an allegory of the embattled situation of the public third-world culture and society*" (Jameson 1986, 69). Aijaz Ahmad critiques Jameson, in short objecting to the reduction of all Third World texts into a unitary response to (capitalist, Western) imperialism.

30. As the portrait of the First Lady reveals, the multiform expression of female embodiment to which *Dogeaters* gives voice are cross-cut by class privileges. Only women of the upper classes survive in the narrative, either through escape, or through joining the nationalist guerrilla movement, or through adopting the position of the neocolonial exploiter. By focusing on the spectatorial gazes to which all women and gay men are subject, Hagedorn does, indeed, understate the class stratification amongst these varied "objects to be looked at."

31. Appadurai's (1992) response to the many "attacks" on nationalism is to call for the construction of a "language" that will encompass nonterritorial, exilic identities (418).

32. Moreover, the threat of rape and torture comes from both sides of the class struggle—the male elite and the "dark, barefoot boys" (the caddies), though opposed in economic and nationalist matters, have in common this trafficking in women.

33. Clearly preoccupied with the issues of class privilege, women's complicity, and the consequences of escape, Hagedorn crafts a similar scene in her 1981 novella *Pet Food*. In this earlier work, the Filipina protagonist, George Sand, envisions a group of guerrillas coming to her father's house and killing everyone but her grandmother: "I hear them in the next room, killing the nurse. . . . I lie in my bed, sweating and staring at the door. Should I try to escape?" (Hagedorn 1993, 108).

34. Biddy Martin both emphasizes the association of the feminine gender with "subjection to a bodily vulnerability" and the ways in which—in a U.S. context—"the construction of race as subjection to a body" coexists with this gendered vulnerability (Martin, 117). In Hagedorn's novel, gendered vulnerability coexists not so much with racialized vulnerability but with class vulnerability, with the impoverished more likely to be buried beneath hastily constructed buildings. My main argument, however, is that in their defensive reactions to gendered vulnerability, Hagedorn's Filipina characters are too often construed as betraying their country—escaping to the United States and so forth. In the terms of this argument, resisting gender subordination is seen as a revolution of lesser importance, even a fractious uprising that must be put down, in order to wage the main war against imperialism and neocolonialism.

35. Scarry also reflects upon the idiom of "betrayal," where the tortured person is made to assume responsibility for his/her own destruction (i.e., pain). Scarry counters "world, self, and voice are lost, or nearly lost, through the intense pain of torture and *not through the confession* as is wrongly suggested by its connotations of betrayal" (Scarry, 35; emphasis added).

36. Interpolating Deleuze, Studlar remarks on how "rituals of suffering show the masochist's contempt for the superego's expectation that punishment could prevent forbidden pleasure" (Studlar, 17–18). Since the superego's punishing logic is coded male—that is, the superego represents the internalization of the father's law held in place by the threat of castration—then this masochistic contempt might be construed as a feminized resistance to the punishing male order (i.e., it refuses punishment as punishment, thus transcending its logic). As Studlar claims in a later section, the fantasy goal of masochism is "expiation of the father and the symbiotic reunion with an idealized maternal rule" (Studlar, 26). One might view Leonor's masochistic suffering, then, not merely as sign of her circumscribed position but also as sign of her perversion of punishment—her contempt for the general's torturing tactics.

37. Hagedorn herself has commented on the "profound sense of 'freedom' as a woman—a freedom of movement and choice" that she associates with Western culture, particularly in her recollection of arriving in San Francisco and being able to "ventur[e] out . . . alone," without older relatives or paid chaperones (Hagedorn 1994, 175).

38. In an interview with Jon Halliday, Sirk characterized the picture as "about the antithesis of Thoreau's qualified Rousseauism" (Halliday, 99). Elaborating on the film, Halliday writes, "[I]t is a tough attack on the moralism of petit bourgeois America. Within the story, and the [melodramatic] genre (and the cast), Sirk has constructed a film which historicizes the lost American ideal of Thoreau and situates the barren ideology of bourgeois America in class terms. He does this by showing the *relations* between people whose roles are already specified—for example, at the country club" (Halliday, 10). Also commenting on Sirk's use of melodrama, Michael Stern states, "Sirk more frequently turned to family structure or small-town stratification as a microcosm of the broader issues [such as the failing social order]" (Stern, 26). Like Sirk, Hagedorn uses the petty tragedies of quotidian life in order to comment upon the national and transnational social forces inscribing Filipinas' everyday politics which include sexual choice and sexual desire.

39. In this respect, Hagedorn's novel appears to abide by "the classic tenets of dominant Euro-American feminism," to use Inderpal Grewal's words. Such feminism privileges the "antagonism between men and women as the primary source of exploitation" and naively celebrates Third World female protagonists' becoming " 'free' individual[s]," with "the West as the site for such 'freedom' " (Grewal, 63). Yet, only Rio's story follows the trajectory preferred by Euro-American feminism. As noted earlier, Daisy challenges Western feminists' presumptions that the West is the sole site of feminist liberation.

40. The phrase is Diana Fuss's, from the title of her article "Fashion and the Homospectatorial Look." However, my allusion to this phrase is indebted to Kim Rowe's excellent undergraduate paper, in which she deconstructs the formation of Pucha and Rio's gendered subjectivity—their learning how to be women—through

"homospectatorship": "When they are older, Rio is the only one comfortable with the underlying homo-sexual meaning of that construction [of womanhood]. Pucha affects a heterosexual identity, while Rio more accurately sees the effects of female homo-spectatorship on the construction of gender" (Rowe, 104). My thanks to Katheryn Rios for bringing the essay to my attention.

41. I allude here to works by Apter, Boone, and Sedgwick (1992) that record the way in which Western enclaves of gays and lesbians at the turn of and early part of the century used Oriental drag to perform queer subjectivity. Yet one cannot simply read the native's crossing into Western identity and space as sign of a similar (queer) performance, since such crossings are often the result of necessity and constraint. One might question, then, the Western exclusiveness of "acting out" and the Orientalism it perpetuates in its celebration of a specifically Occidental queer strategy against a likewise Occidental compulsory heterosexuality.

42. Autonomy and self-determination are themselves privileged notions which spring from Enlightenment philosophies regarding the natural rights of rational men—claims that did not extend to emotional women or superstitious savages. This is not to suggest that women and dark-skinned peoples are irrational, but that the idea of rational autonomy is produced through the (en)gendering of its (female and dark-skinned) Others. See Cora Kaplan for her explication of Enlightenment rationality as disabling to articulations of female pleasure and desire.

43. I am indebted to Viet Nguyen for helping me clarify this nuance. In a previous draft of this chapter, I implicitly argued that Joey's nationalism renders him the only gay hero; however, as Viet argues persuasively, once Joey becomes a nationalist, "[his] sexuality is erased—he either becomes heterosexual or his sexuality is erased as an issue" (personal correspondence).

44. I would further contest the gendered nationalist message that Casper attributes to Hagedorn: that women betray the nation. While Hagedorn most emphatically does focus on Filipinas (and on their at times unendurable marriages), as well as on the compromised nationalism of the Philippines, she does not link them causally in the way that Casper suggests.

CHAPTER FOUR
GLOBAL-LOCAL DISCOURSE AND GENDERED SCREEN FICTIONS

1. Immanuel Wallerstein and Roland Robertson are perhaps the most well-known spokespersons for, respectively, "the world system" and "globalization." Whereas Wallerstein focuses on the "modern world system [as] a capitalist world economy," Robertson defines globalization as " 'the crystallization of the entire world as a single place,' the emergence of 'the global-human condition' and 'the consciousness of the globe as such' " (Wallerstein, 35; Robertson, quoted in King, 11. See also Robertson's *Globalization*). Following Robertson, I distinguish "globalization" as having an economic component but not being reducible to the spread of global capital. Cross-cultural media networks fuel globalization even as the demand for the broadcasting of television programs across cultures is partially attributable to the migration of peoples across borders to feed capitalist profit-taking. Furthermore, when commentators speak of a current phase of globalization they are referring to a distinct time-space compression that is connected to technologies

of high-speed travel and communications (see King, viii; see also Robertson's outline of five phases of globalization [59]; the last "uncertainty phase" is the one in which I am situating Yamashita's novel). Capital may be making use of these technologies (capitalizing on flexible cross-border strategies of accumulation that avoid or slip by national regulations), but it has not necessarily driven this phase of globalization in some coherent logic/plan to which culture and society are merely epiphenomenal effects. See my later discussion of the economy as a means to map globalization for a fuller discussion of the distinct yet overlapping phenomenon of global capital and the cultural modes of conceptualizing globalization.

2. See Neferti Tadiar's "sexual economies" article for a critique of Japan's and America's shared imperialist aspirations vis-à-vis the Philippines.

3. None of the reviews I surveyed characterize *Through the Arc* as an Asian immigrant text, though some do make note of Yamashita's background to emphasize her understanding of cross-cultural fusion (*Los Angeles Times, San Francisco Review of Books, Publisher's Weekly*).

4. Elaine Kim remarks upon this prescribed seriousness of purpose by which Asian American cultural texts were evaluated: "It seemed that every film, every article, and even many novels had to be a uni-dimensional documentary filled with literal and solemnly delivered history lessons. Given the enormity of general ignorance about Asian Americans, it was difficult to do anything but play a dead straight part" (1995, 13). Though Kim characterizes this solemnity as an evaluative criteria favored by *past* (cultural nationalist) critics, to what degree Asian American literary scholarship can wend its way around playfully narrated fictional pleasures remains to be seen. Sau-ling Wong remains much more speculative about whether Asian Americans will be receptive to the "playful artist"; specifically, she leaves open the question of whether Asian American history—at this particular juncture—"may or may not be able to afford such a move [i.e., the urge to play]" (S. Wong 1993, 207).

5. Cumings describes the changed foreign policy attitudes toward East Asian countries, a shift from focusing on those countries along "Red" China's rim as a "defense perimeter" to be invaded/saved for their own good—in essence, as helpless and incompetent "basket cases" (c. 1950)—to seeing them as potential partners and allies. He quotes Nixon in a 1967 article calling the United States a "Pacific power. . . . [O]ur interests and our ideals propel us westward across the Pacific, not as *conquerors but as partners*" (Cumings, 33; emphasis added).

6. There is much debate over the "Asia-Pacific," with Wilson and Dirlik in particular taking issue with what they take to be a narrow view of the " 'Asia-Pacific' formulated by market planners and military strategists." They propose an alternative vision of the "Asia/Pacific"—this time with a slash instead of a hyphen—representing the views of Pacific-Basin populations (Wilson and Dirlik, 6). Despite there being multiple conceptual communities conjured up by "the Asia-Pacific"—from Hong Kong elites jetting to Vancouver, to Pacific Islanders protesting nuclear fallout, to nimble-fingered Asian women working in both Malaysia and downtown L.A.—they are all conceived as fluid, border-crossing, and post- or trans-national in their affiliations.

7. Connery describes Pacific Rim discourse as "an imagining of U.S. multinational capitalism in an era when the 'socialist' bloc still existed, and it is the socialist bloc that is the principle discursive and strategic Other" (Connery, 32), while Bruce

Cumings claims that "Pacific Rim" is a "class-based definition of Asia. The 'community' is a capitalist archipelago, based on indigenous labor power and purchasing power—although mainly labor power until recently" (Cumings, 33). To my mind, Donald Nonini offers one of the most persuasive accounts of the Asia-Pacific: "[T]he 'Asia-Pacific' or 'Pacific Rim' can best be understood as the trope for a set of economic, political, and cultural processes creating relationships within a supraregion of Asian and the United States that have been under way since approximately the mid-1970s—processes arising from what the Marxist geographer David Harvey has called the 'spatial displacements' or 'spatial fixes' of contemporary capitalism" (Nonini, 163). See also Ong and Nonini's characterization of modern Chinese transnationalism as a parallel, yet ethnic-specific (Chinese), rather than pan-ethnic, social formation, likewise associated with late capitalism and arising "out of the new transnational economic processes that transcend the porous political boundaries of nation-states" (Ong and Nonini, 11).

8. According to Dirlik, the Asia-Pacific idea was invented by Europeans somewhat haphazardly, from their discovery of it in the sixteenth century, and more formally since the nineteenth century onwards (Dirlik 1993, 5–6). However, he and the other contributors to his volume are concerned with "the discourse of the Pacific as part of a global discourse . . . the product of a discourse of capitalism" which "began to emerge sometimes in the 1960s" (Dirlik 1993, 7–8). See M. Consuelo León W. for a genealogy of the Pacific image in American minds since the eighteenth century.

9. Dirlik, however, states that the idea "originated in Japan, was picked up in the United States in the 1970s, and has been kept alive over the years by Australian efforts" (Dirlik 1993, 8)—again a hybrid or tribrid cultural diffusion.

10. Despite its incongruency with a geographic region, many critics specify the Pacific Rim through geographical lists. Connery notes that "by 1973 or 1974, it appears to mean the United States and East Asia." However,

> the most extensive geographical definition of the term has been: peninsular and island Southeast Asia; China, Northeast Asia, including the Soviet Pacific region; Australia; New Zealand; Papua New Guinea, the islands of the south Pacific; and the Pacific Coast of South, Central, and North America. For practical discursive purposes, the Pacific Rim consists of the United States, Canada, Mexico (tenuously though . . .), Japan, China, the Four Tigers . . . —Taiwan, Hong Kong, South Korea, and Singapore—and the up-and-coming, or minor-league players: Malaysia, Thailand, Indonesia, and the Philippines. The psychic center of the Pacific Rim is the United States-Japan relationship. (Connery, 32)

Relying less on a geopolitical catalog and more on a geoeconomic one, Bruce Cumings argues that "Rimspeak" ropes in the miracle economics of Latin American, "post-Allende Chile, *maquiladora* Mexico, even Atlantic Rim Brazil (but only in its pre-debt-crisis phase of 'miracle growth')" (Cumings, 31).

11. Interestingly, Dirlik, who is not a long-standing scholar of Asian American Studies, has little difficulty embracing the idea of an Asia-Pacific that extends into America. By contrast, Gary Okihiro, a central figure in Asian American Studies, stresses an American invasive desire that ultimately brought forth Asian American history: "Asians, it must be remembered, did not come to America; Americans went to Asia. Asians, it must be remembered, did not come to take the wealth of America;

Americans went to take the wealth of Asia. Asians, it must be remembered, did not come to conquer and colonize America; Americans went to conquer and colonize Asia. And the matter of the 'when and the where' of Asian American history is located therein, in Europe's eastward and westward thrusts, engendered, transformative, expansive" (Okihiro, 28–29).

12. As examples of the way in which "the mobility and control of some groups can actively weaken other people," Doreen Massey points to the "greater isolation today of the island of Pitcairn," resulting in part from the possibility of air travel over the Pacific and to a more quotidian scenario: "Every time someone uses a car, and thereby increases their personal mobility, they reduce both the social rationale and the financial viability of the public transport system—and thereby also potentially reduce the mobility of those who rely on that system" (Massey, 150).

13. Furthermore, by moving focus away from the miracle economies of the Pacific Rim and scrutinizing a former export-driven "miracle" economy now in a state of tremendous debt crisis—ostensibly located outside "the Asia-Pacific" region—the narrative encourages speculation over the financially determinate, changeable borders of the "Asia-Pacific" region. As noted earlier, Bruce Cumings claims that "sometimes Rim-speak ropes in the Latin American countries [such as] post-Allende Chile, *maquiladora* Mexico, even Atlantic Rim Brazil (but only in its pre-debt-crisis phase of 'miracle growth')" (Cumings, 31). If Brazil can only be a part of the Rim in its miracle phase, then is *Through the Arc*'s portrait of post-miraculous Brazil a harbinger of "the endpoint of Pacific Rim discourse," which Christopher Connery dates in February 1990—the same year of *Through the Arc*'s publication (Connery, 46). While for some "free marketeers" the end of Pacific Rim discourse merely marks the expansion of their economic formulae onto a "global rim" (Connery, 55), in *Through the Arc*'s case, going beyond Pacific Rim discourse is part of a larger critique of the fiction of co-prosperity. The novel wedges apart the seamless portrait of miraculous "development" by underscoring the diversity of social actors participating in co-prosperous growth.

14. See Cheung (1990) for a gendered critique of this heroic subject in Asian American literature.

15. A combination of Japanese technological innovation and Chinese American history, Kazumasa is a truly pan-Asian American invention, a figure whose founding identity myths cross ethnic and national borders. Also, in referring to the Chinese railroad worker as an archetypal figure in Asian American history, I am not suggesting that this figure will or ought to remain at the center of Asian American founding myths. Rather, I wish to emphasize Yamashita's "signifying" (repeating with a difference) on traditional tropes of Asian American literature.

16. While Kingston emphasizes the backbreaking work of her Chinese ancestors on the railroads, Ronald Takaki wishes to dispel the notion that this immigrant population provided only unskilled labor: "The construction of the Central Pacific Railroad line was a Chinese achievement. Not only did they perform the physical labor required to clear trees and lay tracks; they also provided important technical labor by operating power drills and handling explosives. . . . The Chinese workers were, in one observer's description, 'a great army laying siege to Nature in her strongest citadel.' " (Takaki 1990a, 230; 1990b, 85).

17. Many Asians in the nineteenth century did emigrate to South America; for instance, the Chinese in Peru and Mexico and the Japanese in Brazil (Hu-Dehart; Tsuchida; Reichl; Maeyama). However, the Chinese railroad worker in Asian American historiography is most readily associated with building the U.S. transcontinental railroad.

18. To be perfectly clear, I am not pronouncing the fight for national inclusion anachronistic. Sau-ling Wong compellingly argues that making claims vis-à-vis the U.S. nation-state is as legitimate and ongoing a critical practice for Asian Americans as mining the economic, social, and cultural links between Asians in the United States and Asians elsewhere (e.g., Brazil, Japan, the "Pacific Rim"). Wong stresses that Asian American scholars ought to configure these foci, not in a time-line of progression and succession, but as simultaneously occurring modes of redefinition and struggle. I wholeheartedly agree with Wong's argument, especially in relation to the vogue in the postnational trend in Asian American criticism. I use the term "anachronism," then, in a literary-critical sense: to highlight Yamashita's use of a particular icon, object, or technology associated with a particular time and displacing it into another setting to jarring effect (in this case, to relativize temporally the national and global grounds of Asian Americans' political claims and literary subjects).

19. Yamashita's early-1990s novel, thus, foreshadows reformulations of Japanese identity in the Americas that have been aired in this latter half of the decade, for instance in the most recent issue of *Amerasia Journal* 23.3 (Winter 1997–98), entitled *Beyond National Boundaries: The Complexity of Japanese-American History*, where guest editor Yuji Ichioka's introduction clearly enunciates a narrative of Japanese and Japanese American perspectives, on the one hand, linked to the historical watershed of World War II (alternatively the "Pacific War"), yet, on the other, moving beyond the internment as *the* singular meaning of the war for Japanese on both sides of the Pacific.

20. See David Harvey's "The Condition of Postmodernity" and Frederic Jameson's "Postmodernism, or the Cultural Logic of Late Capitalism."

21. Exemplary of this approach are critics of media imperialism who "concern themselves with the structural and institutional aspects of the global media . . . focusing on such issues as the 'dumping' of cheap television programmes in the Third World or the market dominance of Western news agencies" (Tomlinson, 22). See also Tomlinson's critique of Ariel Dorfman and Armand Mattelart's *How to Read Donald Duck: Imperialist Ideology in the Disney Comic* (Tomlinson, 34–67).

22. See Leo Ching (268, 270), who details the resurgence of Japan bashing; also see Woo-Cumings who traces a renewed orientalism in Pacific Rim discourse that portrays "East Asian countries [as] . . . predatory in economics . . . sapping U.S. strength" (Woo-Cumings, 137).

23. Vincent Chin was a Chinese American draftsman in Detroit who was clubbed to death by two recently laid-off American autoworkers who blamed Japanese imports for the loss of their jobs. Chin's killers were sentenced to three years of probation and a fine of $3,780. See S. Chan (176–78) and Wei (193–96) on the way in which the Chin case galvanized the Asian American community.

24. See Schwoch's Manaus article on the extraction economy of Brazil. See also Mitter (70–74) for an analysis of the World Bank's role in the debt crisis of Brazil.

25. As a brief economic historicization of that shift, Masao Miyoshi notes that "in the late 1960s, the global domination of U.S. multinational corporations was unchallengeable" but that "around 1970, European and Japanese transnational corporations (TNCs) emerged rapidly to compete with their U.S. counterparts" (Miyoshi, 734–35).

26. In her 1991 essay, "Heterogeneity, Hybridity, Multiplicity: Marking Asian American Differences," and in her more recent book, *Immigrant Acts: On Asian American Cultural Politics*, Lisa Lowe precisely urges Asian Americans to "affiliate with other groups whose cohesions may be based on other valences of oppression [i.e., valences other than Asian American ethnicity]" (1991, 32).

27. According to Paul Spickard, analyses of intermarriage frequently equate it with "the ultimate form of assimilation, the step by which a minority group finally loses its distinct ethnic identity and is obliterated in a mass of homogeneous Anglo-American culture" (Spickard, 10). See also Fong and Yung's study that seeks to go "beyond the assimilationist interpretation of outmarriage" (Fong and Yung, 78).

28. See Vink's and Lopez's studies of the telenovela. Lopez explicitly calls the telenovela "an essentially melodramatic narrative mode, with roots that can be traced back to prior (Latin American and international) melodramatic forms (in the theater, serial literature, etc.) and their reinscription and recirculation by the mass media in the cinema and radio" (Lopez 1995, 258). Links between American soap opera and melodrama are explored in Modleski and Ang. See also Peter Brooks's work on textual melodrama.

29. As feminists critics of popular culture have pointed out, such dismissals of the soap opera, and other popular feminine narratives, reflect a larger devaluation of modes of expression both written by and having appeal to women (Modleski, 11–15; Geraghty, 1–2.). Rejecting that bias, Tania Modleski, Ien Ang, Nico Vink, Charlotte Brunsdon, and more recently, Martha Nochimson, and Christine Gledhill, among others, analyze the specifically feminine appeal of soap operas and prime-time melodramas, taking seriously the perspectives of their largely female audience.

30. "Soap opera" is the standard translation of telenovela: see, for instance, Mercedes Creel's survey of scholarship on women and the media in Latin America. One web site on Latino TV characterizes telenovelas as "Latin America's most successful programming exports. A genre by itself, telenovelas are similar to American soap operas in that they handle drama conflicts, romance, evil against good paradoxes and are delivered in daily episodes. The difference is that telenovelas are finite, dramatic conflicts with an ending, their average duration is 120 to 200 one hour episodes, they combine exteriors and interior production and constitute pan-regional's broadcast television programming vertebrae" (see "Latino TV").

31. My account of Yamashita's motives in writing *Through the Arc* is drawn from a 1993 interview with the author conducted by Michael Murashige, forthcoming in the volume *Word Matters: Interviews with Twenty Writers of Asian Descent*. My sincere thanks to Michael for sharing his transcript with me, to which all quotes refer. See also the published excerpt of this interview (Murashige 1994).

32. Yamashita first drafted the manuscript for *Brazil-Maru* while in Brazil. When she returned to the States in 1984, the author rewrote the manuscript, and after a third rewrite, Yamashita admits that she "was really tired of doing it and so,

at Ronaldo's suggestion and just my own needs, I started to write *Through the Arc*"
(Murashige 1993, 5).

33. When tied to historical accuracy, even with some interpretive leeway, the
author felt compelled to focus on the stories of immigrant Japanese men who literally took over their wives' interviews. Among the methodological problems Yamashita encountered, her female interviewees, if not widowed, would inevitably invite
their husbands to participate in the interview and the men "would take over [the
conversation]" while the women "stopped talking" (Murashige 1993, 21).

34. See Tsuchida's study on the Japanese in Brazil, specifically his examination of
the Aliança colony, a religious and intellectual community upon whom Yamashita, it
would appear, based her novel *Brazil-Maru*.

35. Roland Robertson outlines five phases of globalization, the first or "germinal
phase" lasting in Europe from the early fifteenth until the mid-eighteenth century
and punctuated by the expansion of Catholicism, heliocentric theory, and concepts
about "humanity"; as distinct from the most recent or "uncertainty phase" of globalization, beginning in the late 1960s, accentuated by "sharp acceleration in means
of global communication. Societies increasingly facing problems of multiculturality
and polyethnicity.... Civil rights become a global issue.... Concern with hu-
mankind as a species-community" (Robertson, 58–59).

36. See Massey's "A Place Called Home" for an overview of these changes in
the world economy, especially pages 158–62. See also Swasti Mitter and Maria Mies
for an account of the specific targeting of women as a "docile" work force and of
the collusion of patriarchy and capitalist accumulation. In fact, Mies argues that
capitalism is an ideology of unlimited growth that depends on the invisibility of
certain types of labor, women in households and colonized peoples, for example,
for its myth of generated surplus.

37. Vink, following Charlotte Brunsdon, writes that "soap operas and novelas
colonize the public world from a perspective of private and personal feelings. The
world of intimate feelings, traditionally (i.e., since the bourgeois revolution) perceived as women's domain, proves to be the strongest, the most valuable" (Vink,
187). Likewise, Lopez argues that "the telenovela exploits personalization—the in-
dividualization of the social world—as an epistemology. It ceaselessly offers its audience dramas of recognition and re-cognition by locating social and political issues
in personal and familial terms and thus making sense of an increasingly complex
world" (Lopez 1995, 261).

38. As Brunsdon tentatively acknowledges in a later article, this broad characterization of women eclipses differences in work habits and domestic confinement
attendant upon race and class distinctions (1995, 51).

39. Moreover, akin to *Dogeaters*'s chronological inconsistencies that result from
the author's tying her stories of female desires to those of nationalist revolution,
Yamashita's novel operates through a deliberate time distortion. That is, unlike
Hagedorn, whose references to Marcos's rule do not exactly match the temporality
of her narratives of female and gay awakenings, Yamashita's novel, set in the future,
avoids such historically verifiable mismatches, even as her chronologies are *a priori*
historically incorrect (transcendent of fixed dates in the past). Setting her novel in
a futuristic, imaginary space thus mediates Yamashita's conjoining of "historical
time" (a projection of the global future as past) with the space-times of the personal

and the everyday, precisely because "history" in futuristic fiction is still up for grabs, its heroes and heroines yet to be determined.

40. Dona Angustia's allusion to a regional difference to make sense of Chico Paco's gender difference may also be a subtle reference to the prevalence of male homosexuals in religious cults in the north and northeast of Brazil. See Fry.

41. At the same time, the novel's muted portrayal of the two men's romance may also be the result of the author's refusal to pathologize or frame Chico Paco and Gilberto's sexual desires as anything but "normal" (191) (in contrast to her characterization of Gilberto's love of movement as transgressive and "traumatic"). In this sense, Yamashita demurs from soap operas' tendency to represent gay characters only in terms of "the sexuality-as-a-problem paradigm" (Fuqua, 208). According to Joy Fuqua, "[I]t is in the representation of the 'everyday' in relation to gay characters which causes the difficulty for soap opera" (Fuqua, 208–209). Yamashita's text, it would seem, does not share this difficulty; in fact, it concentrates almost exclusively on the everyday, rendering sexuality-as-a-problem almost an afterthought.

42. One should note that, while Yamashita follows soap opera's prioritization of romance, emotionality, and domestic feelings, she also strays from the heterosexism of soap operas, representing with equal validity the domestic trials suffered by Chico Paco and Gilberto as she represents the relations of heterosexual pairs, such as Tania and Batista or Lourdes and Kazumasa. According to Vink, "homosexuality and bisexuality are often mentioned in telenovelas, but either with the effeminate male as socially female or very indirectly" (184).

43. Quite relevant here is Doreen Massey's observation regarding different perspectives on time-space compression that arise from one's former sense of mastery over the world situation: "The most commonly argued position . . . is that the vast current reorganizations of capital, the formation of a new global space, and in particular its use of new technologies of communication, have undermined an older sense of a 'place-called home,' and left us placeless and disoriented. But is it really so? . . . Those who today worry about a sense of disorientation and a loss of control must once have felt they knew exactly where they were, and that they *had* control. . . . To what extent [then] is this a predominantly white/First World take on things?" (163, 165). Massey further notes that women in the First World have also not been privy to a sense of control and hence may not necessarily share in the supposedly universal anxiety over the disruption of "a place-called home": "Much of the current disorientation . . . is put down to the arrival in one form or another of the 'Other.' Yet some 'Others' of the dominant definers in First World society have always been there—women. It is interesting to note how frequently the characterization of place as home comes from those who have left, and it would be fascinating to explores how often this characterization is framed around those who—perforce—stayed behind; and how often the former was male, setting out to discover and change the world, and the latter female, most particularly a mother, assigned the role of personifying a place which did not change." (166–67). Massey suggests that what causes the Subject to be disoriented is the capacity of Others— especially the mother who is supposed to stay at home—to travel. Though "mum's" leaving home may cause disorientation for her husband, sons, and brothers who expect to return to a nurturing hearth, this act of leave-taking may in fact signify quite differently for "mum" herself. It may represent the first opportunity to see

"for real" the places brought into her home by way of the media or by way of consumable items. Though perceived as a troubling sense of cognitive anxiety for those interested in locating or containing an individual, for the traveler herself it may offer her a greater material reality.

44. See Mumford on the paradigmatic nature of the paternity plot to U.S. soap operas (94–116).

45. To a certain extent, the flying capacities of Batista's pigeons are also differentiated by gender. Batista notes that " 'the female is usually faster than the male [since] the female goes to sleep later and rises earlier [getting into] the habit . . . from taking care of her babies' " (115).

46. Swasti Mitter's work has also been seminal to the examination of women as the preferred labor of transnational corporations. See *Common Fate, Common Bond.* According to Mies, "[T]he new strategy of obscuring women's productive work for capital is propagated under the slogan of 'flexibilization of labour.' Not only are women pushed out of the formal sector . . . they are reintegrated into capitalist development in a whole range of informal, non-organized, non-protected production relations, ranging from part-time work, through contract work, to home-working, to unpaid neighbourhood work" (Mies, 126–27).

47. Laura Stempel Mumford questions the critical truism that soap operas do not offer narrative closure: "This open-endedness is one of the most discussed aspects of soap operas' narrative form, forming the basis for many theories about soap's narrative structure. Some theorists have discerned ties between irresolution and a specific kind of female viewing pleasure, while others have argued that non-closure undermines the traditional narrative trajectory" (39). Rejecting this critical truism, Mumford asserts that "far from being marked by a unique lack of closure, soaps are actually characterized by just the opposite: an excess of resolving gestures. Paradoxically, it may be this very profusion that has encouraged critics to see soaps as totally lacking in traditional narrative resolution" (72).

48. More recently, Lisa Lowe has characterized a nonlinear, teleologically-disruptive "anti-structure" as a primary feature of " 'decolonizing' writing," to which I referred briefly in the previous chapter. Lowe suggests that "the writing of *different* histories—of nonelites, of insurgencies, of women, from the 'bottom up'—inevitably runs up against representation and linear narrative as problematic categories" (Lowe 1996, 112). In other words, the antiprogressive structure of Yamashita's text might be said to arise out of its revisioning and contesting of official (developmental) history—an impulse linked to subordinated groups such as women, but not exclusive to women.

49. "I [was] at the point where if I [didn't] know what direction this [was] pointing, I really [couldn't] carve this work. . . . And so, at some point, I made some decisions about how the work ends and how I bring all these disparate characters to bear on the story and how that would work out" (Murashige 1993, 6–7).

50. Unlike their American counterparts, telenovelas terminate after a run of six to seven months. The point to be registered is that both kinds of soap opera depend upon erotic suspension, a function of the deferral—sometimes indefinitely—of endpoints and intact meanings.

51. The phrase "less than masterful" is borrowed from Nochimson's study of American soaps (30).

52. In 1990, Cheung characterized such a transformed feminist studies as a prospective formation, possibly suggested in the "recent shift from feminist studies to gender studies" (245). Though Cheung implies that such a transformed gender studies is (morally) imperative, she also leaves ambiguous its present-day realization: "Lest feminist criticism remain in the wilderness, white scholars must reckon with race and class as integral experiences for both men and women, and acknowledge that not only female voices but the voices of many men of color have been historically silenced or dismissed. Expanding the feminist frame of reference will allow certain existing theories to be interrogated or reformulated" (246).

53. Wong aims her critique primarily against the derisive characterization of extravagant acts as wasteful. She deftly catalogs a wide array of instances in which Asian American authors grapple with the (implicit) question of how their artistic, playful works serve their families, clan, or community—in essence, translating extravagance into the logic and language of functionalist necessity. Interestingly, her own essay reenacts this same process of subjecting the concepts of play and artistry to "the trial of usefulness" (S. Wong 1993, 193), even as she dwells on the interdependence of the two terms (189). Ultimately, Wong resolves the disjuncture between codes of necessity and extravagance by turning play into work, in short, establishing a useful function for play within an Asian American context. Thus, she asserts that "even those Asian American authors most drawn to images of free play have never lost sight of the issues of utility and community: that at heart . . . their 'purposelessness' [is] always 'purposive' " (209).

54. In the case of Hagedorn's book, which won the Before Columbus Foundation Award, communal opprobrium has been explicit, detailed in various critics' complaints about its politics imbedded in its form. In contrast, Yamashita's novel has been generally underexplored by Asian American critics, suffering a different kind of opprobrium—neglect.

55. Moreover, as feminist critics of political economy have pointed out, valuations of what counts as work are not gender neutral. Elaborating on the ways in which female labor is rendered "socially invisible," Maria Mies argues that women's work is "defined—by Marxist and non-Marxist theoreticians—as 'non-productive.' It appeared under the form of love, care, emotionality, motherhood and wifehood" (Mies, 31). This casualization of women's work as a natural extension of their biology—for example, mothering, housework, supplemental (rather than primary) income—is a form of gender-based exploitation necessary to capital. Thus, Hartmann and Mies, among others, fault Marx's critique of capitalist productivity for rendering women's labor invisible and for obscuring the distinctiveness of gender-based oppression.

56. See Bruce Iwasaki's early definition of Asian American literature as a literature whose theme was identity.

CONCLUSION
ASIAN AMERICAN FEMINIST LITERARY CRITICISM ON MULTIPLE TERRAINS

1. This list is suggestive rather than prescriptive of the criterion by which Asian American literature has been traditionally incorporated into an Asian American Studies canon. Clearly, the expectations of what work Asian American literature is expected to perform is variable over time and currently under debate, as made

amply clear in the most recent and public arguments over the Association for Asian American Studies's assigning and revoking the 1998 Award for Fiction to Lois-Ann Yamanaka's *Blu's Hanging*. However, even in its variableness over time, Asian American literary criticism has acknowledged the implicit primacy of ethnopolitical critique to interpretations of the literature, with a focus on women, sexuality, and gender too often construed as antithetical or divisive to that primary task.

2. For a sociological analysis of demographic changes since 1965, see Paul Ong, Edna Bonacich, and Lucie Cheng's "The Political Economy of Capitalist Restructuring and the New Asian Immigration," and Yen Espiritu and Paul Ong's "Class Constraints on Racial Solidarity among Asian Americans." For accounts of how these demographic changes have reverberated in the arena of cultural studies and theories of ethnicity, see S. Wong (1995) and Koshy.

3. The tracing of a singular gendered concept, like homosociality, across a wider range of texts, would act as a significant extension of the gendered Asian American literary criticism begun here. Though not the main focus of this study, it is worth comparing in brief how homosociality is defined in Bulosan's, Jen's, Hagedorn's, and Yamashita's novels (e.g., what it defines itself against, the degree to which it shades into homoeroticism, how it is imagined as compatible with certain economic and political programs, and so forth). In Bulosan's text, "brotherhood" is construed in utopian, socialist, nationalist and universalistic terms, as an alternative to racism and intraracial bestial behavior, and as an antonym to social divisiveness. In contrast, Jen emphasizes a capitalist, co-conspiratorial homosociality embodied by Grover and Ralph, a homosociality that abets a masculinist individualist self-discovery and that is counterposed to the work of women behind the scenes. Imagining it both ways, homosociality in *Dogeaters* is glimpsed, not only in the country-club cronies verbally recounting their conquests over women and the poor, but also in the counterhomosociality imagined in Girlie's dream of the serving class—the caddies who rebel against the country-club men. In Hagedorn's novel, as in Yamashita's, homosociality is distinguished from homosexuality, which in the former text becomes explicit and linked to a subjective desire at odds with critical interpretations stressing nationalism. Homosexuality, in *Through the Arc*, emerges as one more category of family life disrupted by development schemes.

4. Though time constraints prevent me from doing so here, I would also point to the need for a fuller elaboration of Asian American "feminists'" still uneasy relationship to feminism: have Asian American scholars moved beyond the point where disavowing feminism is a way of asserting cultural integrity?

5. Feminism, in other words, is likely to be viewed with greater suspicion in communities of color, I believe, if it remains strictly deconstructive (posing the limits of any progress narrative) without posing an alternative liberation narrative. Somewhat paradoxically, what makes feminism less seductive to many Asian American scholars is its refusal to offer a liberation narrative—something along the lines of "Once capitalist processes of working through racialized labor/racialized immigration is revealed and critiqued, once we make this visible, progressive forces and workers can unite to wrest the means of production from the current capitalist owners, and a greater materialist egalitarianism will be achieved in the world." The

promise that a better apprehension of the world (a better way of knowing) can lead to liberation—a change in structures of domination—is indeed seductive; and it is precisely this seduction with which we must negotiate even as we can recognize that the quest for better ways of knowing often solidifies structures of domination (often co-opts social change to the very project of finding ever more correct and inclusive methods of visibility) than overturning them.

Works Cited

Ahmad, Aijaz. 1987. "Jameson's Rhetoric of Otherness and the 'National Allegory.' " *Social Text* 17 (Fall): 3–25.

Alloula, Malek. 1986. *The Colonial Harem.* Trans. Myrna Godzich and Wlad Godzich. Minneapolis: University of Minnesota Press.

Alquizola, Marilyn. 1991. "Subversion or Affirmation: The Text and Subtext of *America Is in the Heart.*" In *Asian Americans: Comparative and Global Perspectives,* ed. Shirley Hune, Hyung-chan Kim, Stephen S. Fugita, and Amy Ling, 199–209. Pullman: Washington State University Press.

Anderson, Benedict. 1988. "Cacique Democracy in the Philippines: Origins and Dreams." *New Left Review* 169 (May–June): 3–31.

———. 1991. *Imagined Communities: Reflections on the Origin and Spread of Nationalism.* Rev. ed. New York: Verso.

Ang, Ien. 1985. *Watching Dallas: Soap Opera and the Melodramatic Imagination.* Trans. Ella Couling. New York: Methuen.

Anthias, Floya, and Nira Yuval-Davis, eds. 1989. Introduction to *Woman-Nation-State.* New York: St. Martin's Press.

"Anti-Miscegenation Laws and the Pilipino." 1976. In *Letters in Exile: An Introductory Reader on the History of Filipinos in America,* ed. UCLA Asian American Studies Center, 63–71. Los Angeles: The Regents of the University of California.

Appadurai, Arjun. 1990. "Disjuncture and Difference in the Global Cultural Economy." *Public Culture* 2, no. 2 (Spring): 1–24.

———. 1993. "Patriotism and Its Futures." *Public Culture* 5: 411–29.

Apter, Emily. 1994. "Acting out Orientalism: Sapphic Theatricality in Turn-of-the-Century Paris." *L'esprit créateur* 34, no. 2 (Summer): 102–15.

Armstrong, Nancy. 1987. *Desire and Domestic Fiction: A Political History of the Novel.* New York: Oxford University Press.

Asian Women United of California, eds. 1989. *Making Waves: An Anthology of Writings by and about Asian American Women.* Boston: Beacon Press.

Bakhtin, Mikhail. 1981. *The Dialogic Imagination.* Ed. Michael Holquist, trans. Caryl Emerson and Michael Holquist. Austin: University of Texas Press.

Balce-Cortes, Nerissa. 1995. "Imagining the Neocolony." *Critical Mass* 2, no. 2 (Spring): 95–120.

Barrett, Michèle. 1985. "Ideology and the Cultural Production of Gender." In *Feminist Criticism and Social Change: Sex, Class, and Race in Literature and Culture,* ed. Judith Newton and Deborah Rosenfelt, 65–85. New York: Methuen.

Bascara, Victor. 1993. "Hitting Critical Mass (or, Do your parents still say 'Oriental,' too?)" *Critical Mass,* no. 1 (Fall); 3–38.

Baym, Nina. 1981. "Melodramas of Beset Manhood." *American Quarterly* 33, no. 2 (Summer): 123–39.

Bhabha, Homi K. 1994. *The Location of Culture.* New York: Routledge.

Boone, Joseph. 1995. "Vacation Cruises; or, The Homoerotics of Orientalism." *PMLA* 110, no. 1 (January): 89–107.

Brooks, Peter. 1995 [1976]. *The Melodramatic Imagination: Balzac, Henry James, Melodrama, and the Mode of Excess.* Reprint, New Haven, Conn.: Yale University Press.

Brunsdon, Charlotte. 1981. " 'Crossroads': Notes on Soap Opera." *Screen* 22, no. 4: 32–37.

———. 1995. "The Role of Soap Opera in the Development of Feminist Television Scholarship." In *To Be Continued . . . : Soap Operas around the World,* ed. Robert C. Allen, 49–65. New York: Routledge.

Buell, Frederick. 1994. *National Culture and the New Global System.* Baltimore: Johns Hopkins University Press.

Bulosan, Carlos. 1942. *The Laughter of My Father.* New York: Harcourt, Brace.

———. 1943a. "Freedom from Want." *Saturday Evening Post,* 6 March, 12.

———. 1943b. "Letter to a Filipino Woman." *New Republic,* 8 November, 645–46.

———. 1973. *America Is in the Heart.* New York: Harcourt, Brace, 1946. Reprint, Seattle: University of Washington Press.

———. 1995. *On Becoming Filipino: Selected Writings of Carlos Bulosan.* Ed. E. San Juan, Jr. Philadelphia: Temple University Press.

Butler, Judith. 1990. *Gender Trouble: Feminism and the Subversion of Identity.* New York: Routledge.

Campbell, John R. B. 1991. Review of *Through the Arc of the Rain Forest,* by Karen Tei Yamashita. *New York Times Book Review,* 10 March, 16.

Campomanes, Oscar V. 1992. "Filipinos in the United States and Their Literature of Exile." In *Reading the Literatures of Asian America,* ed. Shirley Geok-lin Lim and Amy Ling, 49–78. Philadelphia: Temple University Press.

———. 1997. "Asian American Studies beyond California and the Question of U.S. Imperialism." *Positions* 5, no. 2 (Fall): 523–50.

Casper, Leonard. 1990. "Bangungot and the Philippine Dream in Hagedorn." *Solidarity* 127 (July–September): 152–57.

Césaire, Aimé. 1972. *Discourse on Colonialism.* New York: Monthly Review Press.

Cha, Theresa Hak Kyung. 1995. *Dictee.* N.p.: Tanam Press, 1982. Reprint, Berkeley, Calif.: Third Women Press.

Chan, Jeffery Paul, Frank Chin, Lawson Fusao Inada, and Shawn H. Wong. 1982. "An Introduction to Chinese-American and Japanese-American Literatures." In *Three American Literatures: Essays in Chicano, Native American, and Asian-American Literature for Teachers of American Literature,* ed. Houston Baker, 197–228. New York: Modern Language Association.

———, eds. 1991a. *AIIIEEEEE!: An Anthology of Asian American Writers.* Washington, D.C.: Howard University Press, 1974. Reprint, New York: Mentor.

———, eds. 1991b. *The Big AIIIEEEEE!: An Anthology of Chinese American and Japanese American Literature.* New York: Meridian.

Chan, Sucheng. 1991. *Asian Americans: An Interpretive History.* Boston: Twayne.

Cheung, King-Kok. 1990. "The Woman Warrior versus the Chinaman Pacific: Must a Chinese American Critic Choose between Feminism and Heroism?" In *Conflicts in Feminism,* ed. Marianne Hirsch and Evelyn Fox Keller, 234–51. New York: Routledge.

———. 1993. *Articulate Silences: Hisaye Yamamoto, Maxine Hong Kingston, Joy Ko-gawa*. Ithaca, N.Y.: Cornell University Press.

Chin, Frank. 1988. *The Chinaman Pacific & Frisco R.R. Co.* Minneapolis: Coffee House Press.

Chin, Frank, and Jeffrey Paul Chan. 1972. "Racist Love." In *Seeing Through Shuck*, ed. Richard Kostelanetz, 65–79. New York: Ballantine.

Ching, Leo. 1991. "Imaginings in the Empires of the Sun: Japanese Mass Culture in Asia." In *Asia/Pacific as Space of Cultural Production*, ed. Rob Wilson and Arif Dirlik, 262–83. Durham, N.C.: Duke University Press.

Chow, Rey. 1991. *Woman and Chinese Modernity: The Politics of Reading Between West and East*. Minneapolis: University of Minnesota Press.

———. 1993. *Writing Diaspora: Tactics of Intervention in Contemporary Cultural Stud-ies*. Bloomington: Indiana University Press.

Connery, Christopher L. 1995. "Pacific Rim Discourse: The U.S. Global Imagi-nary in the Late Cold War Years." In *Asia/Pacific as Space of Cultural Production*, ed. Rob Wilson and Arif Dirlik, 30–56. Durham, N.C.: Duke University Press.

Constantino, Renato. 1987. "The Miseducation of the Filipino." In *The Philippines Reader: A History of Colonialism, Neocolonialism, Dictatorship, and Resistance*, ed. Daniel B. Schirmer and Stephen Rosskamm Shalom, 45–49. Boston: South End Press.

Coontz, Stephanie. 1992. *The Way We Never Were: American Families and the Nostal-gia Trap*. New York: Basic Books.

Cordova, Fred. 1983. *Filipinos: Forgotten Asian Americans*. N.p.: Demonstration Project for Asian Americans.

Creel, Mercedes Charles. "Women and the Communications Media in Latin America." *Mexican Journal of Communication* 3 (www.cem.itesm.mx/dacs/buen-dia/ingles/mjc/index/html).

Cumings, Bruce. 1993. "Rimspeak; or, The Discourse of the 'Pacific Rim.'" In *What's in a Rim: Critical Perspectives on the Pacific Region Idea*, ed. Arif Dirlik, 29–47. Boulder, Colo.: Westview Press, 1993.

"Curriculum Committee Report." 1975. *Asian American Review* 2, no. 1: 6–15.

De Lauretis, Teresa. 1984. *Alice Doesn't: Feminism, Semiotics, Cinema*. Bloomington: Indiana University Press, 1984.

Delphy, Christine. 1984. *Close to Home: A Materialist Analysis of Women's Oppression*. Trans. and ed. Diana Leonard. Amherst: University of Massachusetts Press.

Denton, Frank H., and Victoria Villena-Denton, eds. 1986. *Filipino Views of America: Warm Memories, Cold Realities*. Washington, D.C.: Asia Fellows.

Desmond, Jane C. 1993. "Where Is 'The Nation'?: Public Discourse, the Body, and Visual Display." *East-West* 7, no. 2 (July): 81–110.

Diaz, Vicente M. 1993. "Pious Sites: Chamorro Culture Between Spanish Catholi-cism and American Liberal Individualism." In *Cultures of United States Imperial-ism*, ed. Amy Kaplan and Donald E. Pease, 312–39. Durham, N.C.: Duke Uni-versity Press.

Dirlik, Arif, ed. 1993. *What's in a Rim: Critical Perspectives on the Pacific Region Idea*. Boulder, Colo.: Westview Press.

———. 1996. "Asians on the Rim: Transnational Capital and Local Community in the Making of Contemporary Asian America." *Amerasia Journal* 22, no. 3: 1–24.

Ditsky, J. M. 1991. Review of *Through the Arc of the Rain Forest*, by Karen Tei Yamashita. *Choice* (March): 1139–40.

Emerson, Ralph Waldo. 1957. *Selections from Ralph Waldo Emerson*. Ed. Stephen E. Whicher. Boston: Houghton Mifflin.

Enloe, Cynthia. 1990. *Bananas, Beaches, and Bases: Making Feminist Sense of International Politics*. Berkeley: University of California Press.

Espiritu, Yen Le. 1992. *Asian American Panethnicity: Bridging Institutions and Identities*. Philadelphia: Temple University Press.

———. 1997. "Race, Class, and Gender in Asian America." In *Making More Waves: New Writing by Asian American Women*, ed. Elaine H. Kim, Lilia V. Villanueva, and Asian Women United of California, 135–141. Boston: Beacon Press.

Espiritu, Yen Le, and Paul Ong. 1994. "Class Constraints on Racial Solidarity among Asian Americans." In *The New Asian Immigration in Los Angeles and Global Restructuring*, ed. Paul Ong, Edna Bonacich, and Lucie Cheng, 295–321. Philadelphia: Temple University Press.

Evangelista, Susan. 1993. "Jessica Hagedorn and Manila Magic." *MELUS* 18, no. 4 (Winter): 41–52.

Fanon, Frantz. 1967. *Black Skin, White Masks*. Trans. Charles Lam Markmann. Paris: Editions du Seuil, 1952. Reprint, New York: Grove Weidenfeld.

———. 1965. *A Dying Colonialism*. Trans. Haakon Chevalier. N.p.: François Maspero, 1959. Reprint, New York: Grove Press.

Flax, Jane. 1990. "Postmodernism and Gender Relations in Feminist Theory." In *Feminism/Postmodernism*, ed. Linda Nicholson. New York: Routledge.

Fong, Colleen, and Judy Yung. 1995–1996. "In Search of the Right Spouse: Interracial Marriage among Chinese and Japanese Americans." *Amerasia Journal* 21, no. 3 (Winter): 77–98.

Francisco, Luzviminda. 1976. "The First Vietnam—The Philippine-American War of 1899–1902." In *Letters in Exile: An Introductory Reader on the History of Pilipinos in America*, ed. UCLA Asian American Studies Center, 1–22. Los Angeles: The Regents of the University of California.

Franklin, Benjamin. 1989 [1791]. *The Autobiography*. In *The Norton Anthology of American Literature*, 3d. ed., ed. Nina Baym et al., 408–523. New York: W. W. Norton.

Fry, Peter. 1995. "Male Homosexuality and Afro-Brazilian Possession Cults." In *Latin American Male Homosexualities*, ed. Stephen O. Murray, 193–220. Albuquerque: University of New Mexico Press.

Fujikane, Candace. 1994. "Between Nationalisms: Hawaii's Local Nation and Its Troubled Racial Paradise." *Critical Mass* 1, no. 2 (Spring): 23–58.

Fuqua, Joy V. 1995. " 'There's a Queer in my Soap! ': The Homophobia/AIDS Story-line of *One Life to Live*." In *To Be Continued . . . : Soap Operas around the World*, ed. Robert C. Allen, 199–212. New York: Routledge.

Fuss, Diana. 1992. "Fashion and the Homospectatorial Look." *Critical Inquiry* 18 (Summer): 713–37.

Geraghty, Christine. 1991. *Women and Soap Opera: A Study of Prime Time Soaps*. Cambridge, England: Polity Press.

Gier, Jean Vengua. 1995. " '. . .to have come from someplace': *October Light, America is in the Heart*, and 'Flip' Writing after the Third World Strikes." *Critical Mass* 2, no. 2 (Spring): 1–33.

Gilroy, Paul. 1993. *The Black Atlantic: Modernity and Double Consciousness.* Cambridge: Harvard University Press.

Gledhill, Christine. 1992. "Speculations on the Relationship between Soap Opera and Melodrama." *Quarterly Review of Film and Video* 14, nos. 1–2 (1992): 103–24.

Goldberg, Jonathan. 1992. "Bradford's 'Ancient Members' and 'A Case of Buggery . . . Amongst Them.' " In *Nationalisms and Sexualities*, eds. Andrew Parker, Mary Russo, Doris Sommer, and Patricia Yaeger, 60–76. New York: Routledge.

Gonzalez, N. V. M. 1976. "The Needle Under the Rock." *The Manila Review* 6: 32–41.

———. 1991. Review of *Dogeaters*, by Jessica Hagedorn. *Amerasia Journal* 17, no. 1: 189–92.

Gramsci, Antonio. 1971. *Selections from the Prison Notebooks.* Ed. and trans. Quintin Hoare and Geoffrey Nowell Smith. New York: International Publishers.

Grewal, Inderpal. 1994. "The Postcolonial, Ethnic Studies, and the Diaspora: The Contexts of Ethnic Immigrant/Migrant Cultural Studies in the U.S." *Socialist Review* 24, no. 4: 45–74.

Grewal, Inderpal, and Caren Kaplan, eds. 1994. *Scattered Hegemonies: Postmodernity and Transnational Feminist Practices.* Minneapolis: University of Minnesota Press.

Hagedorn, Jessica. 1991. *Dogeaters.* New York: Pantheon, 1990. Reprint, New York: Penguin.

———. 1993. *Danger and Beauty.* New York: Penguin.

———. 1994. "The Exile within/The Question of Identity." In *The State of Asian America: Activism and Resistance in the 1990s*, ed. Karin Aguilar-San Juan, 173–82. Boston: South End Press.

Halberstam, David. 1993. *The Fifties.* New York: Villard Books.

Hall, Lisa Kahaeleole Chang, and J. Kehaulani Kauanui. 1996. "Same-Sex Sexuality in Pacific Literature." In *Asian American Sexualities: Dimensions of the Gay and Lesbian Experience*, ed. Russell Leong, 113–18. New York: Routledge.

Hall, Stuart. 1980. "Encoding/Decoding." In *Culture, Media, Language: Working Papers in Cultural Studies, 1972–79*, ed. Stuart Hall, Dorothy Hobson, Andrew Lowe, and Paul Willis, 128–38. London: Unwin Hyman.

———. 1988. "New Ethnicities." In *Black Film, British Cinema*, ed. Kobena Mercer, 27–31. London: Institute of Contemporary Arts.

Halliday, John. 1972. *Sirk on Sirk: Interviews with Jon Halliday.* New York: Viking.

Hannerz, Ulf. 1990. "Cosmopolitans and Locals in World Culture." *Theory, Culture, and Society* 7: 237–51.

Haraway, Donna. 1988. "Situated Knowledges: The Science Question in Feminism and the Privilege of Partial Perspective." *Feminist Studies* 14, no. 3 (Fall): 575–99.

Harris, Cheryl. 1993. "Whiteness as Property." *Harvard Law Review* 106, no. 8 (June): 1709–91.

Harris, Michael. 1990. Review of *Through the Arc of the Rain Forest*, by Karen Tei Yamashita. *Los Angeles Times*, 9 September, 6.

Hartmann, Heidi. 1981. "The Unhappy Marriage of Marxism and Feminism: Toward a More Progressive Union." In *Women and Revolution: A Discussion of the Unhappy Marriage of Marxism and Feminism*, ed. Lydia Sargent, 1–41. Boston: South End Press.

Harvey, David. 1990. *The Condition of Postmodernity: An Enquiry into the Origins of Cultural Change*. Oxford: Blackwell.

Hennessy, Rosemary. 1993. *Materialist Feminism and the Politics of Discourse*. New York: Routledge.

Hing, Bill Ong. 1993. *Making and Remaking Asian America through Immigration Policy, 1850–1990*. Stanford, Calif.: Stanford University Press.

Ho, Cathy Lang. 1990. "Tropical Rainbows: Crossing Japan and Brazil." Review of *Through the Arc of the Rain Forest*, by Karen Tei Yamashita. *San Francisco Review of Books* 15, no. 2 (Fall), 33.

Hu-DeHart, Evelyn. 1989. "Coolies, Shopkeepers, Pioneers: The Chinese of Mexico and Peru (1849–1930)." *Amerasia Journal* 15, no. 2: 91–116.

———. 1991. "From Area Studies to Ethnic Studies: The Study of the Chinese Diaspora in Latin America." In *Asian Americans: Comparative and Global Perspectives*, ed. Shirley Hune, Hyung-chan Kim, Stephen S. Fugita, and Amy Ling, 5–16. Pullman: Washington State University Press.

Hwang, David Henry. 1982. "The Dance and the Railroad." In *Broken Promises: Four Plays*, 59–99. New York: Avon.

Ichioka, Yuji, ed. 1997–1998. *Beyond National Boundaries: The Complexity of Japanese-American History*. Special issue of *Amerasia Journal* 23, no. 3 (Winter).

Ileto, Reynaldo. 1979. *Pasyon and Revolution: Popular Movements in the Philippines 1840–1910*. Quezon City: Ateneo de Manila University Press.

Iwasaki, Bruce. 1971. "Responses and Change for the Asian in America: A Survey of Asian American Literature." In *Roots: An Asian American Reader*, ed. Amy Tachiki, Eddie Wong, Franklin Odo, and Buck Wong, 89–100. Los Angeles: The Regents of the University of California.

Jameson, Frederic, ed. 1983. *Formations of Pleasure*. New York: Routledge.

———. 1984. "Postmodernism, or The Cultural Logic of Late Capitalism." *New Left Review* 146 (July–August): 53–92.

———. 1986. "Third-World Literature in the Era of Multinational Capitalism." *Social Text* 15 (Fall): 65–88.

Jen, Gish. 1991. *Typical American*. Boston: Houghton Mifflin.

———. 1993. Telephone interview with Rachel Lee, 9 September. Forthcoming in *Word Matters: Interviews with Twenty Writers of Asian Descent*. Honolulu: University of Hawaii Press.

Kaledin, Eugenia. 1984. *Mothers and More: American Women in the 1950s*. Boston: Twayne.

Kandiyoti, Deniz. 1994. "Identity and Its Discontents: Women and the Nation." In *Colonial Discourse and Postcolonial Theory: A Reader*, ed. Patrick Williams and Laura Chrisman, 376–91. New York: Columbia University Press.

Kaplan, Amy. 1988. *The Social Construction of American Realism*. Chicago: University of Chicago Press.

————. 1993. " 'Left Alone in America:' The Absence of Empire in the Study of American Culture." In *Cultures of United States Imperialism*, ed. Amy Kaplan and Donald E. Pease, 3–21. Durham, N.C.: Duke University Press.

Kaplan, Amy, and Donald Pease, eds. 1993. *Cultures of United States Imperialism*. Durham, N.C.: Duke University Press.

Kaplan, Cora. 1983. "Wild Nights: Pleasure/Sexuality/Feminism." In *Formations of Pleasure*, ed. Frederic Jameson, 15–35. New York: Routledge.

Kim, Elaine H. 1982. *Asian American Literature: An Introduction to the Writings and Their Social Context*. Philadelphia: Temple University Press.

————. 1984. "Asian American Writers: A Bibliographical Review." *American Studies International* 22, no. 2 (October): 41–78.

————. 1990. " 'Such Opposite Creatures:' Men and Women in Asian American Literature." *Michigan Quarterly Review* 29, no. 1 (Winter): 68–93.

————. 1995. "Beyond Railroads and Internment: Comments on the Past, Present, and Future of Asian American Studies." In *Privileging Positions: The Sites of Asian American Studies*, ed. Gary Y. Okihiro, Marilyn Alquizola, Dorothy Fujita Rony, and K. Scott Wong, 11–19. Pullman: Washington State University Press.

Kim, Elaine H., Lilia V. Villanueva, and Asian Women United of California, eds. 1997. *Making More Waves: New Writing by Asian American Women*. Boston: Beacon Press.

King, Anthony D., ed. 1991. *Culture, Globalization, and the World System: Contemporary Conditions for the Representation of Identity*. Binghamton: State University of New York.

Kingston, Maxine Hong. 1989. *China Men*. New York: Knopf, 1980. Reprint, New York: Vintage.

Kolodny, Annette. 1975. *The Lay of the Land*. Chapel Hill: University of North Carolina Press.

Koshy, Susan. 1996. "The Fiction of Asian American Literature." *Yale Journal of Criticism* 9, no. 2 (Fall): 315–46.

"Latino TV." (www.channel1.com/users/zamawa/tv/laprog.html).

Law-Yone, Wendy. 1993. *Irrawaddy Tango*. New York: Knopf.

Leong, Russell, ed. 1996. *Asian American Sexualities: Dimensions of the Gay and Lesbian Experience*. New York: Routledge.

Leverenz, David. 1989. *Manhood and the American Renaissance*. Ithaca, N.Y.: Cornell University Press.

Li, David Leiwei. 1992. "The Production of Chinese American Tradition: Displacing American Orientalist Discourse." In *Reading the Literatures of Asian America*, ed. Shirley Goek-lin Lim and Amy Ling, 319–32. Philadelphia: Temple University Press.

Lim, Shirley Geok-lin. 1993. "Feminist and Ethnic Literary Theories in Asian American Literature." *Feminist Studies* 19, no. 3 (Fall): 571—95.

Lim, Shirley Geok-lin, and Amy Ling, eds. 1992. Introduction to *Reading the Literatures of Asian America*. Philadelphia: Temple University Press.

Lim, Shirley Geok-lin, and Tsutakawa, Mayumi, eds. 1989. *The Forbidden Stitch: An Asian American Women's Anthology*. Corvallis, Oreg.: Calyx Books.

Lim-Hing, Sharon, ed. 1994. *The Very Inside: An Anthology of Writing by Asian and Pacific Islander Lesbian and Bisexual Women*. Toronto: Sister Vision.

Linden-Ward, Blanche, and Carol Hurd Green. *American Women in the 1960s: Changing the Future*. Boston: Twayne, 1993.

Liu, Lydia. 1994. "The Female Body and Nationalist Discourse: The Field of Life and Death Revisited." In *Scattered Hegemonies: Postmodernity and Transnational Feminist Practices*, ed. Inderpal Grewal and Caren Kaplan, 37–62. Minneapolis: University of Minnesota Press.

Lopez, Ana. 1985. "The Melodrama in Latin America: Films, Telenovelas, and the Currency of a Popular Form." *Wide Angle* 7, no. 3: 4–13.

———. 1995. "Our Welcomed Guests: Telenovelas in Latin America." In *To Be Continued . . . : Soap Operas around the World*, ed. Robert C. Allen, 256–75. New York: Routledge.

Lowe, Lisa. 1991. "Heterogeneity, Hybridity, Multiplicity: Marking Asian American Differences." *Diaspora* 1, no. 1 (Spring): 24–44.

———. 1996. *Immigrant Acts: On Asian American Cultural Politics*. Durham, N.C.: Duke University Press.

Lye, Colleen. 1995. "Toward an Asian (American) Cultural Studies: Postmodernism and the 'Peril of Yellow Capital and Labor.'" In *Privileging Positions: The Sites of Asian American Studies*, ed. Gary Y. Okihiro, Marilyn Alquizola, Dorothy Fujita Rony, K. Scott Wong, 47–56. Pullman: Washington State University Press.

Maeyama, Takashi. 1979. "Ethnicity, Secret Societies, and Associations: the Japanese in Brazil." *Comparative Study of Society and History* 21, no. 4: 589–610.

Mani, Lata. 1990a. "Contentious Traditions: The Debate on *Sati* in Colonial India." In *Recasting Women: Essays on Indian Colonial History*, ed. Kumkum Sangari and Sudesh Vaid, 88–123. New Brunswick, N.J.: Rutgers University Press.

———. 1990b. "Multiple Mediations: Feminist Scholarship in the Age of Multinational Reception." *Feminist Review* 35 (Summer): 24–41.

Martin, Biddy. 1994. "Sexualities without Genders and Other Queer Utopias." *diacritics* 24, no. 2–3 (Summer–Fall): 104–21.

Martin, Biddy, and Chandra Talpade Mohanty. 1986. "Feminist Politics: What's Home Got to Do with It?" In *Feminist Studies/Critical Studies*, ed. Teresa de Lauretis, 191–212. Bloomington: Indiana University Press.

Massey, Doreen. 1994. *Space, Place, and Gender*. Minneapolis: University of Minnesota Press.

May, Elaine Tyler. 1988. *Homeward Bound: American Families in the Cold War Era*. New York: Basic Books, 1988.

Mazumdar, Sucheta. 1991. "Asian American Studies and Asian Studies: Rethinking Roots." In *Asian Americans: Comparative and Global Perspectives*, ed. Shirley Hune, Hyung-chan Kim, Stephen S. Fugita, and Amy Ling, 29–44. Pullman: Washington State University Press.

McWilliams, Carey. 1973. Introduction to *America Is in the Heart*. Seattle: University of Washington Press.

Melendy, H. Brett. 1976. "California's Discrimination Against Filipinos 1927–1935." In *Letters in Exile: An Introductory Reader on the History of Pilipinos in America*, UCLA Asian American Studies Center, 35–43. Los Angeles: The Regents of the University of California.

Merriam, Eve. 1964. *After Nora Slammed the Door: American Women in the 1960s: The Unfinished Revolution.* New York: World Publishing Co.

Michaels, Walter Benn. 1987. *The Gold Standard and the Logic of Naturalism.* Berkeley: University of California Press.

Mies, Maria. 1986. *Patriarchy and Accumulation on a World Scale: Women in the International Division of Labour.* London: Zed Books.

Miller, Stuart Creighton. 1982. *"Benevolent Assimilation": The American Conquest of the Philippines, 1899–1903.* New Haven, Conn.: Yale University Press.

Mitter, Swasti. 1986. *Common Fate, Common Bond: Women in the Global Economy.* London: Pluto Press.

Miyoshi, Masao. 1993. "A Borderless World? From Colonialism to Transnationalism and the Decline of the Nation-State." *Critical Inquiry* 19 (Summer): 726–51.

Modleski, Tania. 1990. *Loving with a Vengeance: Mass-Produced Fantasies for Women.* Hamden, Conn.: Archon, 1982. Reprint, New York: Routledge.

Mohanty, Chandra Talpade. 1991. "Under Western Eyes: Feminist Scholarship and Colonial Discourses." In *Third World Women and the Politics of Feminism,* ed. Chandra Talpade Mohanty, Ann Russo, and Lourdes Torres, 51–80. Bloomington: Indiana University Press.

Morantte, P. C. 1944. "Two Filipinos in America." *Books Abroad* (Autumn): 323–27.

Mostern, Kenneth. 1995. "Why Is America in the Heart?" *Critical Mass* 2, no. 2 (Spring): 35–65.

Moy, James. 1993. *Marginal Sites: Staging the Chinese in America.* Iowa City: University of Iowa Press.

Mukherjee, Bharati. 1989. *Jasmine.* New York: Ballantine.

Mulvey, Laura. 1990. "Visual Pleasure and Narrative Cinema." In *Issues in Feminist Film Criticism,* ed. Patricia Erens, 28–40. Bloomington: Indiana University Press.

Mumford, Laura Stempel. 1995. *Love and Ideology in the Afternoon: Soap Opera, Women, and Television Genre.* Bloomington: Indiana University Press.

Murashige, Michael S. 1993 (Summer). Interview with Karen Tei Yamashita. Unpublished manuscript. Forthcoming in *Word Matters: Interviews with Twenty Writers of Asian Descent.* Honolulu: University of Hawaii Press.

———. 1994. "Karen Tei Yamashita: An Interview." *Amerasia Journal* 20, no. 3: 49–59.

Nguyen, Viet Thanh. 1997. "Writing the Body Politic: Asian American Subjects and the American Nation." Ph.D. diss., University of California, Berkeley.

Nochimson, Martha. 1992. *No End to Her: Soap Opera and the Female Subject.* Berkeley: University of California Press.

Nonini, Donald M. 1993. "On the Outs on the Rim: An Ethnographic Grounding of the 'Asia-Pacific' Imaginary." In *What's in a Rim: Critical Perspectives on the Pacific Region Idea,* ed. Arif Dirlik, 161–82. Boulder, Colo.: Westview Press.

Oerton, Sarah. 1997. " 'Queer Housewives?': Some Problems in Theorising the Division of Domestic Labour in Lesbian and Gay Households." *Women's Studies International Forum* 20, no. 3: 421–30.

Okihiro, Gary Y. 1994. *Margins and Mainstreams: Asians in American History and Culture*. Seattle: University of Washington Press.

Omatsu, Glenn. 1994. "The 'Four Prisons' and the Movements of Liberation: Asian American Activism from the 1960s to the 1990s." In *The State of Asian America: Activism and Resistance in the 1990s*, ed. Karin Aguilar-San Juan, 19–69. Boston: South End Press .

Omi, Michael, and Howard Winant. 1986. *Racial Formation in the United States: From the 1960s to the 1980s*. New York: Routledge.

Ong, Aihwa. 1993. "On the Edge of Empires: Flexible Citizenship among Chinese in Diaspora." *Positions* 1, no. 3 (Winter): 745–78.

Ong, Aihwa, and Donald Nonini. 1997. " Introduction: Chinese Transnationalism as an Alternative Modernity." In *Ungrounded Empires: The Cultural Politics of Modern Chinese Transnationalism*, ed. Aihwa Ong and Donald Nonini. New York: Routledge.

Ong, Paul, Edna Bonacich, and Lucie Cheng. 1994. "The Political Economy of Capitalist Restructuring and the New Asian Immigration." In *The New Asian Immigration in Los Angeles and Global Restructuring*, ed. Paul Ong, Edna Bonacich, and Lucie Cheng, 3–35. Philadelphia: Temple University Press.

Parker, Andrew, Mary Russo, Doris Sommer, and Patricia Yaeger, eds. 1992. Introduction to *Nationalisms and Sexualities*. New York: Routledge.

Pease, Donald E. 1990. "New Americanists: Revisionist Interventions into the Canon." *boundary 2* 17, no. 1: 1–37.

———. 1993. "New Perspectives on U.S. Culture and Imperialism." In *Cultures of United States Imperialism*, ed. Amy Kaplan and Donald E. Pease, 22–37. Durham, N.C.: Duke University Press.

Pettman, Jan Jindy. 1996. "Border Crossing/Shifting Identities: Minorities, Gender, and the State in International Perspective." In *Challenging Boundaries: Global Flows, Territorial Identities*, ed. Michael J. Shapiro and Hayward R. Alker, 261–83. Minneapolis: University of Minnesota Press.

Pfeil, Fred. 1991. "Vine Land." Review of *Through the Arc of the Rain Forest*, by Karen Tei Yamashita. *Voice* 5 (February): 66.

Rabinowitz, Paula. 1991. *Labor and Desire: Women's Revolutionary Fiction in Depression America*. Chapel Hill: University of North Carolina Press.

Radhakrishnan, R. 1992. "Nationalism, Gender, and the Narrative of Identity." In *Nationalisms and Sexualities*, ed. Andrew Parker, Mary Russo, Doris Sommer, and Patricia Yaeger, 77–95. New York: Routledge.

Rafael, Vicente L., ed. 1995. *Discrepant Histories: Translocal Essays on Filipino Culture*. Philadelphia: Temple University Press.

———. 1990. "Patronage and Pornography: Ideology and Spectatorship in the Early Marcos Years." *Comparative Studies in Society and History* 32, no. 2 (April): 282–304.

Rajan, Rajeswari Sunder. 1993. *Real and Imagined Women: Gender, Culture, and Post-colonialism*. New York: Routledge.

Rakesh, Ratti, ed. 1993. *A Lotus of Another Color: An Unfolding of the South Asian Gay and Lesbian Experience*. Boston: Alyson Publications.

Reichl, Christopher A. 1995. "Stages in the Historical Process of Ethnicity: The Japanese in Brazil, 1908–1988." *Ethnohistory* 42, no. 1 (Winter): 31–62.

Review of *Through the Arc of the Rain Forest*, by Karen Tei Yamashita. 1990. *Publishers Weekly*, 20 July, 55.

Robertson, Roland. 1992. *Globalization: Social Theory and Global Culture*. London: Sage Publications.

Rogin, Michael Paul. 1987. *Ronald Reagan, the Movie, and Other Episodes in Political Demonology*. Berkeley: University of California Press.

———. 1993. " 'Make My Day! ': Spectacle as Amnesia in Imperial Politics [and] the Sequel." In *Cultures of United States Imperialism*, ed. Amy Kaplan and Donald E. Pease, 499–534. Durham, N.C.: Duke University Press.

Rouse, Roger. 1995. "Thinking through Transnationalism: Notes on the Cultural Politics of Class Relations in the Contemporary United States." *Public Culture* 7: 353–402.

Rowe, Kim R. 1993. "Female Spectatorship: Constructing Heterosexual Identities with Homosexual Looks." *The Honors Journal* (University of Colorado, Boulder) 2, no. 1 (February): 98–105.

Rubin, Gayle. 1975. "The Traffic in Women: Notes on the 'Political Economy' of Sex." In *Toward an Anthropology of Women*, ed. Rayna Reiter, 157–210. New York: Monthly Review Press.

Said, Edward. 1979. *Orientalism*. New York: Pantheon, 1978. Reprint, New York: Vintage.

———. 1988. Forward to *Selected Subaltern Studies*, ed. Ranajit Guha and Gayatri Chakravorty Spivak. New York: Oxford University Press.

———. 1993. *Culture and Imperialism*. New York: Knopf.

Saldívar, José David. 1991. *The Dialectics of Our America: Genealogy, Cultural Critique, and Literary History*. Durham, N.C.: Duke University Press.

San Juan, E., Jr. 1972. *Carlos Bulosan and the Imagination of Class Struggle*. Quezon City: University of Philippines Press.

———. 1978. "Carlos Bulosan: An Introduction." *Asian and Pacific Quarterly of Cultural and Social Affairs* 10, no. 2 (Winter): 43–8.

———. 1992. *Racial Formations/Critical Transformations: Articulations of Power in Ethnic and Racial Studies in the United States*. Atlantic Highlands, N.J.: Humanities International Press.

Sandmeyer, Elmer Clarence. 1991 [1939, 1973]. *The Anti-Chinese Movement in California*. Urbana: University of Illinois Press.

Santiago, Lilia Quindoza. 1995. "Rebirthing *Babaye*: The Women's Movement in the Philippines." In *The Challenge of Local Feminisms: Women's Movements in Global Perspective*, ed. Amrita Basu, 110–28. Boulder, Colo.: Westview Press.

Santos, Tomas N. 1976. "The Filipino Writer in America—Old and New." *World Literature Written in English* 15, no. 2 (November): 406–14.

Scarry, Elaine. 1985. *The Body in Pain: The Making and Unmaking of the World*. New York: Oxford University Press.

Schirmer, Daniel B., and Stephen Rosskamm Shalom. 1987. *The Philippines Reader: A History of Colonialism, Neocolonialism, Dictatorship, and Resistance*. Boston: South End Press.

Schwoch, James. 1995. "Manaus: Television from the Borderless." *Public Culture* 7: 455–64.

Seaman, Donna. 1990. Review of *Through the Arc of the Rain Forest*, by Karen Tei Yamashita. *Booklist*, 1 August, 2157.

Sedgwick, Eve Kosofsky. 1985. *Between Men: English Literature and Male Homosocial Desire*. New York: Columbia University Press.

———. 1992. "Nationalisms and Sexualities in the Age of Wilde." In *Nationalisms and Sexualities*, ed. Andrew Parker, Mary Russo, Doris Sommer, and Patricia Yaeger, 235–45. New York: Routledge.

Sengupta, Somini. 1996. "Cultivating the Art of the Mélange." *New York Times*, 4 December, C1.

Shah, Sonia. 1997. *Dragon Ladies: Asian American Feminists Breathe Fire*. Boston: South End Press.

Sharpe, Jenny. 1994. "The Unspeakable Limits of Rape: Colonial Violence and Counter-Insurgency." In *Colonial Discourse and Postcolonial Theory: A Reader*, ed. Patrick Williams and Laura Chrisman, 211–43. New York: Columbia University Press.

Sollors, Werner. 1986. *Beyond Ethnicity: Consent and Descent in American Culture*. New York: Oxford University Press.

Spickard, Paul R. 1989. *Mixed Blood: Intermarriage and Ethnic Identity in Twentieth-Century America*. Madison: University of Wisconsin Press.

Spivak, Gayatri Chakravorty. 1988a. "Can the Subaltern Speak?" In *Marxism and the Interpretation of Culture*, ed. Cary Nelson and Lawrence Grossberg, 271–313. Urbana: University of Illinois Press.

———. 1988b. "Subaltern Studies: Deconstructing Historiography." Introduction to *Selected Subaltern Studies*, ed. Ranajit Guha and Gayatri Chakravorty Spivak. New York, Oxford University Press.

———. 1990. *The Post-colonial Critic: Interviews, Strategies, Dialogues*. Ed. Sarah Harasym. New York: Routledge.

———. 1993. *Outside in the Teaching Machine*. New York: Routledge.

Stern, Michael. 1979. *Douglas Sirk*. Boston: Twayne.

Stoltzfus, Brenda J. 1987. "A Woman's Place in the Struggle." In *The Philippines Reader: A History of Colonialism, Neocolonialism, Dictatorship, and Resistance*, ed. Daniel B. Schirmer and Stephen Rosskamm Shalom, 308–12. Boston: South End Press.

Studlar, Gaylyn. 1988. *In the Realm of Pleasure: Von Sternberg, Dietrich, and the Masochistic Aesthetic*. Urbana: University of Illinois Press.

Suleri, Sara. 1987. *Meatless Days*. Chicago: University of Chicago Press.

———. 1994. "Woman Skin Deep: Feminism and the Postcolonial Condition." In *Colonial Discourse and Postcolonial Theory: A Reader*, ed. Patrick Williams and Laura Chrisman, 244–56. New York: Columbia University Press.

Sumida, Stephen H. 1991. *And the View from the Shore: Literary Traditions of Hawai'i*. Seattle: University of Washington Press.

Tadiar, Neferti Xina M. 1993. "Sexual Economies in the Asia-Pacific Community." In *What's in a Rim: Critical Perspectives on the Pacific Region Idea*, ed. Arif Dirlik, 183–210. Boulder, Colo.: Westview Press.

———. 1995. "Manila's New Metropolitan Form." In *Discrepant Histories: Translocal Essays on Filipino Cultures*, ed. Vicente L. Rafael, 285–313. Philadelphia: Temple University Press.

Takagi, Dana, and Michael Omi. 1995. "Thinking Theory in Asian American Studies." *Amerasia Journal* 21, nos. 1–2: xi–xv.

Takaki, Ronald. 1990a. *Iron Cages: Race and Culture in 19th-Century America.* New York: Knopf, 1979. Reprint, New York: Oxford University Press.

———. 1990b. *Strangers from a Different Shore: A History of Asian Americans.* Boston: Little, Brown, 1989. Reprint, New York: Penguin.

———, ed. 1994 [1987]. *From Different Shores: Perspectives on Race and Ethnicity in America.* 2d ed. New York: Oxford University Press.

Tate, Claudia. 1992. *Domestic Allegories of Political Desire: Black Heroine's Text at the Turn of the Century.* New York: Oxford University Press.

Thoreau, Henry David. 1960 [1854, 1849]. *Walden and Civil Disobedience.* Ed. Sherman Paul. Boston: Houghton Mifflin.

Tomlinson, John. 1991. *Cultural Imperialism: A Critical Introduction.* Baltimore: Johns Hopkins University Press.

Trinh T. Minh-ha. 1989. *Woman, Native, Other: Writing Postcoloniality and Feminism.* Bloomington: Indiana University Press.

———. 1991. *When the Moon Waxes Red: Representation, Gender, and Cultural Politics.* New York: Routledge.

Tsuchida, Nobuya. 1978. "The Japanese in Brazil, 1908–1941." Ph.D. diss., University of California, Los Angeles.

Uno, Roberta, ed. 1993. *Unbroken Thread: An Anthology of Plays by Asian American Women.* Amherst: University of Massachusetts Press.

Vink, Nico. 1988. *The Telenovela and Emancipation: A Study on Television and Social Change in Brazil.* Amsterdam, The Netherlands: Royal Tropical Institute.

W., M. Consuelo León. 1995. "Foundations of the American Image of the Pacific." In *Asia/Pacific as Space of Cultural Production*, ed. Rob Wilson and Arif Dirlik, 17–29. Durham, N.C.: Duke University Press.

Wallerstein, Immanuel. 1990. "Culture as the Ideological Battleground of the Modern World-System." *Theory, Culture, and Society* 7: 31–55.

Watanabe, Sylvia, and Carol Bruchac, eds. 1990. *Home to Stay: Asian American Women's Fiction.* Ed. Greenfield Center. New York: Greenfield Review Press.

Wei, William. 1993. *The Asian American Movement.* Philadelphia: Temple University Press.

W.I.C. 1933. "Marriage: Miscegenation." *California Law Review* 22 (November): 116–17.

Wiegman, Robyn. 1995. *American Anatomies: Theorizing Race and Gender.* Durham, N.C.: Duke University Press.

Williams, Patrick, and Laura Chrisman, eds. 1994. *Colonial Discourse and Post-Colonial Theory: A Reader.* New York: Columbia University Press.

Wilson, Rob, and Arif Dirlik, eds. 1995. *Asia/Pacific as Space of Cultural Production.* Durham, N.C.: Duke University Press.

Women of South Asian Descent Collective, ed. 1993. *Our Feet Walk the Sky: Women of the South Asian Diaspora.* San Francisco: Aunt Lute Books.

Wong, K. Scott. 1996. "The Transformation of Culture: Three Chinese Views of America." *American Quarterly* 48, no. 2 (June): 201–32.

Wong, Sau-ling Cynthia. Forthcoming. " 'Astronaut Wives' and 'Little Dragons': Identity Negotiations by Diasporic Chinese Women in Two Popular Novels of the 1980s." In *Proceedings of the 1992 Luodi Shenggen International Conference on Overseas Chinese*, ed. L. Ling-Chi Wang and Gungwu Wang. Singapore: Times Academic Press.

———. 1992. "Ethnicizing Gender: An Exploration of Sexuality as Sign in Chinese Immigrant Literature." In *Reading the Literatures of Asian America*, ed. Shirley Geok-lin Lim and Amy Ling, 111–29. Philadelphia: Temple University Press.

Wong, Sau-ling Cythia. 1993. *Reading Asian American Literature: From Necessity to Extravagance*. Princeton, N.J.: Princeton University Press.

———. 1995. "Denationalization Reconsidered: Asian American Cultural Criticism at a Theoretical Crossroads." *Amerasia* 21, nos. 1– 2: 1–27.

Woo-Cumings, Meredith. 1993. "Market Dependency in U.S.-East Asian Relations." In *What's in a Rim: Critical Perspectives on the Pacific Region Idea*, ed. Arif Dirlik, 135–57. Boulder, Colo.: Westview Press.

Woodside, Alexander. 1993. "The Asia-Pacific Idea as Mobilization Myth." In *What's in a Rim: Critical Perspectives on the Pacific Region Idea*, ed. Arif Dirlik, 13–28. Boulder, Colo.: Westview Press.

Yamanaka, Lois-Ann. 1996. *Wild Meat and the Bully Burgers*. New York: Farrar, Straus, and Giroux.

———. 1997. *Blu's Hanging*. New York: Avon.

Yamashita, Karen Tei. 1990. *Through the Arc of the Rain Forest*. Minneapolis: Coffee House Press.

———. 1992. *Brazil-Maru*. Minneapolis: Coffee House Press.

———. 1995. "A Study of the Novel Siamese Twins and Mongoloids: Cultural Appropriation and the Deconstruction of Stereotype via the Absurdity of Metaphor." Paper delivered at the San Francisco Book Festival, Concourse Exhibition Center, 11 November.

———. 1997. *Tropic of Orange*. Minneapolis: Coffee House Press.

Yogi, Stan. 1990. "An Eco-Fantasy Set in Brazil." Review of *Through the Arc of the Rain Forest*, by Karen Tei Yamashita. *San Francisco Chronicle Review*. 30 September, 6.

Index

Ahmad, Aijaz, 170n.29
Alien Land Laws, 50, 136. *See also* exclusion
Alquizola, Marilyn, 160n.27
America, 3–14, 16–17, 110, 140, 151n.3, 152n.6, 161n.6; as bicontinental expanse, 5, 7, 106, 141; cultural dominance of, 7, 9–10, 16, 73–75, 77, 80, 87, 167n.4; decentering its importance in Asian American Studies, 5–6, 9, 108–114, 138, 152n.4, 152n.6, 154n.13, 154n.17, 155n.19; embodied in women, 31–34, 41, 43; and fraternal community, 18, 23–24, 32–33, 41; gendered terms of, 12, 34–36, 38–41, 146; imperialism of, 6–7, 16, 19, 41–42, 73, 75–77, 81, 86, 106, 109, 122, 140, 152n.3, 153n.7, 157n.6; Latin/South, 7, 112, 114, 121–122, 131, 140, 143, 176n.17; as property, 37–39, 49; racialized domestic policies of, 4, 8, 11, 16, 33–34, 38–40, 49–50, 114, 153nn. 7 and 8, 159n.17, 162n.9; sexual politics of, 29–30, 37–38; as site of desire, 24, 42, 76–77, 98–99, 156n.3, 167n.4
America Is in the Heart (Bulosan), 6, 12, 17–43, 63, 75, 118, 141, 156nn. 1 and 2, 157n.4, 158nn. 9, 13, and 14, 159nn. 15, 16, and 17, 160nn. 24 and 27, 161nn. 4 and 5, 182n.3. *See also* Bulosan, Carlos
American literature, canonically defined, 44, 46–47, 55
American myths and narratives, 44–48, 50–54, 70–71, 140, 143, 162n.12, 163n.17, 166n.32; of accumulation, 48, 54–55, 58–59, 63–64, 72, 164n.22; of the American Dream, 45, 52, 54, 161n.5, 163n.21; of exceptionalism, 6, 8–9, 114, 151n.3, 152n.4; of home-ownership, 49–51, 53–54, 64, 72; of individualism, 48, 54–56, 58, 60–61, 70, 118, 163n.15; of limitlessness, 45, 48, 54–56, 59, 77, 140; of success, progress, and self-enlargement, 48, 59, 69, 162n.13, 163n.13; of self-making, 48, 54–59, 61–64, 69–70, 72, 118, 164n.22
Americanization, 44, 48, 116–117, 153n.6
Anderson, Benedict, 19, 157n.5

anti-miscegenation laws, 30–31, 37–39
Appadurai, Arjun, 94–95
Aquino, Benigno, Jr., 85
Armstrong, Nancy, 139
Asian America, 75, 110, 117, 140, 155n.17
Asian American literature, 15–16, 88, 106–107, 113, 118, 137–146, 153n.11, 175n.14; traditional frameworks of, 107, 113–121, 137, 139, 151n.1, 154n.12, 175n.15, 181nn. 56 and 1
Asian American Studies, 5–8, 10–11, 15, 106, 108, 112, 139–146, 156n.21, 181n.1, 182n.3; emphasis on railroads, 113–115, 119, 138, 175nn. 15 and 16, 176n.17; and ethnopolitical critique, 4, 7–9, 12, 113, 116, 137, 140, 144, 156n.1, 182n.1; and feminism, 4, 8, 10–11, 15, 65, 143–146, 155nn. 18 and 19, 164n.25, 165n.25, 182n.5; prospective frameworks of, 5–6, 9–11, 141, 143, 146, 154n.17, 155nn. 17, 18, and 19; traditional themes and agendas of, 5–6, 11, 15, 107, 113, 117, 119–121, 136–138, 140, 143–144, 146, 152n. 4 and 6, 154n.13, 155n.17, 173n.4, 174n.11, 176nn. 18 and 19
Asian and Asian American feminism, 10–11, 15, 139, 146, 169n.28, 181n.52, 182n.4
Asian immigrants. *See* immigration, Asian
Asia-Pacific region, 9–11, 15, 106–113, 119–120, 138, 152n.3, 154n.14, 156nn. 21, 22, and 23, 173nn. 5, 6, and 7, 174nn. 7, 8, 9, and 10, 175n.13, 176n.22
assimilation, 6, 65, 110, 177n.27

Balce-Cortes, Nerissa, 79, 166n.1
Barrett, Michèle, viii
Bascara, Victor, vii
Baym, Nina, 61, 163n.18
Bonifacio, Andres, 19
boundaries, territorial-national, 7, 9, 11, 75, 122; violation of, 6, 10–11, 109, 111, 113, 121–122
Brazil, 15, 106–107, 110–118, 121, 133, 137, 174n.10, 175n.13, 176n.24, 178n.34, 179n.40